JoAnna Russ

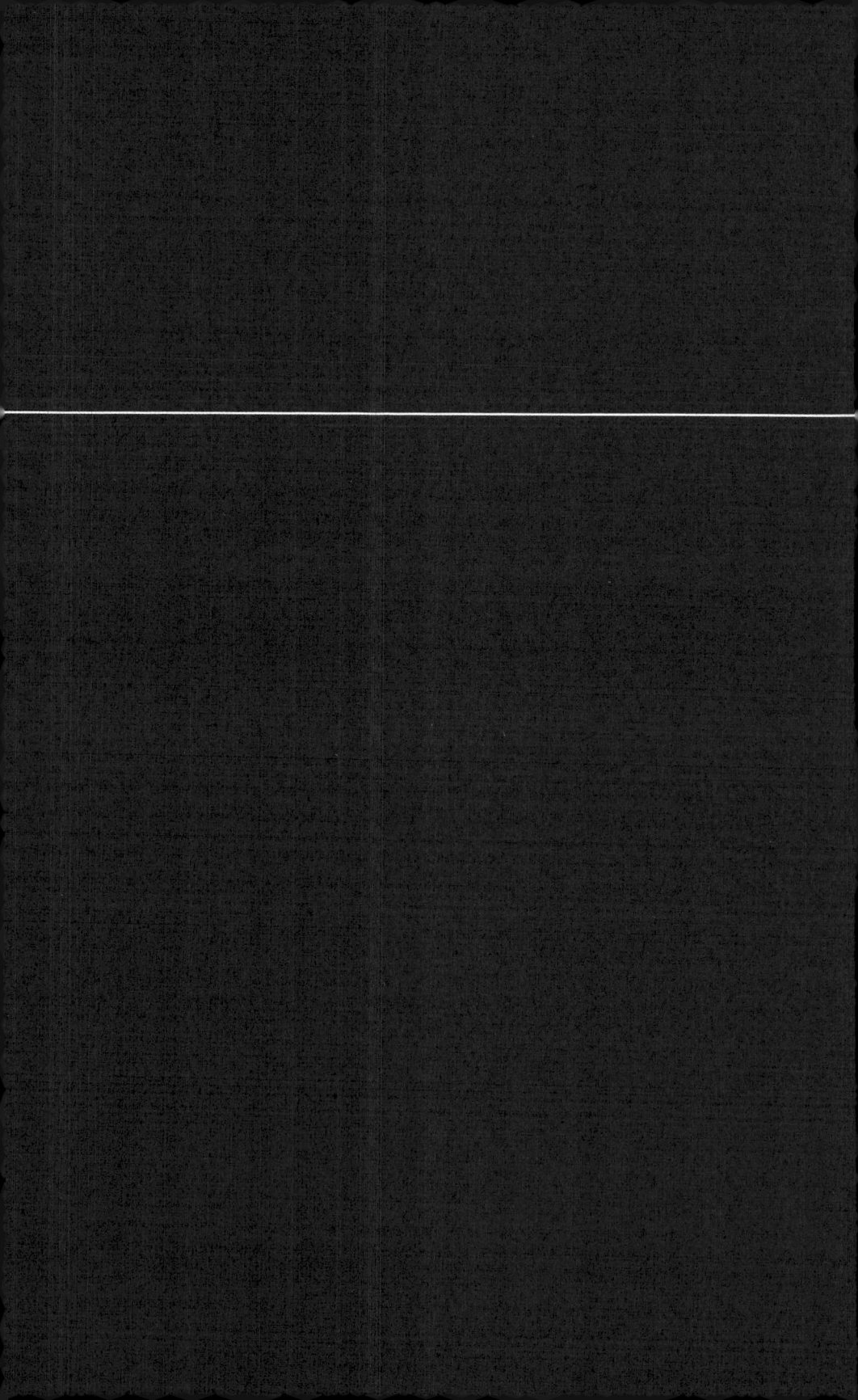

# MODERN MASTERS OF SCIENCE FICTION

Edited by Gary K. Wolfe

Science fiction often anticipates the consequences of scientific discoveries. The immense strides made by science since World War II have been matched step by step by writers who gave equal attention to scientific principles, human imagination, and the craft of fiction. The respect for science fiction won by Jules Verne and H. G. Wells was further increased by Isaac Asimov, Arthur C. Clarke, Robert Heinlein, Ursula K. Le Guin, Joanna Russ, and Ray Bradbury. Modern Masters of Science Fiction is devoted to books that survey the work of individual authors who continue to inspire and advance science fiction.

*A list of books in the series appears at the end of this book.*

# JOANNA RUSS

Gwyneth Jones

UNIVERSITY OF
ILLINOIS PRESS
Urbana, Chicago, and Springfield

∞ This book is printed on acid-free paper.

Library of Congress Cataloging-in-Publication Data
Names: Jones, Gwyneth A., author.
Title: Joanna Russ / by Gwyneth Jones.
Description: Urbana, IL : University of Illinois Press, [2019] | Series: Modern masters
    of science fiction | Includes bibliographical references and index.
Identifiers: LCCN 2019001531| ISBN 9780252042638 (hardcover : alk. paper) |
    ISBN 9780252084478 (pbk. : alk. paper)
Subjects: LCSH: Russ, Joanna, 1937–2011—Criticism and interpretation. | Science fiction,
    American—History and criticism.
Classification: LCC PS3568.U763 Z76 2019 | DDC 813/.54—dc23
    LC record available at https://lccn.loc.gov/2019001531

Ebook ISBN 9780252051487

# contents

# ACKNOWLEDGMENTS

Jeanne Cortiel's study of Joanna Russ, *Demand My Writing*, was an essential resource throughout this project, as was the essay collection *On Joanna Russ*, edited by Farah Mendlesohn. Judith Merril's nonfiction writings (*The Merril Theory of Litr'y Criticism*, edited by Ritch Calvin) gave me deep background and a vivid picture of the American sf genre and community as it was in the 1960s, when Joanna joined the Gang. Helen Merrick's *The Secret Feminist Cabal* was equally valuable, and fascinating, for the feminist seventies.

Special thanks to my patient editor at the University of Illinois Press, Marika Christofides; to Andy Sawyer and the staff of the Science Fiction Collections Library at the University of Liverpool; to Jeanne Cortiel, Samuel Delany, Jeanne Gomoll, Sarah LeFanu, Julie Phillips, Lisa Tuttle, and Luise White; to Charlotte Bunch for permitting me to use the interview with Joanna from *Quest*; and to Kathryn Cramer for her insightful memories of Joanna's later career. Many thanks also, for all kinds of help and encouragement, to Suzy Charnas, Ritchie Calvin, Timmi Duchamp, Diana Finch, S. T. Joshi, Ursula K. Le Guin, Sarah Lohmann, Vonda N. McIntyre, Michelle Massé of the MLA, Jeffrey D. Smith, and Chelsea Quinn Yarbro. Randy Byers gets a special mention for identifying *The Two of Them*'s biblical ending and the Ezekiel reference. So does Gabriel Jones, who introduced me to the "new music"—giving me a context and motivation for Joanna's recklessly radical experiments in fiction.

JOANNA RUSS

# CHAPTER 1

## JOANNA RUSS, TRANS-TEMP AGENT
### From the Death of the Universe to "The Second Inquisition"

The House gave a little tentative shake and then another, and then shivered into a hundred, no, a million, no many, many more atoms, atoms that threw the airy snow up in a great billowing rise. The crisp noon kitchen, the mellow living room, the Real Food chute, the self-renewable rug, the sealed windows—all in a tremendous whoosh into the air. But not into the air, rather into the space above the air, and then it settled down on the frozen air, onto the sluggishly living pools of liquid nitrogen, bounced a little, billowed a little, and finally lay quietly, invisibly, over a radius of some hundred miles.

The House almost *had* lasted forever . . . as such things go.

—"Nor Custom Stale," 1959

I am temperamentally a religious mystic, as I suppose many sf writers are. The "sense of wonder" and all that. Hard to explain—mysticism cannot be expressed directly or analytically in words.

—Joanna Russ, interview with Paul Walker, 1972

Joanna Russ was born in the Bronx, New York, in 1937—a "third-generation Ashkenazy Jew"[1] in a close-knit community. Her mother, Bertha (née Zinner), a grade-school and visiting science teacher, wrote fiction, only giving up when Joanna "came along." Her father, Evarett, taught "shop class." Bertha loved poetry. In a *New York Review of Science Fiction* feature on sf writers' childhood inspirations, Joanna remembered an impressive game: "We'd take *The Oxford Book of English Verse*, pick a first line . . . and ask mother to name and recite the poem."[2] At age five Joanna was making (with her parents' help) illustrated books sewn together with thread. Her earliest science fiction stories include, from 1945 to 1949: "Destination—Moon," "Visit to the Fourth Dimension," and "Thoughts of a Deluded Scientist."[3] Evarett taught her to sew and had a keen interest in popular science. He and Joanna would look at the moon, Jupiter, and Saturn with a 6" mirror telescope he'd ground and cased himself. "The mosquito bites were no fun," Joanna noted. "But we persisted."[4]

Overgrown vacant lots made good playgrounds, and her parents took her often to the Bronx Zoo and the Botanical Gardens. Her upbringing was secular, but her "sense of wonder" was passionate. On a school trip to the American Museum of Natural History she was overwhelmed by the science exhibits: "[I] thrilled to the astronomy, and wept at evolution, no kidding!"[5] At age twelve she "stole" her mother's Groff Conklin anthologies of sf and horror (which Bertha claimed she liked because they put her to sleep). She also recalled reading "at twelve or so" *The New World of Physics*, found on her parents' shelves. *The New World of Physics*[6] hadn't been published in 1949, but the adventure of finding and tackling grown-up books surely shows what Joanna wanted to convey: that as a child she lived with two loving adults, highly intelligent, fascinated by literature and the sciences, who taught her by example that no knowledge was out of reach and no achievement barred to her.

She would only note, later, of World War II, that she'd "absorbed all those wartime posters and movies about heroic women," but in the year peace broke out she suffered a personal disaster. Her father became seriously ill in 1945; he "used to assuage his own fear," says Joanna, "by bullying my mother, and later me."[7] Her lively, loving father became the enemy; her wonderful, enabling mother the "Squashed Woman": "guilty at being intelligent, guilty at having gone to graduate school . . . guilty at having a job . . . guilty at being competent at anything," telling Joanna that "men's egos had to be built up by women" and that "a woman like herself was a dreadful threat simply by existing."[8] Was there a sudden change? Or was Joanna seeing her parents' relationship more clearly? We have only one witness, but we can be sure she was not alone. Without any young-consumer spending muscle, or Marlon Brando posturing; without overt rebellion as yet, this *female* adolescent drama of disillusion was unfolding all over America (and the whole Western world). In one corner was the disappointed, domineering father (he-man manqué), smoldering in resentment against his wife's ladylike "superiorities"; in the other was the mother, compliant and complicit, endlessly failing to appease him. Between them was the angry, bewildered girl-child who has lost *both* her parents.[9] When Joanna grew up, all her friends, "artist-intellectual" young women of the 1950s, were making the same vow: *never to be like their mothers.* It would be decades before Joanna was reconciled (as she recorded, in her autobiographical stories "The Little Dirty Girl" and "The Autobiography of My Mother") with two, at least, of the three combatants. In the interim she would become one of those who spoke for a generation of angry young women, enfranchised but far from emancipated—first as one of twentieth-century sf's greatest writers, critics, and apologists, later also as a radical feminist.

Why did Joanna, with her formidable intellect, choose science fiction—a genre ranked as *almost* the lowest of popular trash?[10] One answer is that as one of the two "leading, in-house academic sf theorists in the seventies" (the other was Samuel Delany),[11] she rejected that dismissal, insisting that sf could be a legitimate, powerful modern art form. Another is that her life and times chose Joanna. She was compelled to write science fiction by Cold War politics, captured by a homemade telescope, inspired by the science exhibits at the Natural History Museum and her mother's Groff Conklin anthologies. Above all, there was her intense response to the subject matter of the benighted genre: "Sf and fantasy seemed to me a revelation, a tremendous widening of the horizons. I had no idea such astonishing things might be going on in the world (or out of it). It was the blend of possibility and high fantasy that was so wonderful."[12]

After skipping three grades at elementary school she "had a place at Science High" (presumably the Bronx High School of Science) but "due to family insanity"[13] made an early, lonely start at the William Howard Taft Public High School instead. At sixteen she was the only girl among ten finalists for the

National Westinghouse Science Talent Search, with a project titled "Growth of Certain Fungi under Colored Light and in Darkness."[14] The credit was dear to her, often cited in interviews, but it marked the end of Joanna's science career. She enrolled at Cornell University, studying English; she published poetry[15] and stories in the university's literary magazines and wrote plays that were produced on campus. In her final year she studied under Vladimir Nabokov, whose modernist style was a lasting influence. In 1957, at age twenty, she graduated with honors and went straight on to Yale to study drama and playwriting.

Joanna was far from being a feminist at this time. On the contrary, timid "Jeannine" in *The Female Man* may be taken as a wry portrait of her younger self: a willowy, awkward young lady, living in a continuum where "women's liberation never happened," whose only rebellion is her unhappiness and a curious reluctance to get married, although she's convinced she *needs* a husband.[16] Joanna felt the same pressures and, by her own account, the same ineffective resentment. But her academic achievements gave her a route out. As an Ashkenazi Jew, however secular, she'd internalized (as she described, years later, for the journal *Lesbian Ethics*) a different set of gender rules from the Gentile version. Ashkenazi women weren't expected to be fragile. Men were not admired for their muscle or their skill at fixing the car. "What [Jewish] men claimed for their own," Joanna noted, "was poetry, philosophy, science and fiction, all the things I loved the most."[17] If, to undo the damage done to her childhood, she needed to surpass her father and avenge her mother (there is no Freudian name for this complex, which possibly explains why "therapy" never seems to have resolved any issues for seventies feminists), she was on her way. But it was not to be—or not by the fast track that had carried her so far. At college, in writing class, Joanna learned that female *experience* disqualified her from becoming a great writer, irrespective of her intellect and talent.

"When male sophomores brought in material about rapes, fist fights in bars, brutality, sperm, etc., the class (mostly male) would receive such writing with respect, even reverence because it was 'deep,' 'raw,' and 'real.' When I wrote about a high school dance, this was considered 'unimportant,' 'trivial.' . . . There was a profound bias . . . as to what was the proper material for 'great' writing. I got the message . . . (after all, I'd never raped anybody or been in a fist fight in a bar)."[18]

At Yale, "pre-Brustein," though she received her MFA in 1960, she did not thrive (works included a version of *The Hobbit* for radio, which J. R. R. Tolkien declined to endorse). She didn't give up on theater easily. Three short plays were staged "off Broadway" in 1969; the most successful, *Window Dressing*, was collected in a feminist theater anthology.[19] She was still citing theater credits in 1970 but in the end conceded that she'd "wrestled with playwriting for three years and lost."[20] She couldn't find a teaching post, either. This was the "domestic revival," when American women, including honors graduates, were strongly discouraged from seeking a career outside the home. The only women teachers in college were prewar appointees: new posts were filled by men. The English Department at Cornell—as Joanna reported, in justified fury, to the *Khatru* Symposium—encouraged her to pursue a PhD yet had never hired a woman. *"Where did they think I would end up teaching? . . . What the students learn is that teachers come in two types—old spinsters and glamorous young men. Which will a female student become? (Answer: faculty wife.)"*[21]

In some résumés it's implied, probably by Joanna's own choice, that she "taught at various universities" from 1960 onward. In fact, she found and lost uninspiring New York office jobs, worked (often for free) in theater and radio, and struggled with the depression she'd suffered since high school (at twelve she'd taken her problem to the school psychiatrist; he told the child she had penis envy). She returned to analysis; the sessions did not help: dreamt of being Alexander the Great, "fell in love" with macho men who didn't notice, and dismissed sexual feelings toward women as pointless, just as she'd dismissed "crushes" on girl friends as a teenager. In 1963 she married Albert Amateau, "a short, gentle, retiring, pleasant man" (*He'll do*, is her bleak comment).[22] Their unhappiness is documented in Joanna's nongenre novel *On Strike against God*. The best thing about this time was that she'd started to write fiction again—*science* fiction, to avoid the invalid-experience trap. Her stories were published, and she was "hailed" by the sf community, a forum where at last she would have a voice.

## "NOR CUSTOM STALE"

"Nor Custom Stale" (in the *Magazine of Fantasy and Science Fiction* [September 1959]) was Joanna's first commercial sale (according to *F&SF* records, "Nor

Custom Stale" was accepted by the magazine on May 18, 1959). The narrative opens a nominal "ten or twelve centuries" in the future and concerns a marvelous, giant gadget, the "forever house"—so insulated from change that it might last forever and furnished with so many modern conveniences that the occupants need never leave. Harry and Freda Allen's "house" has been in their family for fifteen generations, and since lifespans of forever-house owners have been increasing, those "generations" cover an impressive span of years. At Harry's retirement party, one bitter winter's night, irascible Harry argues with "Wilberforce from the office." Wilberforce maintains that life requires risk and change: Harry insists that absence of change is why "forever houses" extend lives. Tempers get heated. Freda diffidently reports that the house has developed a fault (a red light on the futuristic control board, that great dramatic standby of the 1950s and '60s). She's ignored until the guests have departed. Harry then refers to the house's manual and finds there's "a small leak" in their fuel line. He disconnects their "Car" (a component of the "forever house" system) and orders Freda to call "the Company." They won't send anybody out: all repair services are on hold until springtime. Harry, far from finding this response disturbing, seizes the opportunity to triumph over Wilberforce and decrees a winter vacation—which the couple will spend at home, in absolute quiet. He directs Hilda to call their friends to make sure the two of them aren't disturbed, and they settle down to wait for a spring that will never come.

Ostensibly, "Nor Custom Stale" is a straightforward Cold War story. The "real year"[23] is "squarely set" in the America of the fifties, that schizophrenic decade of compulsory domestic bliss and inescapable external terrors. The forever house recalls, remarkably closely, the "electric home" extolled by Vice President Richard Nixon in his debate with Nikita Khrushchev at the American National Exhibition in Moscow (July 1959)[24]—except this is an *atomic* house, powered by a "hot and dangerous heart" buried in bedrock, miles beneath the sleek, semi-hemispherical surface structure, and it provides everything. It chews up rock to create the "Air" that Freda and Harry breathe; which they have learned to prefer to natural air. It synthesizes the "Real Food" they prefer to natural food. How many forever houses are there? We are not told but are instead left to imagine thousands—millions?—of buried miniature nuclear reactors, dotting the U.S. suburban landscape, a prospect that in the 1950s would not have been unthinkable.

Lisa Yaszek comments: "It's surprising to find a Russ story squarely set in ... imaginative space that Russ elsewhere so roundly condemns"[25]—stories of the far future, that is, assuming fifties gender roles will still prevail. But as Yaszek goes on to explore, Joanna's subtext is not supportive of conservatism. Harry and Freda are doomed by their stereotyped, gender-role routines. Harry gives the orders, expects Freda's domestic services, and smugly rebukes her rational alarm, but as the red lights proliferate, the partners are complicit in their folie à deux. The picture windows are set to show recorded images, not the disturbing world outdoors. Freda erases each day's completed crossword so they can do it again tomorrow. Minor components in a self-perpetuating system, they might as well be sealed up in a nuclear bunker, and who is ever going to tell them it's safe to emerge?[26]

As a critique of fifties conformity, the story might be good yet routine. But there's a striking, science / fiction fusion building in these mesmerizing images of erasure and diffusion: Joanna the novice has gone straight for the ultimate end game. Time has stopped for Harry and Freda, while, in the world outside, the universe continues to expand, carrying them *almost* to the limit of existence itself. The finale is beautiful: "awe-inspiring" is a fitting term. The "heat death of the universe" (a final state of maximum entropy) was not a new idea in 1959, but Joanna's human story about hard physics is a fine achievement, resonating splendidly, as good science fiction should, with the social realities of her times. Seasoned critics and up-and-coming younger sf writers took note.

## STORIES, 1960–1966

Joanna published several other genre stories between 1960 and 1966. Surprisingly, none of them was science fiction. "My Dear Emily" (*Magazine of Fantasy and Science Fiction* [July 1962]; collected in *The Zanzibar Cat*) is worth special attention. Joanna's epigraph in *The Zanzibar Cat* reads "Someday Hammer Films [*sic*] will make a movie out of this story, and I will die of bliss."[27] For a discussion of the striking queer / sexuality content, I recommend the reading by Jeanne Cortiel in her lesbian feminist study of Joanna, *Demand My Writing*.[28] Read "innocently" as a nineteenth-century American Vampire story, daringly *suggestive* of homosexual relations, "My Dear Emily" recounts the strange adventure of two young ladies, bosom friends, who return from their schooling in the east to San Francisco to enter the adult social world. Their names are Emily and Charlotte (invoking the literary daring of the Brontë sisters, or perhaps Emily Dickinson, Charlotte Perkins Gilman). Emily is engaged, but like Jeannine in *The Female Man*—though Emily is a much more decided character—her gestures betray a secret resistance to her fate. Martin Guevara, a flashy stranger presumably of Spanish descent who somehow appears in the young ladies' refined circle, is the vampire who recognizes a suitable target in Emily: she (after token resistance) welcomes his wicked embrace. "We like souls that come to us," Guevara remarks complacently, before suggesting they take turns to debauch her friend. But he is matched in ruthlessness, and it's the young ladies who survive to enjoy their unnatural future together (Joanna's preferred ending—not used in the *Magazine of Fantasy and Science Fiction*). The story is told in sharply delineated vignettes that glitter with "eye-kicks" (notably, the rebellious drops of blood that Emily lets fall on Emerson's American Transcendental poems in the first scene). The dialogue is elliptical and realist, as if spoken by living agents rather than contrived to deliver a plot—a technique that would become a Joanna Russ trademark. Unexpectedly (perhaps reflecting her fear of accepting her own lesbian sexuality), the narrative insists on the dehumanizing price Emily and Charlotte pay for their transformation. Emily's view of the San Francisco crowds, post initiation, ("What a field of ripe wheat!") is chilling, and the "language" that bursts from this vampirized young lady ("Damned . . . the whole world's damned . . .") has a ring of sincerity. But it's a real shame that Hammer Horror didn't make that movie.

More uncanny tales followed. In "There Is Another Shore You Know, upon the Other Side" (*Magazine of Fantasy and Science Fiction* [September 1963]) a wistful English ghost, who came to Rome as an invalid and died in 1821 (the same year as John Keats), has lingered, unable to reach that other shore. (Perhaps she picked up the Lobster Quadrille quote from a Victorian visitor?) "I Had Vacantly Crumpled It into My Pocket . . ." (*Magazine of Fantasy and Science Fiction* [August 1964]; collected in *The Zanzibar Cat* and in *Cthulhu 2000: A Lovecraftian Anthology*) is a wintery Lovecraftian gothic, featuring surely an avatar of Lovecraft himself as shabby, awkward Irvin Rubin, an accounts clerk obsessed with the "literature" of arcane fantasy. Narrated by a concerned female colleague, the story recounts Irv's passion for a beautiful lady who haunts a bench in Central Park and shares his wildest dreams. June Kramer, his colleague (a middle-aged, single woman with a happy, all-female social life: rare in the contemporary genre!), fears Irv is going crazy. Unfortunately, she's wrong. June is forced to glimpse eyes that look out from the Pit, and she must find in herself, if she can, the superhuman courage to confront that being; that *thing*, whatever it is. . . .

"Come Closer" (*Magazine of Horror* [August 1965]; collected in *The Hidden Side of the Moon*), though not recorded in the "Cthulhu Mythos,"[29] also draws on Joanna's admiration for the master. Told in Lovecraft's Homespun American mode, it's a simple yet artfully creepy tale about a missing child. "The New Men" (*Magazine of Fantasy and Science Fiction* [February 1966]; collected in *The Zanzibar Cat*) is set in the real world's glasnost era (the internal date is 1985). Here, the Soviet Empire persists. An old monster of the Polish nobility meets a new kind of monster, with unexpected results. It's a neat vampire variation, but more conventional than "Dear Emily." "This Night at My Fire" (published in the Cornell triannual literary magazine, *Epoch* [Winter 1966]; collected in *The Hidden Side of the Moon*) is an eerie mood-piece: a woman beside the fire in a holiday cabin, armed with a pack of Tarot cards, defeats both Death and her "he-man" husband.

In a nongenre, modernist story of this period, "Life in a Furniture Store" (*Epoch* [Fall 1965]); collected in *The Hidden Side of the Moon*), an unnamed narrator has failed to thrive in the world of young ladies with little office jobs. She presents a cubist, shattered sketch of the experience: her boss with the "technicolor blue eyes," so cleverly placed above his pink jowls; the absurdly stilted office furniture. Escaping briefly into the freedom of a city full of rain and promise, she next adopts the persona of a young wife whose husband doesn't understand her, parading around her cage in a scarlet kimono and black stockings, in married idleness. Failing again to maintain the expected charade, she falls into memories of her teenage years, evocatively described as "a room where everything is jumbled together, scraps of the sea, pressed notebooks; flowers"—and confesses her hopeless love for another girl: "I believe she is dead now."

Positioned by these dreamlike, psychoanalytical flourishes, the narrator visits a New York townhouse, crowded with arty-intellectual accessories, watchful furniture, and sly, untouchable cats, that "Laura" shares with two older ladies (tacitly, a lesbian couple). In appearance and appeal, this "Laura" is close to the "Laura Rose" character in *The Female Man*—the all-American teenage daughter of the family visited by "Janet Evason," the woman from feminist utopia. She favors the same outsized, boyish clothing and has the same soft coloring, the same edible-looking flesh: but she's far more intimidating. The interaction between the two women—in theory, friends—wavers between hostility and longing, as the narrative slips between precision, and stream-of-consciousness dissolves. The visit is not a success. Having finally tried to enact *her own* desire, and failed again, the narrator, resigning herself to the "despair of inanimate objects,"[30] "goes to live in a furniture store."

Joanna used autobiographical material ruthlessly throughout her career and with great effect: this story could be the record of an actual day in the life of her wilderness years, intensified by the skewed angles and strange shadows of a contemporary Hitchcock movie. What the narrator tells us, through the world she describes, is not "literal" truth but the truth of a rather terrifying state of mind. An accomplished sketch for some of the content and technique of *The Female Man*, "Life in a Furniture Store" seems to raise the question, Why didn't Joanna follow up her uncanny tales with a disturbing and stylish gothic novel? Perhaps she might have taken that path: she would always be fascinated by the horror/gothic modes. But Joanna in the early 1960s was struggling *not* to be terrified, and to stay away from the verge of madness.[31] Science fiction appealed to her intellect, her sense of wonder, her longing for an escape from the trap she was in—and besides, the sf people invited her in.

The *Magazine of Fantasy and Science Fiction*, Joanna's primary market, was the benchmark venue for artistically ambitious sf. Female writers appeared regularly: Judith Merril, Zenna Henderson, Miriam Allen deFord, Carol Emshwiller, Leslie Bonnet, Jane Rice, Evelyn Smith, and Anne McCaffery all made the cover lineup in the sixties (seriously outnumbered, of course, by the *images* of women featured). Joanna's name appeared there too, for her slight ghost story "There Is Another Shore."[32] The artistically ambitious inner circle was a small world, and Joanna's promise had been noted. Damon Knight, co-founder, with editor and writer Judith Merril, of the "Milford" conference, reached out. In 1966 Joanna shared her first Milford workshop with an intelligent and eccentric gathering of novices and masters at The Anchorage, the rambling home of Knight and his wife, Kate Wilhelm, in Milford,

Pennsylvania (also Judith Merril's hometown). It was an intense introduction: there were forty-two writers that year, according to Samuel Delany, who was also attending his first "Milford."

The year Joanna "ran away" from her husband (they later divorced), 1966 was climactic in other ways too. She found a real job, teaching speech at Queensborough Community College; she "came out" as a lesbian, privately if not publicly ("coming out" can extend over years: Joanna also records "coming out" in 1969 and 1976), and made a momentous, life-changing decision:

> Long before I became a feminist in any explicit way . . . I had turned from writing love stories about women, in which women were losers, and adventure stories about men in which men were winners, to writing adventure stories about a woman in which the woman won. It was one of the hardest things I ever did in my life. These are stories about a sword-and-sorcery heroine called Alyx, and before writing the first I spent about two weeks in front of my typewriter, shaking.[33]

A new Joanna Russ story, "Mr. Wilde's Second Chance," appeared in October 1966 (*Magazine of Fantasy and Science Fiction*; collected in *The Hidden Side of the Moon*). Oscar, having died in poverty and disgrace, is given the opportunity to create a revision of his sorry career and qualify for heaven. He succeeds brilliantly—and then breaks the board that holds this absurd pastiche across his knee.

In 1967 Joanna returned to Cornell as an instructor, and the first "Alyx" stories appeared in *Orbit 2*, the second volume in Damon Knight's prestigious anthology series—"one of the chief expressions of the American version of science fiction's New Wave"[34]

## ALYX STORIES, 1967–1970

C. L. Moore's "Jirel of Joiry" is often cited as the first sword-and-sorcery female hero, but the claim should be nuanced: Jirel is a precursor. The first Jirel tale, "The Black God's Kiss,"[35] is a gorgeous Lovecraftian vision; three further appearances have diminishing effect. In her thigh-length doeskin tunic and metal shin guards, Jirel's a fine pulp-fiction pinup, but Joanna's fearless little pick-lock, ex-missionary, sometimes-pirate, talented amateur accountant was a genuine innovation. In "Alyx" Joanna found expression for her dawning feminism and, crucially, the attractive recurrent character so important to a genre audience. In his chapter "Alyx among the Genres" in Farah Mendlesohn's essay collection *On Joanna Russ*, Gary Wolfe lists all the many editions and appearances of these stories, to make the point: Alyx was a familiar figure in the sf field not only in the 1960s but for "much of the 1970s and early 1980s"[36]

The Alyx stories published in *Orbit 2* (1967) were "Bluestocking" and "I Thought She Was Afeared, before She Stroked My Beard." Damon Knight reversed the order of the two stories and changed both titles (sf writers had little control over the text of their books and stories: a situation Joanna hated[37]). "Bluestocking" became "The Adventuress"; "I Thought She Was Afeared . . ." became "I Gave Her Sack and Sherry." Joanna's order was restored in the Alyx collections, starting with the Gregg Press edition (1976), for which Samuel Delany wrote an introduction.

Knight probably felt that "Bluestocking" was obscure, but if one reads the viewpoint character as an avatar of Joanna herself (a safe bet in her longer fictions), the allusion to a proto-feminist intellectual movement makes sense. Alyx, we are told, arrived in Ourdh, the "richest and vilest of cities," as a missionary, "a neat, level-browed governessy person." She now trades, without apology for her sex, as a successful thief, open to any shady job opportunity. Joanna had arrived in the genre world as a ladylike writer of sad, uncanny tales: with the appearance of "Alyx" she announced herself as a gender-bending player of the male-ordered sword-and-sorcery game. The story was an instant classic: expert, warm-hearted, and very stylish. The city here called "Ourdh," with its jeweled courtesans and abject beggars, was already a (sub)genre staple. The plot couldn't be simpler, but the treatment is a revelation, transforming the sword-for-hire formula into internally realist fiction, with a dashing turn of speed, an ironic edge, and an "anomalous streak of quiet humanity." Edarra, a brattish teenage heiress, thinks she needs a rescuer. Our female hero mocks her, but they meet again at a splendid and ghastly society party. Alyx learns that Edarra really does need rescuing, and she gets herself and the young woman (plus a hefty sum in loot) safely out of town by commandeering a leaky fishing boat she finds unattended. The rest of the story comprises their seafaring exploits, Edarra's learning curve, and Alyx's tenderness for the girl who could be the daughter she's left behind. There's a monster (who startled the genre audience by being explicitly female). There are pirates, who board the vessel bent on rape and are summarily dealt with. There's the accidental fire that almost kills Alyx and completes Edarra's transition to competent adulthood. Just when the "unlikely couple" in this buddy movie are casting sidelong glances and wondering where their flirtatious closeness might be going, a handsome fisherman (unmarried, by the symbols painted on his boat) appears. Wise Alyx decides to recollect, with lip-smacking delight, a glorious, red-gold-bearded pirate she once enjoyed,[38] and the buddies go their separate ways.

In "I Thought She Was Afeared, until She Stroked My Beard" (Joanna's title), the wild hill-girl who will become "Alyx" is seventeen. Her husband is brutal and stupid: she mildly resents the beatings but rebels against the stupidity. One day she insists on telling him he's being cheated by the local smugglers. A fight ensues—and suddenly Alyx is free, an unexpectedly dead husband at her feet. She boards the pirate (or smugglers') vessel with a knife in her teeth, out-faces the rape-happy crew, and is adopted by the luxuriously bearded captain as a fierce, human pet and then (but he waits for her to come to him of her own free will) as a lover. But when she wants to become his business partner, she runs up against the same senseless barrier. ("Damn it. I am cleverer than you!" cries Alyx, bewildered). An exuberant and bloody shipboard battle interrupts the quarrel, and then she's off—to become, some years later and with minor inconsistencies, the Alyx in episode 1.

The third story, "The Barbarian,"[39] appeared in Knight's Orbit 3 (1968). Alyx is approaching age forty (in episode 1 she was thirty, the same age as Joanna), still plying her trade in Ourdh but now married to a "good man" who will play the damsel in distress role: a cypher used to propel the plot. Alyx agrees to work for a repellent "fat man" (unnamed) who claims to be immortal and wields "magical" devices: a pocket weapon that can vaporize walls, a cube that shows images of distant scenes. One night they invade the palace. When Alyx refuses to kill the governor's infant daughter (the fat man claims the baby will grow up to be a monster), things go badly wrong. Alyx evades capture but finds her husband struck down by a hideous fever, and she knows it's the fat man's revenge. Rapid deductions lead her to his lair, where strange lights play around the upper room of a ruined tower—but the stairway is blocked by an invisible barrier. Invoking an sf device first deployed in "Arena," by Fredric Brown, and also featured in a Star Trek episode,[40] she deduces that the barrier will let "nothing conscious" pass, and she falls forward through it, having briefly knocked herself out by applying pressure to "an artery at the back of her neck."[41] The fat man now claims he's a super-powered time traveler, invulnerable because he's wearing *in-er-tial dis-crim-in-ation* armor (another borrowing). Alyx employs the low-velocity tactic of sticking her fingers in his eyes and then smothers him with a cushion. She returns to Ourdh to find her man safely recovered.

The first Alyx story plays with the idea of lesbian, intergenerational desire between a young girl and a mother figure, a recurring signifier of alluring trespass in Joanna's fiction. The second pits teenage Alyx's wits and daring against the muscle power and gender superiority of the sexually alluring male pirate, forcing her to admit not defeat but incompatibility, and shifts her from fantasy into the real world by citing the Bosporus strait between modern Greece and Turkey, so named since ancient times.[42] The third completes the positioning of Alyx as female hero by providing her with a male heroine to defend. The character development is satisfying: Alyx at forty is older in self-knowledge, committed to her personal morality, and (less convincingly) instantly able to construe the fat man's limitations. In other ways this is the weakest story. The borrowed devices seem lazy, and the denouement needs too many "rapid deductions." Finally, we see a *settled* Alyx, perhaps on the brink of increasingly formulaic, sword-and-sorcery series success. But true to the only pattern in her career, Joanna's next work and her first novel, *Picnic on Paradise* (New York: Ace, 1968—the same year as *Orbit 3*), was a new beginning.

## PICNIC ON PARADISE

Alyx's fourth adventure scoops her out of science-fantasy land (snatched from execution by drowning in the ancient Mediterranean by the mysterious "Trans-Temporal Military Authority")[43] and deposits her in a wilderness of ice and snow. It's the winter-sports sector of a "resort planet" where a group of tourists, stranded in a warzone, need to be couriered to "Base B," a safe evacuation point. Alyx, as the story opens, has stepped through a sci-fi "portal" (conventionally, a doorway that connects two locations, irrespective of time and space) into a space-port first-class lounge full of eye-hurting futuristic décor and weirdly decorated naked giants. The officer in charge, a lieutenant, can't believe this tiny, middle-aged woman is the "Trans-Temp Agent" he was expecting. Alyx convinces him by tying him in knots (Alyx frequently proves that weight and height don't count against skill and daring, in her adventures) and strips off her own shift in polite response to her charges' nakedness, revealing a worn, scarred little body. The tourists are horrified! This isn't their kind of nudity. "You have on your history," says the artist, Raydos. "We're not used to that."

Alyx's abrupt shift into the far future succeeds, Gary Wolfe believes, because her transition to sfnal "modernity" had been established in "The Barbarian."[44] Taking the initiative, she tells the decorated giants that she's a "Murderer" by trade and accepts the lieutenant's explanation of her mission without a trace of bewilderment. The resort planet, a disputed asset in a "commercial war," is under automated surveillance "up and down the electromagnetic spectrum." The slightest perceived threat will be obliterated. That means no fires, no weapons (but Alyx is allowed plastic substitutes for her knives), no transportation, no food processing, nothing airborne. But Base B is not too far away, and the terrain, though snowy and icebound, is easy. If anything moves in the sky, their best bet, advises the lieutenant, is to get down on hands and knees and "pretend to be yaks." When Alyx learns that the party is to be joined by a renowned outdoors expert, she wonders why (the expense of that scooping operation!) she's being wasted on a picnic. The lieutenant reveals that despite rumors, Alyx is so far the *only* "Trans-Temp Agent." Forget the tourists; this could be a test of her potential.

Provided with miraculous snowsuits, plastic crossbows, and luxury trail food, the party sets out. Gunnar, the media-star specialist, challenges Alyx's leadership, but when she's proved she can hurt him, he develops an irritating crush instead. The older woman, Maudey, deprived of her rejuvenation drugs, is fretful. Her daughter Iris (a relationship they hate to acknowledge) is an insufferably bouncy, thirty-three-year-old adolescent. Raydos, the decent and friendly artist, uses an eye implant that gives him problems, Gavrily the "Conaman" (or corporation man) never stops defending his war profiteering, and the smug post-Buddhist nuns have a forbidden stash of dangerous drugs. The going is easy: the difficulty, for Alyx, is putting up with these "affluent drug-saturated technology junkies, whose primary activity is psychologizing each others' smallest interactions."[45] For peace she walks with Machine, an appealing young man who wears a "Trivia" helmet to shut out a media-saturated world. They reach Base B—only to find that it's been obliterated. Gunnar says there's a Control Embassy three hundred miles farther into the mountains. Alyx directs a raid to capture fresh rations (from the robots restoring the base for the other party in the war), and on they go. There's nothing else to do.

When James Blish, editor for the first "Alyx" collection, pointed out a few continuity problems, Joanna's response was a cheerful "The hell with it."[46] Stories are not blueprints, but an inconsistency in this episode may be a warning to the reader. Alyx should be forty, if she was "scooped" after the events of "The Barbarian," but though her body is scarred and there's grey in her hair, she's now "twenty-six"—a female hero still young enough to make terrible mistakes.

The tourists hate their new rations but nevertheless have to be physically restrained from gobbling a week's supply in a meal. The cold increases, the paths are dangerous; they don't even have spikes on their boots. One night, Alyx has to kill a giant white bear—nobody told her dangerous Earth animals have been introduced to Paradise for sport. Her exploit restores morale, but then Maudey, the weakest of the party, falls to her death. Iris is devastated—until the nuns drug her into giggling oblivion. Alyx, to whom grief is necessary and right, is outraged, and she takes to sneaking off at night to make noisy love with Machine—*Picnic's* male heroine. It's a failure of judgement: Gunnar's jealous resentment is soon obvious. At the final pass, in hellish weather and zero visibility, disaster strikes. Machine falls in an ice chimney, and Gunnar makes sure he dies. Alyx kills Gunnar in a rage of grief and swallows a suicidal handful of the nuns' evil pills.

Iris and the nuns nurse Alyx through her breakdown, and all the women reach safety. Despite the fatalities, the mission is declared a resounding success. As Alyx walks away, undaunted, saluting the ghost of her lost lover, we learn that the Trans-Temp Military Authority has great plans for her.

Schematically, the action of *Picnic on Paradise* is a reprise, in more challenging conditions, of Alyx and Edarra's voyage in "Bluestocking." Alyx takes grown-up babies on a "voyage" punctuated by escalating challenges; a young woman (Iris) transitions to adulthood in her care. But there's a major step up in technique: vividly delineated secondary characters, gripping interpersonal conflicts, and a tense, unexpected, yet inevitable working out of consequences. Standard in construction, superb in execution, this is an immensely satisfying fantasy adventure. Alyx herself is more convincing, more individual than ever, and if the commercial war the "ebony-skinned" lieutenant describes doesn't make much sense, the same could be said for a real, proxy war in Southeast Asia, in which many dark-skinned young Americans were dying for no good reason, when *Picnic* was written and published.

"What really differentiates Alyx . . . *is not her sex, but her character.* Unlike Fafhrd, Alyx is not callow; unlike Elric, there is no doubt Alyx is a hero: tough, smart, practical, competent, brave. (And, notably, explicitly not conventionally beautiful, unlike most contemporary tough, smart, etc., female leads.) . . . Nor does she suffer much internal anguish in these tales. In short, unlike her male counterparts, Alyx is not only someone you can root for, but someone you might actually be able to stand being."[47]

Niall Harrison's "non-sexual" point of difference captures, better than I could express it, "Alyx's" sexual-political impact. Much of Joanna's fictional and critical work in sf was still to come, including all her explicitly feminist fiction, but *Picnic on Paradise*, so absorbing, so undeniably excellent, may be the best work she ever did, simply for the cause of female writers and readers of sf.

## THE SECOND INQUISITION

Years later, Joanna would bring Alyx of Ourdh out of retirement for "A Game Of Vlet" (*Magazine of Fantasy and Science Fiction*, February 1974), an atypical adventure not included in the collections. But first there was "The Second Inquisition" (*Orbit 6*, ed. Damon Knight, 1970),[48] an "Alyx" novella set in the real world's recent past, in which Alyx does not appear, and a female hero from the future is cast as a psychoactive fantasy: the violent yet consoling daydream of a lonely young girl.

The year is 1925, on the eve of the birth of genre science fiction.[49] The story, told in dramatic vignettes, like "My Dear Emily," opens with a young girl's fascinated observation of the summer visitor in her home—apparently a paying guest. Uncannily tall, like the far future humans in *Picnic on Paradise*, with coppery skin and dark hair rough as a pan scourer, the stranger is probably lucky nobody in this small town really knows what "colored people" look like (in 1925 the Ku Klux Klan, largest fraternal organization in America, staged a march forty thousand strong in Washington, D.C.). She gives the girl a notorious 1924 bestseller, *The Green Hat*, advising her that it's a very bad book. That night, in her dreams of "Hispano-Suizas, shingled hair and tragic eyes,"[50] the girl feels the visitor's disapproval, and it spoils her fun. Next morning there are parental reprisals, which the visitor defuses by claiming she recommended *The Green Hat* to the girl. She adds that she destroyed some shocking "drawings" hidden in the novel's endpapers. The girl's bullying father and submissive mother, whose plaintive cry, "Oh, the poor woman, the poor woman," is the tragic chorus of this story, are defeated, confused by the suggestion that one of them has been drawing dirty pictures.

In the next scene the girl and her new friend talk about H. G. Wells's *The Time Machine*. The girl has invented a game, asking people "whether they are Eloi or Morlocks."[51] The visitor is a Morlock: a murderer, that is, who lives a terrible life. Her black uniform is in the wardrobe. She's one of "half a thousand Morlocks" who rule the worlds. But the realist-seeming *Green Hat* episode is overturned when our narrator admits that the visitor is imaginary. She's talking to her own reflection, in the black glass of a window at night.

In "Alyx among the Genres" Gary Wolfe observes that "The Second Inquisition" has "a great deal to do with the kind of fantasies available to young girls, in the popular mainstream fiction of the day."[52] Teenage fantasy stories, sometimes science fictional, typically enact a rite of passage. When the fantasy emerges in response to a major life problem, boundaries are blurred: careful reading shows it *was* the girl herself who sneaked *The Green Hat* from her parents' adults-only shelf.[53] Fantasy steps in again when the narrator is doomed to miss her first country-club dance because her father is unwell. In reality, family friends agree to take her. Our narrator gives the role of rescuer to the thrilling visitor. The dance is an excruciating failure for this shy teenager until another weirdly tall, dark-skinned stranger turns up. A deadly enemy has tracked the visitor down. The girl is whisked away in a stolen car, helps to booby-trap the kitchen of her home, and lingers (when ordered to leave) to witness an expert, brutal execution.

The next escapade is equally exciting: the visitor acquires a boyfriend, a Polish garage mechanic called Bogalusa Joe, who has advanced ideas about "colored people." The girl spies on them having sex, in the dark on the garden swing, as scared and thrilled as when she saw murder done.

One day she comes downstairs to find her parents in a trance. The visitor appears "wrapped in my mother's spring coat." Throwing off this disguise, she's in black from head to foot: it's the uniform of the Trans-Temporal Military Authority (an organization that has clearly grown, hugely, since Alyx was their first "agent" in *Picnic on Paradise*). Other "Morlocks" arrive. The Authority is at war with itself; this modest home is the unlikely venue for a violent sorting-out. The visitor, accused of presuming "on being that woman's granddaughter," loses an eye in a duel and is dragged off, defeated, by an angry Morlock who warns our narrator to keep her mouth shut. Her parents wake to find blood on the rug: their daughter's had a nosebleed.

The visitor is then reported as having left town on a train ("to join the circus," says our narrator's mother). But she appears once more, just before high school starts, looking out of the mirror inside the girl's closet door. Dressed in black and silver, her lost eye replaced by a dazzling implant, she talks about decadent Eloi, sinister Morlocks, alien worlds, and gulfs of time and space. "My dear," she says, "I wished to take you with me but that's impossible." But the figure in the mirror is the girl herself, in the "Trans-Temporal Military Authority" costume she made, and she can no longer cling to belief. She must face her father's temper and his heart disease, and her defeated mother's sick smile, all alone. No more stories.

"The Second Inquisition" is the most puzzling of Joanna's fusions of life and art, but if the consoling visitor is or will become a relative of Joanna's female hero (the "Alyx" cycle is a serpent that eats its own tail[54]), then the "Trans-Temporal Military Authority" may be read, here and elsewhere, as an avatar of the genre and community of science fiction itself. Was Joanna, in 1969, already planning to renounce her dream worlds? In a sense, perhaps. Her next new beginning (after *And Chaos Died*, the stand-alone novel also published in 1970) would transform science fiction into modern art for a cause.

The John Jay Chapman epigram,[55] when set beside the title, suggests that for Joanna there *is* another challenge, after we outface our neighbors. Perhaps the "second inquisition" arrives from the future and asks (if we accept the mission), "How do you plan to change the world?"

# CHAPTER 2

## JOANNA RUSS AND THE NEW WAVE
Experiment and Experience in the World of *And Chaos Died*

> For many composers the crisis is both aesthetic and sociological. . . . [F]
> or other[s] . . . the two dimensions cannot be separated. . . . From this
> perspective, the evidence of profound public antipathy to serialist music
> cannot be ignored and must be translated into a transformed composi-
> tional practice or risk a music that cannot communicate, because no one
> will listen.
>
> —Georgina Born, *Rationalizing Culture*

> [O]n the nineteenth day he threw himself against one of the portholes,
> flattening himself as if in immediate collapse, the little cousin he had
> lived with all his life become so powerful in the vicinity of its big relative
> that he could not bear it. Everything was in imminent collapse.
>
> —Joanna Russ, *And Chaos Died*

Modernism can be hard to pin down. For Baudelaire modernity was in the
stamp that *time* prints on our feeling, the moving edge of the present moment.
Virginia Woolf said writers had to get off their pedestals and describe the very
ordinary character of life itself. Georgina Born sees serial music striving for

such ideological perfection it almost ceases to function as music, while Paul March-Russell sticks with the classic modernist project of finding new kinds of transcendence in a godless world (a task for which science fiction should be well suited). Perhaps modernism has meant something different to every artist or thinker to whom the label has been applied. Thankfully, the mid-twentieth-century iteration of this cultural revolution reached American sf in a fixed form and on a precise date: in January 1966, when Judith Merril, "the first lady of sf,"[1] devoted her "Books" column in the *Magazine of Fantasy and Science Fiction* to the U.K. magazine *New Worlds*, and a literary / sf movement, soon to be enshrined in Merril's 1968 anthology, *England Swings SF*, essentially comprising writers Michael Moorcock, J. G. Ballard, and Brian Aldiss.

Merril, by far the most influential woman in American science fiction of the mid-twentieth century, was the books editor and frequently also wrote the "Books" column from 1965 to 1969. It was her dream to see *literary* science fiction accepted as mainstream literature, but her hopes had been dashed time and again. The atom bomb and the space race had changed nothing, nor did the McCarthy era, when sf became "for a time, virtually the only vehicle of public dissent."[2] The "New Wave" (a term Merril may never have used) offered a fresh approach. Instead of aspiring to become respectable, sf could be *more* challenging, *more* experimental, and join the mainstream via the 1960s avant-garde. But the U.K. writers' moving-edge science fiction (according to its detractors) was nihilistic, pornographic—often extremely violent and detached from any traditional form of imaginary future. Algis Budrys, writing for *Galaxy*, spoke for many in the sf establishment when he expressed his indignation:

> A story by J. G. Ballard, as you know, calls for people who don't think. One begins with characters who regard the physical universe as a mysterious and arbitrary place, and who would not dream of trying to understand its actual laws. Furthermore, in order to be the protagonist of a J. G. Ballard novel . . . you must have cut yourself off from the entire body of scientific education. In this way, when the world disaster—be it wind or water—comes upon you, you are under absolutely no obligation to do anything about it but sit and worship it.[3]

Although the literary mainstream remained elusive, the American "New Wave," more diverse than the British model, enriched and energized the genre: improving style, loosening taboos, and generally bringing the imaginary future up to date. But a cultural revolution of a different order was about to combine with the British influence and bring greater changes. In the dismal 1950s Joanna and her friends, "artist-intellectual" young women, had few dreams beyond that glum determination *not to be like their parents*. By the time Merril launched her avant-garde campaign and Joanna—now teaching at Cornell, where Second Wave feminism was brewing—joined the progressive, literary cadre of the sf community, everyone seemed to be dreaming, and (as if in Brian Aldiss's "psychedelic" novel *Barefoot in the Head* [New York: Faber and Faber, 1969])[4] dreams and nightmares were inextricably entangled.

Race riots and insurrection riots, fueled by poverty and hopelessness, erupted in black ghettos. Civil rights marches and antiwar protests swept aside the barriers between young people and government, and the young were appalled at what they saw and learned. Contraceptive pills became safe and available; mind-expanding drugs, allegedly, opened the doors of perception; and in the party atmosphere between bouts, the music was inseparable from the revolution.[5] By the end of the decade homosexuals had found the courage to fight back against persecution, in the Stonewall riots, and radical feminism (it's hard to establish a single foundation event) was a visible political entity.

Fatal casualties on American soil were highly significant but relatively few. In the general population, support for the protest culture was never great, but for a while, in the moment, it felt as if that favorite sf trope, a world utterly changed, was possible, was actually happening.

REVIEWS, 1966–1971

Joanna's first professional review appeared in the *Magazine of Fantasy and Science Fiction* in December 1966. The book was *Strange Signposts: An Anthology of the Fantastic*. She dismissed the collection as lazy and disappointing: "This is one of that damned flood of anthologies that do nothing but cheapen the market." It was a bold beginning, but she clearly knew the Lovecraftian barrel the anthologists were scraping. On her second outing, in October 1967, she didn't notice that the disappointing James Blish novel she'd been sent (*The Warriors of the Day*) was a reprint of an early title, and she could not take the adventures of Elric of Melniboné (in Michael Moorcock's *Stealer of Souls* and *Stormbringer*), seriously. The cloud-capped palaces were nice, but Elric was just an unusually moody sword-and-sorcery puppet, innocent of "the common operations of intelligence." In January 1968 she praised Roger Zelazny's *Lord of Light* for its imaginative transposition of Western sf tropes into Hindu/Buddhist mythology and culture while regretting the weakness in plot and characterization (typical of Zelazny):

> Kali, who is as beautiful as rainclouds, whose feet are covered in blood, and who wears a necklace made from the skulls of her children whom she has slain . . . is only a tepidly conventional bitch without even the force to be genuinely destructive, let alone the "disfiguring and degenerative disease" that Sam calls her.[6]

*The Mind Parasites*, by Colin Wilson, was a "Lovecraft novel," according to the publishers; it was Lovecraft "in the *Boy's Life* Gee Whiz tradition," according to the reviewer: "One of the worst books I have ever read, and very enjoyable, but then I didn't have to pay for it."

In July she reviewed *Ashes, Ashes*, by René Barjavel, translated by Damon Knight (unintentionally funny, and "not worth waiting twenty years for") and *A Torrent of Faces*, a semi-aquatic utopian world-building project by James Blish and Norman L. Knight. The world-build was fascinating; there were thrilling set pieces, but the storytelling was inadequate. Judith Merril's *The Best of the Best* anthology—the editor's choice from her "Year's Best" collections, 1955 to 1960—should perhaps have been handled with tender care, given Merril's position. Joanna admired J. G. Ballard's "Prima Belladonna"; stories by Fritz Leiber, Carol Emshwiller, Avram Davidson, Cordwainer Smith, and Damon Knight were also excellent. But the editor had so consistently favored the human factor and the "poignant" over hardware, hard science, or speculation that the effect was "surprisingly monotonous." Happily, the book was nice and fat, and nobody would have to read all twenty-nine stories at once.

Previously, in the November 1967 column, the queen of literary sf (defending her territory as the prophetess of the "New Thing") had taken a solid swing at Damon Knight's *Orbit* series, with the cunning stroke that *Orbit 2* was practically devoid of science fiction and only notable for "literary merit." Joanna's fine and highly original Alyx stories (not named) had been caught in the crossfire as "delightfully literate but . . . routine." If Joanna intended to revenge a snub, she was swiftly punished. Merril soon delivered a deviously tepid review of Joanna's terrific *Picnic on Paradise* that must have been a stinging blow to the new writer.[7]

Joanna would contribute twenty-five review articles to the *Magazine of Fantasy and Science Fiction* between 1966 and 1980, "the bulk of her reviewing in the field." She covered "some 110 books of all descriptions," providing, according to Edward James, "a minicourse in how to write science fiction . . . and how to review science fiction, too."[8] With one definite exception she seems never to have chosen the books she covered. She reviewed what she was sent, often warmly appreciative, never intimidated. Her style was entertaining and analytical rather than "evaluative."[9] She could be severe (or worse, wickedly funny) but always gave her reasons and examined her own opinions,[10] consistently meeting the great William Atheling Jr.'s magisterial criteria in every respect but one.

> Obviously then, I think a good critic in any field is a useful citizen who is positively obliged to be harsh toward bad work. By a good critic I mean a man with a good ear, a love for his field at its best, and a broad and detailed knowledge of the techniques of that field.[11]

Despite the anthologies flame war (and misgivings over Elric's firmness of character) Joanna treated the U.K. "New Wave" with respect and understanding. She had no time for Ballard's recycled motifs in "You: Coma: Marilyn Monroe," but his "Prima Belladonna" was the real thing and "retrospectively justified" Merril's pet project. She admired "everything about" Aldiss's Robbe-Grillet-meets-Harold-Pinter novel, *Report on Probability A* except its length, and Moorcock's *Final Programme* inspired lyrical praise for "a kind of literary Cubism: a shifting, unstable, shallow foreground in which every element is constantly entering into new associations with every other."[12] Yet in many respects she had the profile of a seasoned "fan" critic: combining stubborn affection for the old good stuff (Poul Anderson, Hal Clement) and an insistence on "real hard science," with a guilty passion for the romanticism of the humanist fantastic. Some of her highest praise is awarded to Jack Vance's graceful planetary romance, *Emphyrio*, Keith Roberts's post-Renaissance alternate history, *Pavanne* (*Magazine of Fantasy and Science Fiction* [April 1969]), and James Blish's "terrifying" *Black Easter* (December 1968). Ray Bradbury "does everything wrong," but her response to his collection *I Sing the Body Electric* (July 1970) borders on reverence.[13]

Between 1966 and 1971 Joanna encountered few female writers. Carol Emshwiller, Kit Reed, and Katherine MacLean were praised for anthologized stories. *Transplant* (April 1969), by U.K. writer Margaret Jones, was, sadly, a mess: "When the British are bad, they are very bad." Kate Wilhelm's *Let the Fire Fall* (September 1969) was "a book that shows uncommon intelligence," "brimful of the details of ordinary life," impressive, and subtly, radically *different*. Wilhelm writes "in a style Henry James once defined as feminine: that is, the accents never fall where you expect them, big events are over in a flash or revealed obliquely, and the novel always presses on to something else," and though not the usual thing in sf, it works. Anne McCaffery's *The Ship Who Sang* (July 1970) was a fix-up.[14] The early stories, published when McCaffery was "just a pup" (she was ten years older than Joanna), really should have been revised. Joanna interrogates the "deformed baby grows up to be the imprisoned heart of a starship" conceit mercilessly, dwelling on developmental problems and suggesting the idea needs a lot more work. She then admires the book's "contagious joyfulness" and wants McCaffery to write "more of the same" now that she's got the hang of it. It's a condescending review that exactly mirrors Judith Merril's dismissal of *Picnic on Paradise*: probably provoked here not by factional rivalry but by McCaffery's choice of an assimilated, *feminine* sf style.

Typically, Judith Merril, in her columns, would set a topic, which she would illustrate with evaluative assessments (reticent of "spoilers") of new books that suited the theme. Joanna took the riskier approach of *criticizing* science fiction: applying the analytical skill, the patience (and the cutting wit) of a demanding teacher. Unlike Merril—or Merril's archenemy, the waspish Algis Budrys—she had no agenda (or none she wanted to announce), aside from her drive to eradicate the crime of leaving the gender roles of midcentury USA intact in the distant future. Frederik Pohl's *The Age of the Pussyfoot* (the example she would also use in her "The Image of Women in Science Fiction" essay)[15] was a typical sinner. She was not partisan about genre classification—regretting that Moorcock's *Final Programme* had been published as science fiction ("which it is not") and happy that Blish's *Black Easter* came out on a mainstream list—but fake-sf blockbusters, like Robert Merle's *The Day of the Dolphin*, and Ira Levin's massive, "smooth as Crisco" *This Perfect Day*, sequeloid to Huxley's *Brave New World*, made her furious.

How many times can one take apart a commercial mechanism? Readers are timid, so the book is very slow. Readers want value for money, so the book is very long; readers have no background, so the book avoids explaining anything technical, readers are not literate, so the style is very simple; readers like sex but are conservative, so the sex is very mild. Readers (you, dear reader) are stupid, so the hero's final sophistication barely approaches that of the feeblest member of the audience.[16]

In the same column, February 1971, Joanna sees Poul Anderson's *Satan's World* as "a sad example" of what happens when an author writes "more of the same" too often. The quirks of Anderson's series characters, Nicolas Van Rjin with his whores and his "motley crew," were once fun, but they've become distasteful. Or it might be that Joanna herself had changed and could no longer accept the endemic sexism she had ignored for so long. After an excursion to the *Village Voice* in September (reviewing books about magic and introducing readers to Aleister Crowley's instructions for sacrificing a frog), in the November 1971 "Books" column Joanna "outed" her own sexual politics: "Knowing my radical feminist tendencies, the Kindly Editor only sent me good books (by men) this month."[17] The good books were *The Light Fantastic*, edited by Harry Harrison, *Partners in Wonder*, a Harlan Ellison anthology with the "cherry-and-whipped cream" bonus of a quirky Ellison introduction, and James Blish's *The Day after Judgement* (part 2 of the Black Easter Apocalypse, with a neat twist in the devil's tale)—but the star of the column, examined at length, was Shulamith Firestone's *The Dialectic of Sex*. Her *Magazine of Fantasy and Science Fiction* reviews would continue for another decade, but a watershed (or a Rubicon) had been crossed.[18]

## ESSAYS, 1969–1971

Around twenty of Joanna's essays are collected in *Magic Mommas, Trembling Sisters, Puritans and Perverts* (1985); *To Write Like a Woman* (1995), and in *The Country You Have Never Seen* (2007). Some first appeared in feminist journals and engage with sexual politics; others are foundation works of academic sf theory or treat specific authors or works in depth. Two that date from her highly productive early period consider the nature of genre writing.

"Daydream Literature and Science Fiction" (*Extrapolation* [December 1969)]; collected in *The Country You Have Never Seen*), asks why certain works of the fantastic, including the science fiction pulps, are loved and revered, when the essentials of fiction writing—plot, characterization, a realized setting, narrative progression—are vestigial or absent? What do readers find satisfying, and why are the writers getting fiction so wrong? She discusses four authors: A. E. van Vogt, Edgar Allan Poe, David Lindsay (Scottish author of *A Voyage to Arcturus* [London: Methuen, 1920], a classic interplanetary fantasy),[19] and the Welsh sf writer David Redd[20] (at the time, author of two published stories, "Sunbeam's Caress" and "Sundown"). Her conclusion, after close reading of these texts, is that both readers and writers are indifferent to the quality of the telling because, like users of pornography, they bypass the printed story to create their own vicarious experience. Fans who love to fantasize about being "Slans"—A. E. van Vogt's persecuted, discreetly tentacled, superior posthumans—don't need fully realized fiction from van Vogt. As long as Poe uses emotive words—"thrilling," "awful," "horrid"—his big scenes need be no more than "a mist of strange, twangling instruments . . . and overblown rhetoric." The fiction need only be a matrix—*schematic*, like her college students' bad writing. "Daydream literature," Joanna observes, "requires a lot of imagination—in the reader." But this insight into genre's appeal is not pursued. The direct link with actual pornography is not (yet) explored,[21] and the rationale for including Lindsay and Redd—creators, as Joanna shows, of unorthodox but original and compelling poetic effects—is not clear. Her final judgement—that seeking vicarious experience is bad, and daydreamers should grow up—is disappointingly bland.

In "The Wearing Out of Genre Materials" (*College English* [October 1971], collected in in *The Country You Have Never Seen*), a rich and interesting essay, the issue is built-in obsolescence. Here the central conceit of *any* story is, originally, a daydream. The finished work is a compromise between this germinal, "wished for situation, action or scene"[22] and constraints the author is forced to accept, by "reason and conscience," to create believable fiction. (References to Sophocles's *Oedipus Rex* and observations from George Bernard Shaw may or may not help the reader along here). Exposed to the changes of the real world, these *real-izations* of the author's "emotional highpoints" must start to decay. The fictional accretions that made the "conceit" representative of human life wear out and no longer serve their purpose; but this depreciation inspires new writers, attracted by the original conceit, to invent fresh circumstances. Joanna takes her examples from Damon Knight's collection *A Century of Science Fiction* (New York: Simon and Schuster, 1962),[23] in which Knight has helpfully placed three "Robot Revolt" stories in chronological order: Ambrose Bierce's "Moxton's Master" (1899), Isaac Asimov's "Reason" (1941), and Brian Aldiss's "But Who Can Replace a Man?" (1958). All Bierce has to do is propose that (on some dark and stormy night) a robot might rebel!—and this is a central conceit in its "Innocence." Asimov is pleasurably compelled to invent mechanisms for the revolt and its success or suppression; this is "Plausibility." For Aldiss in 1958, revolt is redundant. Man is no longer mighty, but the bewilderment of the confounded rebels is so touching that the artist has recovered all the original value of the conceit—and perhaps more. But this is the "Decadence" of an idea, and after decadence there is only the death of endless repetition. The "wished for situation" has no potency left.

Joanna proposes that in contemporary fiction the "emotional highpoints" of genre are wearing out at an alarming rate. Detective stories are "dead," Romance is "dead," and so on. For the artist who can only find satisfaction at the moving edge, working with a living *novum* (a "new thing": Croatian sf scholar Darko Suvin appropriated this Latin term, now widely used, to describe any science fiction innovation), she offers science fiction as a resort safe from the "graveyard of dead narrative."[24] Science fiction cannot, by definition, run out of "Innocent" ideas . . . and here the proposal fails. "Reason and conscience" compel us to admit (as Joanna would recognize in a later essay, "Towards an Aesthetic of Science Fiction") that science fiction "is, of course, literature." Its novel conceits are as liable to decay, if the "wearing out" process is inevitable, as any others.

Joanna does not seem to have revised her essays. If she couldn't remember a date or the source of a quotation, her footnote text will read, even in the collected edition, "Sorry, can't remember."[25] If she changed her mind, she published the change but did not suppress or condemn the earlier statement. The impression, very different from her reviews, where she rarely offers an unsupported opinion, is of a quick-witted, erudite scholar of the genre tossing out ideas for her friends—*here, have a look at this*—with careless immediacy. Her nonfiction, like her fiction, records a "moving edge" of ideas: few of them sacred, none set in stone.

Joanna's short story output in these years, aside from the Alyx cycle, was slim. In "This Afternoon" (*Cimarron Review* [February 1968]; collected in *The Hidden Side of the Moon*) an American tourist meets an otherworldly creature in a French forest; with more than a hint of homosexual desire, the satyr comes off worse in the encounter. "A Short and Happy Life" (*Magazine of Fantasy and Science Fiction* [June 1969]; collected in *The Hidden Side of the Moon*) mocks multiple-choice exams and the idea that creativity can be quantified. In "The Throaways" (*Consumption* [Summer 1969]); collected in *The Hidden Side of the Moon*), a slightly more substantial satire, two ladies who lunch, a Traditionalist and her friend, the Fashionable, meet at a ca-*fet*-eria and score style points off each other, as the food of the moment—a glob of steaming "fet" (the story is full of absurd word play)—squirms between them. They are united on the inconceivable eeriness of waking up "with the same décor as the night before around you," but a daring mention of actual "Things," or "Permanents," panics the Traditionalist, who hurries off to a reassuring Demonstration. The Fashionable is left weeping for the impossible dream of a trendy culture that is not disposable. The sharp-edged "Window-Dressing" (*New Worlds of Fantasy 2* [New York: Ace, 1970]; collected in *The Hidden Side of the Moon*) is the story form of Joanna's most successful short play. A class-conscious storefront mannequin, hoping for true love, is kidnapped by the boy who stares at her through the plate glass, and she suffers a tragic awakening. He's not a Princeton man and knows nothing of F. Scott Fitzgerald! She attempts to flee and literally falls apart. Her decapitated body becomes a joke décor item in a painter's studio.

"The Man Who Could Not See Devils" (in *Alchemy and Academe*, edited by Anne McCaffery [New York: Doubleday, 1970]; collected in *The Zanzibar Cat*), more fantasy than sf, is set in a medieval-style world where everyone sees angels and devils, and magical curses are effective. The narrator, blind to supernatural policing, is a danger to society. He escapes from his family before they kill him but becomes an outcast, invulnerable and miserable. The story ends happily when he finds his way to a city, where a gang of thieves recognizes that a criminal who can't be touched by magic is a major asset. We leave the narrator as he wonders if his immunity might one day become commonplace and speculates (like Alyx in "The Barbarian") about a scientific and rational future.

Four nongenre stories are marked by a new, feminist consciousness. "Visiting" (*Manhattan Review* [Fall 1967]) and "Visiting Day" (*South* 2, no. 1 [1970]), both collected in *The Hidden Side of the Moon*, though appearing in different venues three years apart, are closely linked. In the short, elliptical "Visiting" two women walk in a wintery public garden in Manhattan. The narrator's internal monologue, about the music she's composing—"I want four voices, tenor, soprano, bass and trumpet; baroque trumpet"—runs in counterpoint with her judgement on poor Lispeth, "a poetess at seventeen," who has since "ground out, from the mill between her thighs," a husband, three children, and a desirable three-quarter-acre plot in the suburbs. Lispeth's only topic is that she's desperate to get away from her children. In "Visiting Day" the same points are made in a more conventional and more dramatic narrative. It's winter again. The narrator is divorced. Lispeth is a faculty wife—a grown up child who "looks seventeen" and wears "pink velour bell-bottomed pants" with "a white crocheted blouse that leaves her arms bare." Eager to talk intellectual feminism, she banishes her children and the nanny, but soon she's tipping brandy into her coffee, and then dispenses with the coffee. She wanders into the snowy garden, where she falls, and there is suddenly a tragic crisis. The self-congratulatory tone of these pieces is more sympathetic if the "Lispeth" character is read as a grim fate avoided rather than a real, fictionalized friend.

"The View from This Window" (*Quark* 1 [New York: Paperback Library, 1970]; collected in *The Hidden Side of the Moon*) could be the sketch for an abandoned campus novel. A junior academic, shivering through the winter in her rented room, meets Alan, a student actor, via a theatrically inclined male colleague (who gropes the narrator at every opportunity, behavior she pretends she enjoys). She falls in love with the boy, woos him with tickets for the circus, and wins him (responsibly! They've both brought condoms!) in a quirky New York apartment she's borrowed for the overnight trip. The romance is faintly impersonal: "Alan" is charming but (like many literary heroines) essentially the distillation of a beloved time and place. The "wished for situation" seems to be university life itself: the happiness the narrator finds in her scholarly penury; medieval music solos; student conversations and experimental movie shows; a bold girl student in a crackly black vinyl dress. The "view" is the view at night from the glass block of the Students' Union (a cliché of campus architecture of the time); an extension of light into darkness; an intoxicating sense that wish and actuality, interior and exterior life, have become one.

Elation bubbles through the "The View from This Window" but comes packaged with sexual harassment, privation, and job insecurity, and is strangely contradicted in a preface of proto-quotations from *The Female Man* (already written, or drafted, at this time):

> Whoever I am and wherever I come from, I am certainly not going to tell you.
>
> I really spring from a people who embed sapphires surgically in their foreheads, whose lips are set with metal foil, who have no teeth, no hands and no eyelids. . . .
>
> On the other hand, I materialized in a laboratory rented from the Harvard Special Researches Project and had to be taught the words for bed, table, chair, while they took my knife away from me, and looking warily into each other's eyes, we wondered which was the less civilized.[26]

"The Precious Object" (*Red Clay Reader* 7 (November 1970); collected in *The Zanzibar Cat*) is another celebration of a time and a place, rich in sensory detail (the Polish Bakery with the 15-watt bulbs, the garbage on the staircase), and also defined by a "precious object" of desire, but even less stable: full of multiple choices and contradictions. The narrator, frankly known as Joanna, lives with Rose (who will appear again in *On Strike against God*), a "wise fat girl" trapped in an apparently sexless relationship with a married man. A homosexual neighbor, "Tay," offers Joanna a better job than her current "typing and filing." He's lovely: she decides to fall in love. The real Joanna is, of course, a lesbian (but not exclusively, it seems). "Tay's" motives are unclear; maybe he has an open mind and an easygoing partner! More probably (as is signaled in the foreword and an insistently unreliable narrative), the "not-quite-fantasy" of a sexual affair with a gay male friend adds the shine of intensity to scenes from *La Vie Bohème* in 1960s New York.

Samuel Delany, in an online memoir, identifies Baird Searles as the object of desire and the "better job" as Joanna's role in producing a radio play version of Delany's *The Star Pit*, by WBAI-FM, a noncommercial New York radio station.[27]

The domestic, romantic concerns in these nongenre fictions, the clothes as signifiers (Lispeth's girlish lace blouse and pink pants; a student's vinyl dress), the unstable, associative narrative style all seem a willful defiance of Joanna's discovery, at college, that "female" concerns had no place in great literature. Her second novel also embraces domestic themes: nursing and nurturing; the coded-feminine ability to perceive and meet others' needs. But this hot female core is safely buried in layers of New Wave style, bravura sf exposition, and dispatches from the turbulent, idealistic American culture wars.

### AND CHAOS DIED

In Joanna's second novel, Jai Vedh, a far-future professional "decorator" with a vacuum in his soul, meets a colony of insouciant superhumans and learns to "turn on, tune in and drop out."[28] He was created by a Joanna who has almost vanished from the record—the hip, bohemian young woman trying to make a living in the minor arts in New York in the Swinging Sixties: never a flower child, definitely a wild child. Published two years after *Picnic on Paradise*, as another Ace Special, *And Chaos Died* was a Nebula Award nominee, fourth runner-up in the annual Locus poll, and reprinted several times in the first edition. Robert Silverberg's cover copy for the Gregg Press hardcover (1978) sums up the appeal: "I wouldn't really call it a novel at all; I'd call it a trip." But the book has not aged well in public opinion. Rigorously imagined experiences of telepathy and other psi powers were challenging even for the times,[29] and a perceived sexual-political crime in the first pages has proved a roadblock for Russ's twenty-first-century audience.[30]

Jai Vedh, a "desperate, quiet, cultured man" from Old Earth, of partly Hindu ethnic origin, suffers a nervous collapse on his first interplanetary journey. The vacuum in his soul overwhelms him, in the presence of the huge vacuum outside the starship's fluctuating hull. When he's sedated after his breakdown, the ship "explodes." He wakes in an escape capsule he's sharing, bizarrely, with the ship's Captain (he remembers the face from a brochure). Jai, the professional decorator, recognizes their landing spot as a designer pleasure garden (there's a path around a lake, going nowhere: people always like those), but there's no other sign of sentient life until a woman appears, greets them without surprise, and offers, speaking "Galactica" (aka American English), to take them to her house. She's wearing a short, deceptively simple dress, beautifully cut, and no underwear. Choosing her words with difficulty (Jai somehow sees images of this difficulty, in his mind), she tells Jai, "I like the way you fit together," and that "no ship is wrecked."

The "house" is a small clearing among trees, where they spend the night. Next morning the Captain, excited by the sleeping woman's unprotected body, attempts rape. Jai stops him—saying he's a homosexual and doesn't like women, but he likes the Captain less. The woman takes them back to the capsule, where more "natives" have gathered, silent and naked. (Jai sees, or hallucinates, that they are shrugging on odd assortments of clothes as the strangers approach.) The first woman takes armloads of *books* out of the capsule: "This is a grammar," she remarks casually, examining one. "It looks interesting." It's a Mandarin Chinese grammar, from Jai's baggage. . . . When did she learn to recognize Chinese? How did all those antique *books* get into the escape pod?

Settling for the night, the two men lie thigh to thigh in the tiny capsule, the Captain appalled at the proximity of a homosexual, Jai meditating vindictively on a "seduction" he's sure would succeed, because he knows the type. Violence erupts between them, at which the first woman bursts in, now wearing ostrich plumes and diamonds. She drags Jai off to a wild, wet festive gathering on the lakeshore, in the middle of a lightning storm. Terrified by the crowd's affectless faces and incomprehensible feats, he flees. She follows and, suddenly so exhausted she can barely stand, apologizes incoherently, seeming to say that Jai, or somebody, needs a "witch doctor"—or a psychiatrist?

Here chapter 1 ends. Confusingly, chapter 2 begins with a reprise of the escape capsule "touch-down," with more convincing details. The capsule makes an impact crater. The same woman appears: but now she's "Evne," the community doctor, welcoming them to a human colony that's had no contact with Earth for 150 years. She shows them a hut they can live in and gives them vegetables to eat (plant cancers, she calls them). Soon she's helping the Captain build a radio beacon so he can "call home." The Captain seems unaware that this is their *second* arrival, but Jai knows something very strange is going on. There was no shipwreck, he realizes. The two of them were *taken* and *brought* here by people who can control both time and space. But why? What for? He asks doctor Evne if he is sick. She replies that both Earthmen are very sick—in the head; Jai says, "Then cure me."[31]

This is the incident that has been read, most influentially by Samuel Delany,[32] as Joanna Russ's endorsing a "cure" for male homosexuality. It seems more likely that Jai, kidnapped by benign superbeings, is asking to be cured of the vacuum in his soul, and the sickness Evne discerns has to do with the *sickening* place Old Earth has become—but the words on the page are ambiguous, and it doesn't help Joanna's case that Jai's own nascent psi powers will later burst into flower after sex with a good woman. But there are further complexities. *And Chaos Died* dates from 1968[33] and features the same lawless daydream as "The Precious Object"; Jai's musings on homosexual experiments at "youth camp" recall Joanna's own sexual history (later described in the essay "Not for Years but for Decades" (1980)). Experiencing orgasm with Evne, Jai's physical responses and his astonished cry, "I'm no longer a virgin!" could refer us to nonconsensual, nonpleasurable, juvenile sexual "relations" on Old Earth, but they also code him as a delighted woman. The best reading, I believe, is Jeanne Cortiel's perception that "Jai Vedh" has *no* fixed physical or sexual identity.[34] All of which is not to deny that distressing sexual scenes, apparently "condoned" by the author, feature in this narrative.

Other characters are introduced: Jai experiences the ungraspable daily life of this "lost colony" as he encounters a little girl who tries to seduce him and a disturbingly cuddly twelve-year-old boy who communicates in prime numbers. Flowers talk, and Jai forgets to speak aloud. The Captain is convinced his homemade beacon will summon rescuers. Jai fears he's right, and that this is what the "natives" want, for reasons he begins to guess. Conflicted and scared, he tries to run away—but the people bring him back and explicitly, tenderly claim him: he's one of their own.[35] His initiation into psi-powered humanity continues with a trek to a "library," on foot into the wilderness, alone with Evne. Away from the colony, his awakened mind can't shut out the myriad consciousness of being. Everything, from rocks to microbes, is aware and invading him. He fights back, rants at Evne's slack-faced silence (telepaths don't need facial expressions); he surrenders, and all is calm:

> The grass rolled to the horizon, whispering . . . feathery around their ankles, concealing small things that chirped, rustles, movements, insects hopping high . . . into the sun, then back into the little world. The sky was pale and enormous. *If one lost one's soul in this*, he thought, *it would fade out in a great fan, into vapor, right out of one's breast.*[36]

The "library" really is, essentially, a big building full of stored knowledge, where Evne is blissfully at home. But for Jai it's another appalling cognitive overload. Evne has to drag him, panicking, outdoors again. They struggle together—the *struggle* to submit to desire, one of Joanna's tropes—and Jai "loses his virginity" (twice on this trip!) in a rapturous psychosexual coupling.[37] When they return to the settlement (via another lyrical, hypersensual trek), Old Earth agents have arrived. The Captain has identified Jai as a renegade: he's shot with an anesthetic dart and wakes up imprisoned on a quantum starship called the Big One. Using his new powers to slip between the molecules of the hull and bulkheads, he meets Evne, who has been teleported to the ship by the combined efforts of "eleven thousand people." They have materialized, naked, in a luxury cabin, where grotesquely enhanced "Mrs. Robins" (possibly a gibe at the movie *The Graduate* [1967]) decides they must be sex-performers from the shipboard entertainment team, and she hops on her "masturbation cycle" to enjoy the show.

As an example of the degradation of Old Earth, this incident misfires.[38] (If Mrs. Robins is guilty of poor taste, Jai and Evne didn't have to stay around.) Their next encounter, with the "professionals" sent out to interview them (the Big One is now close to Old Earth), is more convincingly unpleasant. Evne scares the agents with her abilities, lies through her teeth on important issues (to Jai's bewilderment), lists the problems her people plan to cure, and itemizes the Old Earth exports that are spreading poison: "craziness, disease, drugs, pretty clothes, Art, homosex, and Visions . . ." (an eclectic mix, bound to offend over a wide spectrum). Incarcerated but unharmed, she disappears from her cell between sessions. Jai suffers a hands-on and heavy-drugs interrogation but finally manages the same trick, worming his way through the molecules again. He lands in Canada, in a park: a naked, disoriented superhuman, sensing the hives of humanity beneath him as moving drops of contaminated water.[39]

Joanna's superbeings are not gods or angels. The lost colonists have ordinary lifespans; it took thousands of them to "boost" Evne to the Big One. There's nothing magical going on, just an upgrade. The novel's epigram, the parable of the Death of Chaos,[40] is an atheist fable (attributed to anarchic Daoist philosopher "Chung Tzu"). The only "magic" in *And Chaos Died* is sixties mystic-physics.[41] (Readers may note that the starship, constantly disintegrating and reintegrating itself and all its contents, is performing the same order of miracles as the superbeings). The environments, or stage settings, are equally stripped down. The nameless colony[42] is as bare as a *Star Trek* alien planet set: parkland, a library, and a scrubby "wilderness"—oddly recalling Joanna's childhood environment in the Bronx. Old Earth's surface (where every place is like every other place,[43] all nightmarish) is a vast, degraded suburb, pullulating with aimless humanity, where everything is toxic, everything is "dead," and the ubiquitous signage warning against Poison Ivy is a sick joke.

As Delany notes,[44] the story is not "told in flashback," the usual form for fiction. Jai, our viewpoint, knows only what he learns as events happen. Much of the "plot" is opaque to him, and to the reader, right to the denouement (or beyond). Alone on Earth, disoriented but resourceful, he descends to the executive levels—"Morlocks" rule Old Earth from below, of course, while hapless "Eloi" party on the surface. A minor display of his powers convinces a government official ("government" meaning "criminal," Jai notes)[45] to provide him with the ID he needs, but the official then tries to double-cross him and ends up dead when Jai, warding off a bullet, accidentally stops his heart. The name on Jai's new Old Earth ID wristplate is TELE LANDRU; ironically referencing, as Jai appreciates, both his psi powers and his capacity for murder.[46]

Unable to connect with Evne, he wanders, revisiting his past. The billions, drugged to the eyeballs, prey on each other, set fire to their own homes and bodies, and stumble from one "party" to the next. All the food tastes of yeast and algae (unsurprisingly), and everyone Jai meets, including the fascistic young boy, Ivat, with whom he forms a bond, is psychotic. Only a "feeble-minded" girl, trained to offer sex to any passing stranger—whom he fucks, soused in drugs himself, after escaping from an Aztec heart-excising party—seems like a *good* person (nice to know!). After four days of confirming for himself and the reader that Old Earth really is hell, he gives himself up, and the plot resumes. There's a curious shopping expedition to Cornwall before the casual, crowded denouement plays out, like a Bond movie finale, in a spectacular setting—a luxury hotel in the high Altai desert, where "nature" still survives in naked rock and salt pans. Jai, reunited with Evne, meets a negotiating team from the colony (they hitched their way to Earth in plasma form, from one quantum starship slipstream to another). The "psi-people" make Bambi eyes, offering peace and cooperation. The bad guys (chortling at such naivety) attempt to annihilate them and are utterly annihilated themselves—which is about what Jai expected, by this stage.

It was very simple, really. Old Earth's criminal government had become too dangerous, on a galactic scale, but Evne's people felt obliged to give them a chance, before swatting them (the no-first-strike diplomacy of *Star Trek*). Jai, with his latent powers, and the Captain, with his useful rank and stupidity, were hooked out of a "passing" ship, nudged into setting the necessary trap, and everything has turned out as planned. The colonists return to their nameless home, taking Jai along. The suggestion that *all* Old Earth's "Eloi" will be recuperated is hard to believe: but maybe the rescue of Ivat, a single, psychotic child, provides the moral. People can't be saved en masse, only one at a time. But Jai has escaped to live happily ever after, and that's the end of the fairytale.

In his 1985 essay, Delany suggests that *The Female Man* (1975) is "a radical critique [of *And Chaos Died*] on every level."[47] I see *And Chaos Died* as the end of one path for Joanna and *The Female Man* as a new beginning, and I would be more inclined to compare *And Chaos Died* with Delany's *Dhalgren* (1974), in which a "dramatic depiction of the blighted, broken, urban US"[48] is treated far differently.[49] But if *Dhalgren* is the least science fictional of Delany's sf novels, *And Chaos Died* is all about genre: a modernist novel by a *Star Trek* fan, and a gonzo, baroque classic of the American New Wave.

Judith Merril, deeply engaged, politically and morally, in the cultural wars, and "farther and farther removed from the whole science fiction scene,"[50] resigned from the *Magazine of Fantasy and Science Fiction* in 1969. The "Books" editor job was offered to Joanna, who declined.[51] (The offer, which Merril must have approved, suggests that though they were certainly rivals with serious political differences, there was mutual respect between Judith and Joanna).

The British "New Worlds" trio (Aldiss, Moorcock and Ballard) didn't provide U.S. sf with a ticket to the high-culture enclosure, but they had very successful careers. American "New Wave" titles that shocked Asimov and Budrys are now counted as classics. But what happens when the (secretly rather cozy) relationship between the avant-garde, public taste and market forces genuinely breaks down? According to Stephen Jones, elite modern composers (notably Karlheinz Stockhausen and Pierre Boulez) felt they had no choice, after 1945. In the face of the Nazi death camps, they must turn the clock back to zero: "If composing music was to continue at all, it must cut all its ties with the past—and begin again."[52] The New Wave writers were never at risk of creating sf so "new" that it had no audience. Radical feminists were a different case, as bound by tragic ideology, and as certain of their moral *right* to astound and bewilder the audience, as the iconoclasts of serial music. Everything must go. Every convention must be re-invented, there could be no compromise. For Joanna, the challenge was irresistible.

# CHaPTER 3

# YEAR ZERO ART
## A Lost Generation Finds Its Voice in *The Female Man*

> This interplanetary exploration of Feminist inner space, this sophisti-
> cated, playful fantasy book . . . is, of course, all about reality.
>
> —Phyllis Chesler

> The unburdening began. Piece by heavy piece, Seja took the armor
> from the body of the stranger: the greaves, the thick belt, the monstrous
> helmet—so the long hair flew in the wind—then with some difficulty
> the chest mail. . . . Seeing she wore nothing beneath the chestpiece, Seja
> immediately removed her own shirt, baring her breasts in equal fashion.
> They stood looking at each other for a long moment. Then the face of
> the strange woman broke into an amazing smile.
>
> —Sally Miller Gearhart, *The Wanderground*

It was science that drew American women to science fiction in the 1920s
and 1930s.[1] Newly enfranchised, still struggling against prejudice, they saw
the future as a utopian project in which they would take an active part. In the
lockdown[2] that followed World War II this dream finally died, as Cold War

politics imposed the strangest, most repressive gender roles of the twentieth century on the American people. To serve capitalism's triumph over Communism, men in offices and factories must lose their independence and become cogs in a machine. To drive the material prosperity offensive and keep those men masculine at home (sexual "deviance" was inextricably associated with Communism[3]) women must become acquisitive homemakers, their ambitions restricted to child-rearing, husband-nurturing, and successful marital sex. Boys and girls, segregated from infancy by "masculinity" and "femininity" training, met as sex-hungry teenage enemies in the newly invented rituals of "dating." Adult women were discouraged (by social pressure, vanishing jobs, and low wages) from seeking a career. Wives who couldn't perform relied on tranquilizers or a drugged stay in a mental hospital; female graduates were indeed, as Joanna discovered, expected not to find college posts but to become faculty wives.[4] The harsh costs of this program in suburbia were exposed in Betty Friedan's *The Feminine Mystique* (1963).[5] A much later, more objective report, examining the impact of the "domestic revival" on a wider range of classes and groups, can be found in Elaine Tyler May's *Homeward Bound: American Families in the Cold War Era*.

It's beyond the scope of this study to examine the Cold War reversal of women's emancipation in detail, but it's important to understand that the instigators of Second Wave feminism in America, including Joanna and her cohort in feminist sf, grew up in a stifling world,[6] and their rebellion was driven by desperation as much as by sixties radicalism. Reform movements rise from immediate causes, as well as long term injustice. The "cloud of talking gnats"[7] that bars the way to utopia in *The Female Man* was, to a great extent, created by Cold War politics.

It's equally important to recognize that "domestic revival" policies heightened the covert fear and resentment of women already harbored by the averagely liberal, mid-twentieth-century male sf writer. Fritz Leiber's 1943 horror novel, *Conjure Wife* (a junior male academic is attacked by the vicious, occult powers of the senior faculty wives, who secretly run the university), captures the impasse vividly. A good wife is man's best friend: she keeps his house, manages his career, gives him sex, matches his socks, and mixes his drinks. But to any man smart enough to realize that so much confined power is dangerous, she's as threatening as an unexploded bomb. An unattached woman, not made safe by a husband, is even worse. In this poisonous atmosphere, the "Second Wave" of feminism, in science fiction as in the rest of America, was far from being a continuation of the "First Wave." It was a new and bitter struggle, bitterly opposed, and this is the reality that informs Joanna's major polemic works of the 1970s.

REVIEWS, 1971–1975

Joanna had finished writing *The Female Man* in 1971. In December that year she reviewed two books on "Utopia and Science Fiction" for the academic journal *College English*. In her preamble she observes that academia's interest in sf[8] may "turn out to be the equivalent of being nibbled to death by ducks." *Into the Unknown: The Evolution of Science Fiction from Francis Godwin to H. G. Wells*, by Robert M. Philmus, made a poor impression. Philimus wants to show that science fiction isn't just nonsense, but his style is "so barbarous as to be impenetrable," and the study was "almost as hard to review as it is to read." Robert C. Elliott's *The Shape of Utopia: Studies in a Literary Genre*, a "scattered collection of pleasant, modest, clearly written essays," was more interesting. Elliott's "glancing suggestion" that the proper mode for utopian fiction is *lyric* echoes both Joanna's discussion of the lyric mode in her essay "Why Women Can't Write"[9] and her treatment of Whileaway, the utopian strand in *The Female Man* (an idyll, technically, is a short poem descriptive of rustic life, limited to a small, intimate world). The "lovely distinction" between longing and possibility, which "glimmers and is gone" in Elliott's study, is very suggestive of Whileaway.

Between 1972 and 1975, Joanna provided eight "Books" columns for the *Magazine of Fantasy and Science Fiction*. James Blish, her new editor, although he'd pioneered active female *helpmates* in his sf, wasn't sympathetic to feminism, but there's no evidence that Joanna wanted to promote feminism, the way Judith Merril had promoted the New Wave and was discouraged. She simply covered the books she'd been sent, and in the early seventies, as before—representing the genre accurately—almost all were male-authored.

The old-style humanist fantastic and the "old good stuff" of traditional hard sf are largely absent in this new "season," while New Wave works are prominent: literary and experimental, with plenty of sexual frankness (not always positive for women). Intrigued by ventures into *male* sexual politics,

Joanna was delighted by David Bunch's *Moderan* (December 1972): a fix-up of absurdist fairytales about masculinity training, rich in dark, hilarious images, like the penis-machines that stamp Earth's surface into majestic uniformity: "huge black cylinders . . . swinging between gigantic thighs of metal."[10] She praised Barry Malzberg's *The Falling Astronauts*—depicting everyone involved in the mythology[11] of the Apollo program as literally insane (except for the astronaut's wife). His second novel, *Beyond Apollo* (February 1973), another space-program voyage into inner space in which the paranoid, sexually repressed survivor of a failed Venus shot is our unreliable witness to his own debriefing, was even better: "a passionate, fine, completely realized work." Did Harry Evans murder the captain of his ship? Or is he the captain's alter-ego? He really can't tell: "The Captain had always had homosexual impulses, and by God now he was going to act on them: *if you couldn't do what you wanted to do thirty million miles from Earth, when were you going to get to do it?*"[12]

Charles W. Runyon's *Pig World* ("infantile Marxism and cardboard revolutionaries") was notable for the author's obsession with female anatomy: "Since she wore the medallions of her sex right out in front, I decided to take her on those terms." (Where else would she wear them, asks Joanna. On her head?) Itemizing Runyon's obsessive count of breasts, hips, and pubic hair, she decides to adopt this policy in the novel she's currently writing: "He was a medium-sized man with round buttocks and lumpy testicles, one longer than the other. They swayed as he walked. Sometimes they swayed freely. His penis hung down in front. I decided to take him on those terms."[13]

Bruce McAllister's promising first novel, *Humanity Prime* (December 1972), was rebuked for a poorly conceived undersea sci-fi reproductive system (only one Eve: that's never going to work). M. John Harrison's *The Committed Men*, yet another British, rubble-heap, end-of-the-world story, seemed overly familiar to Joanna the Moorcock fan. Lloyd Biggle suffered a famous put-down for his first novel *The Light That Never Was* (February 1973): "It's narsty to beat up on artists who are probably starving to death on a crust in a garret, but critics ought to be honest."

In June 1973 Joanna reviewed, for the *Village Voice* (under the title "Mystification about (gulp!) Marriage"), *The Future of Marriage*, by Jessie Bernard, and *Marriage: For and Against*, edited by Harold H. Hart. Writing as if on two guidebooks for a country she wishes she could understand but never wants to visit again, Joanna notes that nobody seems to know what "marriage" might be, beyond the economic contract that feminism has torn to shreds, and she complains that writers on the issue always assume there are no forms besides the all-American one-man–one-woman norm. But any real discussion vanishes into the morass that swallows all modern American controversy, ruled by the dreadful prevailing assumption is that "if there are two points of view, the truth must lie exactly between them."[14] She condemns both texts and recommends instead *Woman's Estate*, by Juliet Mitchell, or *Marriage Is a Bad Habit*, by Ruth Dixon (picked up at a secondhand stall).

In the "Books" column for July 1973, James Gunn's *The Listeners* was "two books": an intense, scientific treatment of first contact with far distant aliens, and a dismal novel about fake characters in dull "human interest situations." "When will science fiction learn that we love it for itself alone?" asks Joanna. On two collections of sex stories (original and reprints), *Eros in Orbit* and *Strange Bedfellows*, she comments that "writing about sex" seems to bring out the worst in sf writers. Chelsea Quinn Yarbo's "False Dawn," in *Strange Bedfellows*, deserved a special mention: "a rape told from the point of view of the victim—it's not good clean fun, kiddies." Miriam deFord's story was "pleasant, but not sf." Robert Silverberg gave the best value with his "In the Group" (in *Eros in Orbit*), "a splendidly pathological future of group sex."

Silverberg, the quintessential male, literary sf writer of the seventies, made several appearances in Joanna's columns in this period. His best story, "Some Notes on the Pre-Dynastic Epoch," in Thomas Disch's anthology of "political forebodings," *Bad Moon Rising*, achieved "extraordinary poignancy," but her response to his longer works is equivocal. *Dying Inside*, about a present-day telepath losing his gift, is witty, solid, and "as close to the mainstream as science fiction can get." *Born with the Dead*, a fix-up of three novellas about death, has a great title story (the beloved dead are not gone, they're just living in their own gated communities), but the final effect is "interesting but not moving." Silverberg didn't write the fake-sf blockbusters Joanna hated, but his smooth, conventional novels on sf themes were frustrating, when her dream was to see sf *techniques* invading the mainstream.

Disch's *Bad Moon Rising* was the star of the February 1974 column, with several female writers: Carol Emshwiller, Raylyn Moore, Kit Reed; Kate Wilhelm's impressive treatment of the war in Southeast Asia, and poems from Marilyn Hacker. *Paradox Lost*, from the late Frederic Brown, was "often charming": "raw wonders-and-marvels . . . and large holes in the science." *Complex Man*, a female debut, was a failure, but Maria Farcia's "uncontrolled imagination" showed she might be a real writer one day. In January 1975 (the column in which she called the prolific Silverberg "a sossidge factory trying to become an artist"[15]) Joanna discussed a reviewer's hardest task, setting standards: "Good" can mean almost anything, from "it won't poison you" through "if you like this sort of thing, this is the sort of thing you will like" to "intelligent, thoughtful and interesting"; ambitious books that fail their own high promise may be rated lower than a book that's merely competent. Her examples are John Brunner's *Total Eclipse*: a dazzling scientific puzzle, embedded in dull padding (Joanna suspects Brunner is paid too poorly to give his books the time they deserve), and Philip K. Dick's *Flow My Tears, the Policeman Said*: negligible in content, superb on detail (though the lesbian who is married to her brother *and* a drug freak *and* an undefined fetishist *and* an electronic sex freak *and* lobotomized in some way *and* a collector of bondage pictures might be going too far).[16]

In March 1975 Carol Emshwiller's collection *Joy in Our Cause*, Ursula K. Le Guin's *The Dispossessed: An Ambiguous Utopia*, Brian Aldiss's *Frankenstein Unbound*, and Judy-Lynn del Rey's anthology *Stellar 1* finally brought feminist material to Joanna's seventies columns. *Stellar 1* was poor—with a preface full of "vague, sinister assertions" about "second-class academics who are taking all the fun out of sf." In *Frankenstein Unbound*, Texan retired presidential adviser Joe Bodenland reality-slips from a weird nuclear armageddon in 2020 to the Villa Diodati in 1816, where he beds teenaged "Mary Godwin," influences her sf origin story, and runs into Victor Frankenstein himself, plus a mating pair of monsters. This "definitive failure"[17] was clearly fun to review, but Aldiss's annexing of the female founder of sf and a gratuitous attack on feminism pass without comment: "You are an early example of Women's Lib, baby, just like your Mom. Your cause will grab more power as time passes, boosted by the media. . . . But most of those fighting girls . . . work the male kick themselves, clitoris or no clitoris."[18]

Carol Emshwiller's collection rates the usual unqualified admiration (Emshwiller must have become resigned to this fate) despite, or perhaps because, although it was labeled feminist, "it isn't, it's only absolutely faithful to the center." *The Dispossessed* was not so lucky. Having defined the immoveable problem—"No Utopia can provide a genuine blueprint for social change, only a poetic image of what we need or want"[19]—Joanna subjects the novel to severe political criticism. In the end we learn that (for all its faults) *The Dispossessed* is a superb, grown-up sf novel by a woman, written in marvelous prose, that "has earned the right to be judged by the highest standards." Yet how strange it seems to indulge Aldiss's sexism while castigating *The Dispossessed* for weak gender politics and calling it the work of a junior writer "still in the process of finding her own voice."[20] But though Joanna could, and did, set aside the blow to her own chances delivered by Ursula's different excellence, she couldn't ignore a mission-critical problem for feminist sf: the fact that the only truly first-class, popular, female writer put male central characters, and male-identified ambisexuals, in the center of her works.

In April 1975 Joanna tackled, rather wearily, an assortment of high school text books. "It's important to kill mosquitoes, especially the malaria carrying ones," she says of *Science Fiction: An Introduction*, by L. David Allen (Cliff Notes), which she proceeds to eviscerate in mordant, entertaining detail. Two books from Prentice Hall were less toxic but horribly dull. *Modern Science Fiction*, edited by Norman Spinrad, was "subtle, sophisticated, intelligent and accurate"; *Science Fiction: The Classroom in Orbit*, by Beverley Friend, was the pick of the bunch, a gloriously inventive, classroom-based handbook. The column includes an appreciative review of Michael Moorcock's *The Last Assassin* and Joanna's "repentant Silverberg note," which reads in part: "I wish to apologize publicly for my ghastly fumble. Silverberg is a *very-ex-sossidge-factory still in the process of developing as an artist.* . . . And *that* is what I really meant." Apparently, Silverberg was mollified.[21]

## ESSAYS, 1971–1973

"What Can a Heroine Do?: or, Why Women Can't Write" (*Images of Women in Fiction, Feminist Perspectives*, edited by Susan Koppelman Cornillon [1972]; collected in *To Write Like a Woman* [1995]), the first of two entries in Susan Koppelman's indispensable collection, is regarded as a foundation work of feminist literary scholarship. Joanna analyses a list of templates (classic plots), showing how difficult it is to use a female character as the protagonist in novels, movies, or drama. The equation that Culture = Male is inescapable.

Any woman's role in fiction is passive, if she exists only in relation to a male character. The famous "heroines" we might cite (Juliet? Emma Bovary? Anna Karenina?) are women invented by men and perceived by the reader via male assumptions. The only female role as an active protagonist is the Bitch Goddess, an inexplicable destructive force who ruins male lives. But certified female, or feminine, forms suffer their own disadvantages. A female writer either accepts the template (Jane Austen, Charlotte Brontë) and does her best with the subordinate position allotted to her, or she "writes like a woman" and her works are seen as lacking structure and decision: Virginia Woolf's associative prose is formless; George Eliot can't bring her stories to a firm conclusion.

Engaging in itself, groundbreaking at the time, the essay intersects with Joanna's science fiction both directly and indirectly. Joanna's conclusion is that women's writing *can* be independent of male assumptions, but only "in those genres which already employ plots not limited to one sex—i.e., (cultural) myths which have nothing to do with our accepted gender roles." Genre fictions—detective fiction, supernatural fiction, and, of course, best of all, science fiction—although perhaps not (yet) great art, are examined as escape routes and a way forward.

### "WOMEN CANNOT WRITE—USING THE OLD MYTHS. BUT USING NEW ONES?"

The gender-swapped list of summaries (illustrating the point that classic plots are not gender neutral) has intriguing entries, in relation to Joanna's own science fictions:

1. Two strong women battle for supremacy in the early West.
2. A young girl in Minnesota finds her womanhood by killing a bear.
3. An English noblewoman, vacationing in Arcadia, falls in love with a beautiful, modest young shepherd. But duty calls, she must return to the court of Elizabeth I to wage war on Spain. Just in time the shepherd lad is revealed as the long lost son of the Queen of a neighboring country: the lovers are united and our heroine carries off her husband, and lad in waiting, to the King of England.

On Joanna's utopian "Whileaway" strong women fight to the death with dueling rapiers (apparently, since that's the kind of scar Janet Evason has to show—though we never see the rapiers).[22] Whileawayan girls trek alone into the wilderness as a rite of passage; Janet Evason killed a wolf on her trip.[23] The third plot, a version of Shakespeare's *The Winter's Tale*, recalls the cross-dressing ambiguity of Joanna's later stories, "The Mystery of the Young Gentleman" and "Bodies." Later in the list, a sixth gender-swapped topic "Alexandra the Great" recalls young Joanna's fantasies about "being Alexander the Great." (Her only story of Alexander, "Poor Man, Beggar Man," noted in chapter 4, was nominated for a Nebula Award in 1972). Joanna received the Florence Howe Award for feminist scholarship in 1974. This essay is included in the award's anthology.[24]

"The Image of Women in Science Fiction," (*Red Clay Reader* 7 [November 1970]; reprinted in *Images of Women in Fiction*, edited by Susan Koppelman Cornillon [1972], and in *Vertex Science Fiction Magazine* [February 1974]; collected in *The Country You Have Never Seen*) addresses the silencing and subordination of women's voices in the context of science fiction. Written for a nongenre audience in the casual, "thinking aloud" style of her early theoretical sf essays, this was another ground breaker. Joanna describes science fiction as "What if" literature—where things "not as they are, but as they might be," are seriously depicted. She distinguishes fantasy from science fiction, identifies science fiction as *potentially* the ideal mode for speculation on the future of gender roles, and details the barriers in the way.

Near-future sf (such as *On the Beach*), can be excused for leaving social conditions as they are. But many sf stories are set, allegedly, hundreds or thousands of years in the future, yet even "intelligent and literate" American science fiction depicts relations between the sexes as "those of present day, white, middle-class suburbia." Taking Frederik Pohl's satire, *The Age of the Pussyfoot* as her example of this "Intergalactic Suburbia," she suggests that if you "look more closely" at the novelty-packed worlds of science fiction, you see that women are still homemakers and child-rearers, earning less than their husbands; their talents, if any, are denigrated as unconscious (the hero's wife in *Pussyfoot* is so extraordinarily ordinary that every woman will want to buy the products she likes: how this early consumerist influencer manages to earn less than her husband, I don't know!). "Less sophisticated" sf is worse. The American variety (distinguished from the more respectable British genre) is dominated by the "adventure story cum fairytale called Space Opera"; *Flash Gordon* is cited as a relatively nontoxic example. A feudal economic and social structure is assumed. Women are prizes, or they are motives for the action: supernaturally beautiful, weak, and passive if "good"; evil if ambitious, and *the real focus of interest* (Joanna's emphasis) is rivalry between "strong, rugged, virile he-men." Young fans, predominantly male and shy, are "understandably attracted" by the mode's "absence of real women" and "its tremendous overrating of the 'he-man.'" Adult writers should know better, but instead the "he-man ethic" (illustrated by a quote from her 1968 presentation, "Alien Monsters") is reinforced. "Masculinity equals power, femininity equals powerlessness" is the dominant stereotype of the literature of the future.

This overview (with its deceptive implication that male sf writers simply need to catch up) is supported by brief sections on different aspects of the problem. Progress has been made over the last decade: in the popular TV show *Star Trek* female crew members work alongside the men (in support roles, a footnote concedes), a heartening contrast to all-male spaceships of fifties movies, and John W. Campbell's[25] suggestion than prostitutes should be provided for space explorers. But "two-sexed worlds" of this kind are "colorless and schematic." Gender-differentiated roles, such as childcare, simply don't appear. Socialist sf writer Mack Reynolds and Samuel Delany's group marriages and communal child rearing are cited as positive exceptions. So, bizarrely, is Robert Heinlein, for the "everybody is married to everybody else" set-up in *The Moon Is a Harsh Mistress*.[26] In male-authored "Matriarchy" stories (treated in more depth in the later essay "Amor Vincit Foeminam"), women in power are shown as disorganized and brittle; only dominant because *they are taller and stronger* (Joanna's emphasis). When "he-men" arrive, or return, they overthrow the Matriarchy "with a minimum of trouble" and the women happily revert to their natural, powerless status. Joanna suggests there are more thoughtful, British examples: societies embodying the feminine, peaceful virtues;[27] a Great Mother who rules both sexes by primal authority, but John Wyndham's "Consider Her Ways" is the only title noted.

Women who write science fiction, still a minority, may choose from a list of options:

1. Ladies' magazine fiction—"in which the sweet intuitive little heroine solves an interstellar galactic crisis by mending her slip" (a notorious reference to Zenna Henderson's "SubCommittee"[28]).

2. Galactic Suburbia (the lesser form of male-authored Intergalactic Suburbia, presumably) covers most women writing in the field. Today's genders roles are unchanged, male characters are likely to predominate.
3. Space opera, such as works by Leigh Brackett. Female secondary characters will be submissive, even if the protagonist is a sword-wielding, muscular, aggressive woman.
4. Avant-garde, experimental, and close to the mainstream. "Avant-garde" sf takes us out of the field of science fiction altogether. (Joanna cites Carol Emshwiller; she does not add her own name.)

Sf by women, Joanna concludes, features lively female characters and worlds where men and women *may* be equals, but "the conventional idea that women are second-class people is a hard idea to shake," and "while it is easy enough to show women doing men's work . . . it is in the family scenes and the love scenes that one must look for the author's real freedom from our most destructive prejudices."

The last section is a detailed review of Ursula K. Le Guin's *The Left Hand of Darkness*, "a fine book that won the Science Fiction Writers of America Nebula Award for 1969." Poetic and forceful, written by a woman and all about sex, set on a planet where the inhabitants have an "estrus" cycle "modeled on the human menstrual cycle," and told from the reader-friendly viewpoint of a bewildered, male, Earthling observer, this novel ought to be the perfect riposte to the absence that inspired Joanna's essay. But, notoriously, there are no female characters in *The Left Hand of Darkness* (except the Hainish official who provides a brief afterword). Life-defining sexual gender is unknown. Any Gethen human being may get pregnant, bear children, and (even at the same time) rule as king or take any other position of power or suffering in society. But they all use the male pronoun.[29] This is the "whole difficulty" of science fiction. All the tools and materials necessary for the reinvention of gender and the building of equality are here, yet the actuality remains elusive. "There are plenty of images of women in science fiction," says Joanna. "There are hardly any women."

"Alien Monsters" (a presentation for the Philadelphia SF conference in 1968, published in *Turning Points*, edited by Damon Knight [1977]; collected in *The Country You Have Never Seen*) gives a vivid impression of Joanna in action. She jokes that she's been given the breakfast slot because she's a teacher and can be relied on to get up early; she's pleased with the audience she's drawn, despite the hour. Addressing college-educated fans, most likely nearly all young males, she warms up by flattering them with her "warning" that academia is about to invade sf, and the genre had better get ready for these sneaky people, always seeking new worlds of criticism to conquer. Next year, for the first time, she will be teaching an sf course at Cornell. The lecture proper commences with a rather daring anecdote about Joanna reading an sf magazine story about male homosexuality on Mars, in a Cornell cafeteria. The illustrator, depicting the man who killed another spaceman who made advances, and keen to make sure the murderer doesn't look effeminate, has created a monster: a massive, snarling, beetle-browed megalith of muscle. This "alien monster" (sounding a lot like the Incredible Hulk,[30] except green skin is not mentioned) is the iconic "he-man" of science fiction:

> The real He-Man is invulnerable. He has no weaknesses. Sexually he is superpotent. He does exactly what he pleases, everywhere and at all times. He is absolutely self-sufficient. He depends on nobody, for this would be a weakness. Towards women he is possessive, protective, and patronizing; to men he gives orders. He is never frightened by anything or for any reason. He is never indecisive and he always wins.[31]

Complaining that this notional ideal human being is "absolutely closed" to her as a woman (fantasies about being Alexander the Great tacitly excepted, but of course Alexander was a celebrated beauty, and bisexual), Joanna then claims that "he" is also worthless as a fictional character. He stops every storyline in its tracks. He can have no rivals, no internal conflicts; he turns every female character into cardboard. He is the personification of a specifically American myth about absolute power and ideal masculinity as the uncontrolled, unconditional exercise of power. The problem with this symbol is the problem of all mythology: we don't believe he's real, but we somehow believe he ought to be. The problem with he-men in sf is that science fiction writers like either/or situations, hence the all-powerful male is inevitably balanced by completely powerless women. Moreover, the ideal of absolute masculine power leads to a pornography of violence (which, like the pornography of sex, is liable to erase the *reality* of violence altogether). What's the alternative? Definitely not the equivalent feminine superlative. The feminine equivalent of the he-man is a simpering weakling (here Joanna invokes, as in her "Image" essay, the long-suffering heroine of "SubCommittee"). What Joanna wants to see (with a respect for the pulps absent from the "Image" essay) is an American science fiction faithful to its origins in "real, popular trash" and the "daring, the wildness, the extravagant imagination that we got from starting out in the pulps, but without the . . . attitudes that we got from the same place." This stirring call for sf to unleash its inner Bruce Bannon—which could stand as a manifesto for Joanna's 1968 novel *Picnic on Paradise*, with its subtle critique of toxic masculinity—ends the lesson.

When the editor David Hartwell asked Joanna to take on the task of writing the introduction for *Mary Shelley's Tales and Stories* [1975] (a piece finally titled "On Mary Wollstonecraft Shelley"; reprinted in *To Write Like a Woman*), she protested that she knew nothing about the writer. Hartwell insisted, so she did the necessary reading. The result—despite Joanna's reservations about the repetitive, sentimental descriptions of soulful heroines and heroes ("chestnut hair is a detail one learns to anticipate with trepidation")—is a concentrated, insightful survey of Mary Shelley's works, including *Frankenstein* and *The Last Man*, sensitive to the effect of her tragic life on her art. Reflecting Brian Aldiss's fresh appraisal in *Billion Year Spree* (1973), which she must have seen, Joanna supports Aldiss's assertion that *Frankenstein* is *the* original sf novel, with a quote from the 1831 edition, in which Shelley states that she knows her novel is something unprecedented:

> The event on which the fiction is founded . . . [is] not of impossible occurrence; yet . . . [it can afford] a point of view to the imagination . . . more comprehensive and commanding than any which the ordinary relations of existing events can yield.[32]

The discovery of Mary Shelley must have been extremely heartening for another stubbornly idiosyncratic female author determined to create a new field of her own—or at least a new kind of sf. Joanna's final comment in the *To Write Like a Woman* foreword for this piece sums up her response: "So science fiction had a mother. Well!"

"Somebody's Trying to Kill Me And I Think It's My Husband" (*Journal of Popular Culture* 6, no. 4 (Spring 1973); collected in *To Write Like a Woman*). Back in 1966, when she was writing her uncanny tales for the *Magazine of Fantasy and Science Fiction*, Joanna noticed a line of paperbacks on sale alongside the groceries in her supermarket. The covers were nearly identical: a brooding landscape, a big house, a young woman fleeing in fear. She decided to investigate (assisted by Ace Books editor Terry Carr), and her essay on the modern gothic is the result. Far removed from the original gothic novels of the eighteenth century (the genre that evolved into modern horror) a modern gothic requires a "Heroine," young and virginal, lonely and poor, or otherwise mildly disadvantaged. She's not too pretty (or not in her own estimation), has never had a job or a profession, and is plunged into a new situation (or vacation) involving a "House" (large, brooding, intensely attractive, mysteriously threatening); a "Super Male" embodying the same characteristics (invariably older than the heroine, he treats her brusquely and she finds him frightening); and often a sophisticated, immoral "Other Woman," possibly dead or absent, who is, or was, attached to the "Super Male" somehow. The plot involves an "Ominous Secret" and a cascade of perils, mysteries, murders, and other criminal acts. Scenery painting is the strongest element in the writing; a troubled "young girl" may provide the heroine with secondary interest; often, a "Shadow Male" who seems kindly turns out to be the villain. Written for women and by women, and chosen by female editors, the modern gothics, extraordinarily faithful to their formula, are not love stories (although marriage is the goal) and not thrillers (although "the commonest emotion in these novels is fear"). Adventure fictions in which the protagonist is entirely passive, yet endlessly concerned with details of dress, furnishings, and elaborate meals, these stories are comfort food for women who spend their lives cooking, decorating their own houses, shopping for clothing for themselves and their children—and investing (like the modern gothic heroine) huge efforts in studying the emotions of that feared enigma, the stranger they married. They avoid, glamorize, and vindicate the label "Occupation: Housewife" and "provide precisely the kind of escape reading a middle-class believer in the feminine mystique needs." Entertaining, incisive, and not overly serious, "Somebody's Trying to Kill Me" has become, like its big sister "Why

Women Can't Write," a classic. For further reading, I recommend Tansy Rayner Roberts's excellent "Girl Meets House: Kitchen Sinks, Joanna Russ, and the Female Gothic."[33]

## STORIES RELATED TO *THE FEMALE MAN*, 1971–1975

"Gleepsite" (*Orbit 9*, edited by Damon Knight [1971]; collected in *The Zanzibar Cat*) is a glimpse of what's left standing after the Manland/Womanland conflict. It seems that Manland eventually lost the war—not that it matters much: before the end, the two tribes had made a poisoned desert of eternal night out of their battleground. A bat-winged, shape-shifting version of "Jael,"[34] the super-powered "angry Joanna" character from *The Female Man* visits a former office block where two "watch-ladies," identical blue-rinsed twins, name tags on their breasts, clean and dust the ghosts of travel agencies and other offices. Jael offers them a device that will give them the power to change their environment. After guilty hesitation they accept. Having made her sale, Jael melts a "vitryl" window with the corrosive palm of her hand and returns to the awful night. It is a story notable for the deconstructed, layered-realities technique also used throughout *The Female Man*. Feminism has failed. The world, littered with sci-fi jargon detached from meaning, is a terrible place. But the ladies who clean the office might still decide to "tinker a bit" and make things better. "Gleepsite" is defined, in the note for this story in *The Zanzibar Cat*, as a building material invented by architecture students, with "zero mass, infinite tensile strength, and any other properties you like to give it."[35]

"When It Changed" (*Again, Dangerous Visions*, edited by Harlan Ellison [1972]; winner of the Nebula and Locus Awards, Hugo nominee; collected in *The Zanzibar Cat*) is described by Joanna as "very different" from *The Female Man* but is obviously related to the novel. Cornell legend has it that Joanna Russ wrote "When It Changed" soon after she "became consciously radicalized" at the conference on women hosted by the university in January 1969, attended by Betty Friedan "and other prominent feminist thinkers." The legend seems largely true.[36] Viewpoint character Janet Evason also stars in *The Female Man*, but "When It Changed" is a more conventional story, in which an all-male expedition from Earth returns to a lost colony planet. Having survived a plague that killed the male population, the women of Whileaway (the women changed the name, which was originally "For a While," after the plague), have been building their civilization for six hundred years. It's still a frontier world: everyone has to "live on the farm," and the two landmasses are mostly wilderness, but computer-helmet–mediated "induction" technology is highly developed, and the women long ago perfected "merged ova" IVF (in our continuum the first successful "fused ova" conception was a mouse called Kaguya, created in Japan in 2004; a process safe for humans has not yet been developed). The famous story is short and wonderfully immediate. Earthmen return, out of the blue. They keep saying "sexual equality has been re-established on Earth," but their manners tell a different story, and they let slip that they need to "use" the women for their nice clean genes. The men are significantly larger and stronger, and they have the resources behind them. On this night of first contact, in which the story is set, the Whileawayans—depicted not as faultless but as fully human, friends and enemies, politicians and lovers—know they are doomed. A poignant, valedictory: "When It Changed" speaks not only to women who want to be free from male oppression but to anyone who knows what it means to have been free, and to lose your freedom.

"Nobody's Home" (*New Dimensions*, edited by Robert Silverberg [1972]; collected in *The Zanzibar Cat*) was suggested, according to the author's note in *The Zanzibar Cat*, "by Larry Niven's speculation about teleportation." In the far future the human population of Earth will be much smaller. The social unit will be supranational extended families, with intersecting group marriages and with children reared in common. Everyone will zoom around the world incessantly, using teleportation booths; everyone will be extremely intelligent, speak several languages, and will spend their time gossiping inanely, playing high-IQ word games, and having sex. Computer-helmet automation, just as in Whileaway, though this is a very different treatment, takes care of everything, including the "tax work" that does the global chores. I find the Komarovs vapid, and my sympathies are with Leslie Smith—the throwback "ordinary person" who does not fit in; perhaps this is what Joanna intended.

"An Old-Fashioned Girl" (*Final Stage*, edited by Edward L Ferman and Barry N. Malzberg [1974]) is an extract, adapted from *The Female Man*, part 8, 184–98.

## FEMALE-ORDERED UTOPIAS

How do you design an ideal, female-ordered world, when all the models of utopia are manmade? In Margaret Cavendish's remarkable seventeenth-century novel *The Description of a New World, Called the Blazing-World*,[37] Margaret herself (a character in her own fiction) confesses to her patron, the Empress of the Blazing World, that she'd love to rule a world of her own. But all the many worlds, "as many as stars in the one we inhabit now," have rulers already, so Margaret (or "Margaret") settles (rejecting conquest) for an ideal, immaterial world. After considering the existing models, ancient and modern, she decides to invent an entirely new world, "strictly according to her own desire."

Margaret Cavendish, Duchess of Newcastle, polymath and aristocrat, solved the problem of patriarchy simply by ensuring that talented women (like herself) took the precedence they deserved. Less privileged female writers following in her footsteps struggled with the issue of unjust male rule for centuries, as successive generations of "New Women" found their education wasted and their hopes of liberty dashed—but their feminine "ideal worlds" remained private enclaves or temporary retreats. Even in nineteenth-century America, female utopians found the conviction that a woman's story ends with a wedding hard to shake.[38] "Amazon" legends of ancient, all-female societies are suspect—possibly male authored, for male reasons;[39] Mary E. Bradley Lane's *Mizora*, (1880–1890) and Charlotte Perkins Gilman's *Herland* (1915) relied on magical, spontaneous parthenogenesis for reproduction and were tainted by racism. Lilith Lorraine and others—New Women of the twentieth century—took the social reforms and the benign technology of female utopian thinking with them into the new genre called science fiction. But Lorraine and her sisters put their trust in sf's capacity for "cutting the imaginative patterns for better social conditions, more mature systems of government, more advanced biological research,"[40] without challenging male dominance directly. It was men who imagined problematic, science-fictional "worlds of women"[41] until Joanna devised a new approach in *The Female Man*.

The novel can be read, legitimately, as a feminist science fiction, "about four women, or four versions of what could be the same woman," who pass in and out of each other's realities; one of whom is "Janet Evason," a visitor from the utopian, all-female world of Whileaway. Its other, more coherent identity is radically avant-garde and arguably takes Joanna "out of the field of science fiction altogether."[42]

## THE FEMALE MAN

The first chapter is our introduction to utopia, with no bridge (at this point) from our own reality. The narrator is Janet Evason—like, but not identical to, the character in "When It Changed." Janet was born on a farm, the daughter of two mothers. She made her wilderness trek and killed a wolf at age thirteen. As a young woman she worked where she was needed: mining, farming, running a radio station; she was once a librarian, "after I broke my leg." Now married with two children, she's the S&P (Safety and Peace) officer for the county—she's the sheriff! Her idyllic account of a long journey, implicit with the quiet freedoms of a world without men, introduces the pervasive technologies and the self-sufficient, co-operative customs of this hardworking, ideal society. Janet is a good-natured American frontiersman with a calm, confident affect, who happens to be female. She's fought four duels and killed four times.[43]

The second viewpoint is Jeannine Dadier (Jeannine never narrates; her passages are all in the third person)—a three-day-a-week librarian in New York City who wears the ankle-skimming skirts of the fifties. In her world, where the Depression never ended and World War II never reached the United States, she worries about getting hold of scarce items, like cat food, that can't be had from the government store. On March 17, 1969, she barely notes a headline about a strange woman who has appeared on Broadway and a policeman who vanished (like for like?) at the same time. She's thinking about sex with Cal, her gentle boyfriend: a chore she won't enjoy. She'll watch the ailanthus tree outside her window while he ploughs between her uncomfortably raised knees.

There will be four "Js" in total. One of them is also our omniscient narrator, who interrupts at this point to tell us that Janet Evason, snatched from a campout in a forest on Whileaway, changed places with a New York policeman very briefly. Janet thought someone had been "mucking about with my head." The policeman, who landed in a farm-machine maintenance shed, would have been puzzled by the workers there: "smooth-faced, smooth-skinned, too small and too plump, their coveralls heavy in the seat." But he was sent straight back and won't remember a thing.

A third narrator, emphatically identified as the author ("me, Joanna") takes over, telling us she was "at a cocktail party in Manhattan" when Janet briefly appeared in Jeannine's timeline, and at that very moment she turned into a man. "I mean a female man, of course; my body and soul were exactly the same."[44]

*The Female Man* has been described as an sf story about "four genetically similar women, in four different continuums"; or, in nongenre terms, "four aspects of the same woman." Joanna didn't challenge these descriptions, but the next vignette explains the fascinating fusion of fiction and Joanna's beloved "real science,"[45] which actually informs this novel—based on the "many worlds" interpretation of quantum mechanics, posited by Erwin Schrodinger in 1952, developed by Hugh Everett in 1975. If we all have many histories, really happening, simultaneously, says Joanna, perhaps "there's no such thing as one clear line or strand of probability, and we live on a sort of twisted braid, blurring from one to the other without even knowing it."[46]

Back to the "twisted braid": "Joanna" has come to a cocktail lounge, in her version of 1969, "to watch Janet Evason on television." Jeannine, in elaborate fifties costume, is also present, but she's very nervous and soon disappears. The (male) interviewer ignores the confusing fact that Janet thinks she lives on Earth (confusing for the reader too: she's supposed to come from another planet) and brushes aside the "genetic mixing" that allows an all-female society to have children. He wants to know how the women cope without *sexual love*. The interview is replaced by a commercial when Janet gets started on a helpful explanation. "If you expect me to observe your taboos," she complains (off camera, but we are privileged), "you will have to be more precise about what they are." In Jeannine Dadier's world, adds the omniscient narrator, Janet was (or would be, or might be) asked how the women of Whileaway do their hair. She would respond, "They hack it off with clam shells."

Another exposition of utopia (prescient of twenty-first-century ideals), follows, announced by the assertion "Humanity is unnatural!" from Whileaway's legendary polymath, Dunyasha Bernadetteson. The planet's landmasses were reduced to two continents, North and South; that is, the whole world turned into America, in a "Golden Age" (the term "Golden Age" is ironic: clearly Earth suffered cataclysmic losses in the last empire of Man), *before* the plague (or Catastrophe) that eliminated the male population, nine hundred years ago.

The women have "merged ova" IVF, genetic surgery, and heritable high intelligence. Few structures are permanent; farms are mechanized but not industrialized. Wilderness is precious, and animal welfare is high priority. Mineral-rich solar-system outposts, lost in the Catastrophe, have been reestablished, and the new "induction helmet" technology allows "one workwoman to have not only the brute force but also the flexibility and control of thousands." The human population is small; animal species lost in the Golden Age are being recreated. The goal is to create a garden world "without any artifacts except what we would call miracles" (recalling the "lost colony" in *And Chaos Died*).

Meanwhile, "the ecological housekeeping is enormous" and everyone accepts a centrally controlled working life. A woman can expect only one five-year break, when she has her child, to devote to work or study of her own choice, until she gets a sedentary job at age sixty. Of course it's not enough!

From a Whileaway brimming with energy and purpose, we return to Jeannine in her shabby 1969, daydreaming about Mr. Right (a college professor) who'll one day sweep her off her beautiful feet. She gets up only to feed her cat, and hurries to meet Cal in the street, to avoid having sex. Six months ago, she stood in the cold at the Chinese New Year. Cal was beside her, watching the Dragon Dance.

Next Janet Evason, promoted to a Broadway motorcade and a limousine, is telling her secret agent escort to pick "Joanna" out of the watching crowd. Jeannine, presumably snatched from the Dragon Dance, makes a flash visit to Whileaway, where she's repulsed by the unfeminine femaleness of "Chilia Ysayeson"—and an interjection from the narrator, telling us *"Son,"* as in Evason, is a mistranslation: it should be "Daughter"—ends the first chapter.[47]

A new and sinister voice opens part 2. Describing herself as a "blond Hallowe'en ghoul" (in an S.S. uniform), with grotesquely altered hands, she complains of the "idealistic children who lived downstairs."[48] She's "not Jeannine," "not Janet," and "not Joanna," but she seems to know them. Then "Joanna" (seeming to know the nameless ghoul) takes over, to remind us that she turned into a man. But this time the climactic date is "the seventh of February 1969," not "the third Monday in March". And she was in Chicago, or possibly in a hotel in Los Angeles, not at a party in Manhattan.

We return to the limousine. Janet is driving; she's given her escorts the slip. "Joanna" is a passenger; Jeannine an "evasive outline" in the back seat. It's night. Janet drives confidently, without lights, on dirt roads into the woods. She pulls up, gets out, and vanishes into a private house. A second car arrives. Secret Service men surround the limo. Jeannine has disappeared. As Janet emerges from the house with a "nuclear family" (father, mother, teenage daughter, family dog), "Joanna" is protesting: "Who are you looking for? There's nobody here. There's only me."

It's the author who announces herself here, reminding us that Janet, "Joanna," Jeannine, and the sinister mystery voice *are not independent entities*. The novel's séance-like structure of competing voices is fiction laid bare: every viewpoint character a strand "blurring in and out" in the twisted braid of the author's mind, "the great, grand palimpsest of me"[49]—like the superposition of outcomes, in Schrodinger's mental experiment about that cat in the box. Her past, still part of her, is Jeannine. Her feminist present (and our omniscient narrator) is "Joanna"—although not identical with the real Joanna Russ. Janet is her ideal future, and we don't yet know the character of her shadow self. But we can be sure that in reality there is always, only the author, trying out different treatments of her important scenes (as we all do, in memory); adjusting her "facts" to reflect new thoughts; progressing awkwardly, because there's so much to tell that can't be rendered in linear form. No wonder Joanna told Samuel Delany, in the *Khatru* symposium, that autobiography "is absolutely the hardest thing in the world."[50]

Having "committed myself rather too idiotically" as the author, "Joanna" swiftly retreats behind a veil of science fiction, with Janet's account of her (second) arrival, lying across someone's desk inside the Pentagon. Horrified by the appearance of her first *man*—like a woman, but withered away by a life of unremitting toil—she accosted the only woman in sight, a female secretary: "making a little joke" with the iconic words "Take me to your leader" (mocking "first contact" clichés was already a sci-fi staple in the seventies). And now "Janet Evason" becomes famous all over the media—but she's also "Joanna's" roommate: "That woman lived with me for a month," boasts our narrator, perhaps evoking the real Joanna's first engagement with feminism: no longer watching tv or reading newspapers but living the experience. But "Jeannine" (the ghost of Joanna's past) is still around: peering out of misted mirrors; a missing person in dreams; once calling Joanna "*Janet.*"

Meanwhile, in "Jeannine's" strand, the Dragon Dance reference of the previous chapter has been corrected: it didn't belong in her "Endless Depression" timeline. At a "Chinese New Festival," commemorating the founding of "New China," ruled by Chiang Kai-shek's widow,[51] her presence is stable, and Janet can pick her up successfully. "Jeannine" scripts the event herself, adding some feminine flourishes and two "jowly, thick-necked, determined men" in pursuit, for added excitement. Cal is left behind, holding two Chinese lunch buns, as his girl deserts him: "some haunted Polish ancestor looked out of his eyes."

The three "Js" have come together.

In part 3 "Joanna" announces "the lecture" (on feminism, of course), which readers are invited to skip, and lists the iron-bound rules of the domestic revival's feminine code, which she sincerely tried to accept for so long—

dress for the Man
smile for the Man
talk wittily to the Man
sympathize with the Man
flatter the Man
understand the Man
defer to the Man
entertain the Man
keep the Man
live for the Man[52]

But everything's changed now. Janet Evason is living with her, singing Handel's *Messiah* in the shower: the utopian feminist as a true Redeemer. Playing with the tropes of a "naïve alien" movie, "Joanna" embraces feminism as an anarchic, affectionate alter-ego from another world: Janet using lipstick to draw on the yellow wallpaper in their hotel suite (how could she have known it wasn't washable?); Whileaway calluses catching in the absurdly fluffy rug; Whileaway's bemusement at femininity's undergarments; Whileaway's friendly but alarming sexual advances. Finally, crucially, they go along together to the Manhattan cocktail party that has been trailed, since the story's first pages,[53] as the scene of "Joanna's" transformation and the moment when Janet Evason, the utopian, first appeared.

The "party" is a meat market. There's no trace (from "Joanna's" point of view, or "Janet's") of friends getting together to have fun. It's a hostile mating ritual, nothing else. The women, dressed for display, perform stereotyped routines to attract the men and to dominate each other (Aphrodissa, Little Naughty Girl, Saccharissa, Lamentissa . . .). The men prowl and pounce. When "Janet" politely resists being pounced upon, resistance swiftly becomes an outright struggle with a sex pest who won't back down. Identities, and pronouns, blur. It's "I" ("Joanna") who pushes the pest away; it's "our" wrist he snatches,[54] but it's "Janet" who fights back; while "Joanna," panicking, vanishes into the furniture and begs her not to make trouble. It's "Janet" who breaks the man's arm, by accident, and refuses to back down. He attacked her and "called her a baby," a deadly insult. How was she to know he didn't know how to fight? She won't say sorry. Why should she?

Was a real incident in Joanna's life the germ of this extraordinary novel? Maybe, maybe not, but something like a liberating form of multiple personality disorder seems to emerge here,[55] and we have already seen the consequences unfolding: four characters in a multicontinuum science fiction; four aspects of one woman, flying apart and challenging each other.

A restorative visit to utopia is called for, this time looking at social development. In "When It Changed" sheriff Janet Evason and her partner Katy Michaelason were pair-bonded, a lesbian married couple on the wild frontier, with three children nobody had torn weeping from their arms (nobody better try!). The Whileaway of The Female Man permits few human ties that bind. Five years of cosseted infancy (the mother's career break, already mentioned) end in a forcible separation, desperately resisted, and children never rejoin their parents. Adolescents wander, inventing rites of passage. Young adults, after years of compulsory state labor, join or create new "families." Sexual relations begin at puberty, only taboo with "someone considerably younger or older"; marriage is common, but monogamy is unthinkable. It's an inflexible-sounding program, confirming Joanna's definition of "utopias" as a negative prints of what we lack rather than ideal societies—sexual permissiveness made compulsory "to separate sexuality from questions of ownership, reproduction and family structure";[56] family life outlawed, to comply with Shulamith Firestone's insistence that childhood (dependency) must be abolished.[57] We're told that old age, as in ancient China, is a longed-for time of freedom, but the law will still follow you, and "dropping out" of society incurs the death penalty, even if you're over eighty. (Solipsism, the opposite of womanly devotion, is Whileaway's besetting sin: perhaps everyone would run away from their duties without the lethal sanction. And then there'd be no garden of miracles.)

In part 4 Janet is staying with the family glimpsed in part 2. "Joanna" and Jeannine are almost absent, though we are told that Joanna (in her role as narrator) has "settled in the attic" and "infects the whole house." Janet sketchily maintains her character as the visitor from another world, inspecting cakes at the women's club, but this chapter is all about lesbian first contact. Laura Rose,[58] the honor-student tomboy daughter, with her dreams of "being Genghis Khan," her passion for mathematics and her "cinnamon and apples" sweetness, has fallen in love. Janet tries to resist—the girl is far too young! But they come together passionately over some fascinating math. (Someone invisible and unidentified, clawed and furious, watches the lovers until [she] can't stand it and flees, shrieking.) The lesbian sex scene was astounding for its time, and undoubtedly a factor in *The Female Man's* success.

Janet the utopian is no angel (maybe a feminist angel wouldn't be very liberating). Here she is, in bed with a minor, in the cheerful confidence that the culpable relationship isn't culpable here and won't bother Vittoria, her wife of many years. A tale of careless love closes with another, elegiac utopian journey, and the famous *Female Man* safety manifesto: "You can walk around the Whileawayan equator twenty times (if the feat takes your fancy and you live that long) with one hand on your sex and in the other an emerald the size of a grapefruit. All you'll get is a tired wrist . . . While here, where *we* live—!"[59]

In part 5 Janet has arranged to pick up Jeannine for her (second?) trip to Whileaway. But "Joanna" has also arrived in Jeannine-world, embarrassed by her short skirt next to Jeannine's expansive costume, staring at a tired, strange version of her own city. Someone's messing up the probability mechanics. Who can it be? Jeannine is disgusted when they arrive in an empty field (What if they were bad guys? Where's the army?) and gets into an argument she can't win with the calm utopian. But the willowy young woman is used to being defeated: "That long, young, pretty body loves to be sat on and I think if Jeannine ever meets a Satanist, she will find herself perfectly at home as his altar at the Black Mass, relieved of personality at last and forever."[60]

The omniscient narrator, magically able to describe the whole world of the dream, shows us around in the most affirmative of our introductions to this utopia. We see homes of extruded foam like "white caves hung with veils of diamonds," where women can live comfortably in the icy Polar Regions; we meet workers using induction-helmet technologies "indistinguishable from the women's own bodies"[61] and encounter beloved, comic statues of God. We glimpse how the removal of binary *gender* (more significant, even, than the removal of the sexual threat that men present) is transforming human beings, in a society where reproduction is technological and humanity is no longer "natural," into benign creators and curators of the natural world—and nobody we meet seems overly burdened by doctrinaire politics.

Like Margaret Cavendish, and like other seventies feminist utopians, Joanna sees utopia as a process, not a refuge or a stasis. But Whileaway, more than any of the other "feminist utopias" (except perhaps Mattapoisett in Marge Piercy's 1976 *Woman on the Edge of Time*), is insistently *not* an independent construct. A world radically cleansed of male dominance / sexual threat, and the pain that drives all feminist polemic are explicitly occupying the same space. Jeannine's resistance to utopia should remind us that it was *as "Jeannine"* that Joanna suffered the daily humiliations of Manland, with no defense but a stubborn denial of her plight. Jeannine's starved little life in her one-room apartment—with her three-day-a-week job, Mr. Frosty the cat; gentle, unappreciated Cal, and the ailanthus tree—is the locus in this novel probably most real to readers, and maybe also to the author. Now we see why: because it was *as Jeannine* that Joanna rebelled, changed, and conceived this book; although she had to become "Joanna" to write it.

In Janet's family dome, when Vittoria is showing them around, a little girl (stirring boiling sauce with her finger, protected by an induction helmet) tells the visitors a wandering, nonlinear story about a girl brought up by bears, and the moral of the story is: "Anyone who lives in two worlds is bound to have a complicated life."[62]

In part 6 Jeannine "wakes from a dream of Whileaway"—the previous chapter, that is—with a profound sense of loss (the stairwell says "You can't"; "You can't" says the street) that propels her last-ditch attempt to secure a husband. Even "Joanna" the author (Janet is absent) tells her it's for the best. There are no jobs for women in Jeannine's world. Unmarried women end up on "Menopause Alley," with teenage boys jeering at them. A desperate chorus of "Happily Married Women,"[63] straight out of Betty Friedan, chants awful warnings. The rubric "Men Succeed; Women Get Married" hammers home the solution. Though the only possible man—on a family vacation by the lake—is not even divorced, just "separated," Jeannine is ready to grab him; but at the last minute she chooses Cal instead.

And there, but for the grace of God, go I (comments "Joanna").

In part 7, in a change of mode, Joanna addresses the reader directly with a different story about turning into a man (a female man, that is). Like "coming out," the transformation was a long, complex process. For years she strove to create a neuter persona, in the vain hope that her breasts would not precede her wherever she went, as if she wore a sandwich board shouting LOOK! I HAVE TITS! At last, in floods of tears, she realized what she had to do, to "resolve the contrarieties":

> Take in your bare right hand one naked, severed end of a high-tension wire. Take the other in your left hand. Stand in a puddle. (Don't worry about letting go; you can't) . . . [I]f you interfere in this avalanche by accident you will be knocked down dead, you will be charred like a cutlet, and your eyes will turn to burst red jellies, but if those wires are your own wires, hang on.[64]

Having grasped the wires and declared, once more, that her female humanity is as valid as male humanity, Joanna steps out of the narrative entirely, to anticipate, with angry relish, the trashing "this shapeless book"[65] will suffer. But the story isn't over yet.

We have reached part 8, and in "Joanna's" modest apartment, utopia has been founded. Laura Rose, now a cheerfully bloodthirsty young lesbian, with a red rose embroidered on the crotch of her jeans, wants to hear about the time Janet the Sheriff tracked a solipsistic old lady into the wilderness and shot her dead because she wouldn't come home. Jeannine finds a Whileawayan sex toy (with the attachment for vaginal penetration that "hasn't been used much"): "Joanna" tells her the device could "explode her brains" by introducing her to the female orgasm. Janet explains that she was appointed sheriff because, with her "Stanford-Binet corrected" score of 187," *she is stupid* by Whileaway's standards.[66] At night, when the three "J"s gather in the kitchen, the mellow mood has changed. Jeannine is never happy, no matter how hard she tries.

"Joanna" broods on "the (male, sexual) predation you have to screen out so unremittingly." Janet, whose only regret is that life isn't endless, embarks on a meandering Whileawayan fable.

But suddenly they are somewhere else.

The sinister fourth voice (possibly forgotten by most first-time readers) has returned as a terrifying apparition, all in black (like an agent of the Trans-Temporal Military Authority): bodiless against the black drapes of her apartment, only the ghoul-head and crippled hands visible. Her hair is silver (but she's not old—she's forty-two, born just "before the war"). Silver nails distract the eye from retractable talons; her grin reveals "one fused ribbon of steel" (a problem she quickly hides behind false teeth). She names herself Jael Reasoner, the agent of another "probability mechanics" enabled world. She's collected the three of them, variants genetically identical to herself; she complains that Janet's world was "almost impossible to pinpoint" (but later she will claim to know a great deal about Whileaway). On Jael's Earth the battle of the sexes has been militarized for decades. The two blocs, Manland and Womanland are locked in stalemated conflict, and Jael wants to shake things up. She alludes to "tourist trade" opportunities for the worlds of the three "Js"; she's hinting at something more sinister, however. Jeannine, targeted by Jael as the weak link, is excited.

Jael's East River view is fake. The apartment is underground (Jael is a Morlock!) and a long way from New York. She takes the Js to the surface, disguises them in biohazard suits, and leads them through the rubble of a ruined city, built on seven hills (it's Rome, Italy) to a brothel, or "recreation center." They need to see what Manland is really like. Some of the male infants the Women sell to the enemy are forcibly feminized, surgically or cosmetically, to serve the needs of Men (since real Men can't possibly have sex with each other). Jael's contact, Anna, a beautiful "half-changed" (Jeannine thinks she's wonderful), gets them past the brutish bouncers and takes them to the Boss. Ignoring the biohazard-suited strangers, he reacts only to Jael, working himself up from a fake speech about "equality" into a frenzy of sexual hatred until Jael, drawing on her induced "hysterical strength," lets rip with steel teeth and talons, and he lies at her feet pumping blood like Sisera, the great general slaughtered by the biblical Jael: "at her feet he bowed, he fell, he lay down dead."[67]

The Manland/Womanland scenes are very casually sketched. The fiction barely hangs together, but the metaphor is powerful. Men are completely hateful here, *and Women are complicit*. Jael, the personification of female anger, is an incandescent, fantastical invention. The women in the stairwell—the *nice* women we met in the first "Jael" fragment—are handing over male babies to the war machine, and they are all too real. Could Manland survive if women were ever to band together, perhaps with their allies on the other side, and stop feeding the monster?[68]

Jael takes the "Js" back across the Atlantic to her luxury secret-agent "palace" in the Vermont woods.[69] The lonely, natural setting recalls Whileaway; Jael's house is a fairytale globe on stilts (it's a forever house, with a nuclear core). They meet Davy, a silent, naked, blond servant boy. Jael talks about her life: how she looked down on girls who would be brought up as woman-women (the child bearers?) and was beaten for it; her "slow, steady, responsible work" of murder and mayhem. Garrulous with afterburn, she describes a mission—a summarized novel, a story not yet written?—on a stranger world than we've met yet and then abruptly takes herself off to sleep. She wakes from a nightmare of guilt (the guilt of inanimate objects)—with a memory of feeling shamed and soiled, just by *being* a little girl, that seems to belong to the real Joanna, rather than the futuristic assassin.[70] To clear her head she visits Davy. The pornographic scene that follows is weirdly reminiscent of the boy-debauchery fantasies in Burroughs's *Naked Lunch*. A naked, male adolescent living doll, roused with clinical, voluptuous skill, "begs"—silently, as Davy is incapable of speech—to be mounted. Jael mounts, "swallows him whole like a watermelon seed," brings him to climax by stimulating his anus, and, grasping him internally with all her architecture, *has* her sex toy in an orgasm that leaves her "discharged down to her fingertips." She looks up. The Js are standing around Davy's pen, they've watched the whole thing.

Jael wickedly tells them Davy is a real boy, lobotomized, then that he's a construct: "the original germ-plasm was chimpanzee." Nobody (including the reader) knows what to think, except that this is a vicious turning of the tables—as Jael muses that it's "theoretically possible" her lovely Davy has a form of consciousness, and that "Beauty is always empty."

But the question is, will the three Js do business?

Subtitled "The Book of Joanna," *The Female Man*'s last chapter turns to everyday sexism. The little boys who know before they're ten years old that women drive *like girls*, while real men strive to pass every other man on the road. The little girls who learn to find supporting men's shaky egos irresistible. The women "too intelligent" to be women who are encouraged to be fascinated by (male-ordered, male-enacted) politics and baseball—and if they're not, it's a sign of incapacity. Recently, to her own horror, Joanna deliberately shut the door on a man's thumb in a "rapture of hatred," as a revolutionary act: Jael's rage is real in her. Every single professional she has to deal with is male.[71] Where are all the women? Most of them are mothers: hidden away, sacrificing themselves for their children.

At thirteen Joanna dreamed of being a hero, a poet, a mystic. At sixteen she tried to become a woman, the personification of selfless love, intuition, and purity. As a little girl she was herself: adventurous, curious, determined, bossy. But another of her selves, "Laura Rose"—who fell in love with another girl at summer camp and dreamed of being Genghis Khan—was *different*. Different how? Nobody would say. As an adult, after much "Brynhildic"[72] fantasizing, she finally dared to kiss another woman—a kiss that tore reality itself wide open. And this is the denouement: what we've read is a true story. *The Female Man* is both an authentic record of feminist awakening (as many readers have found) and Joanna's own, raw, personal testament.

Finally, the four "Js" are in New York, at Schrafft's[73] for a Thanksgiving dinner none of them has cooked. Jael asks her question, openly this time. Will the others allow Womanland military bases on their "probability worlds"?

Jeannine agrees without a second thought.

Janet refuses—provoking Jael, who suddenly claims the "plague" that wiped out the men of Whileaway is a lie. The men were killed in a long and dirty war. It was *Jael*, in other words, and the savagery she represents, who built Whileaway's thousand years of peace. Janet rejects this revision. Jeannine and "Joanna" stare accusingly at the utopian—unmasked as no magical redeemer, just a possible outcome of the usual bloody mess of history, and as Janet weeps in dignified silence, grieving for poor Jael Reasoner, the author casts a vote for Jael as the best of them: "twisted as she is on the rack of her own hard logic."

Then it's over. The wave function has collapsed; there is only Joanna, inhabiting all her selves. A Chaucerian envoi, sending her "little book" on its way, encourages *The Female Man* not to be downhearted, when it finds itself no longer relevant. "For on that day we will be free."

*The Female Man* is Year Zero art: an antifiction, with all its fictive effects vivisected. There is only one character, the writer, deconstructed. There is only one story: how she came to embrace radical feminism while retaining a feminine past, still living inside her, whose alter-ego is a fury of repressed rage, and a present identity as a battle-weary female academic and writer, goaded by incessant sexism, whose alter-ego lives in a future cleansed of gender-role dominance. Bringing these four to life and letting them fight for attention in an extended, fascinating, complex single image has been a thrilling modernist (or postrealist) experiment in the art of compelling fiction to tell the truth—the whole truth, in all its immediacy and complexity—about a human experience.

Joanna knew her trade, and her dire predictions about the reception of "this shapeless book" were sound: but though the novel failed to find a mainstream publisher, Frederik Pohl bought it for his science fiction list at Bantam "as soon as he saw it," and even in science fiction world, not the intended audience, *The Female Man* (despite plenty of trashing) was a sensation. Published in 1975—the same year as *The Stepford Wives* movie came out—it became Joanna's greatest critical and commercial success, with "over 500,000 copies sold in paperback" before 1987.[74]

# CHAPTER 4

# THE SECRET FEMINIST CABAL
SF's Sexual Politics and the *Khatru* Symposium

> Joanna was saying that the idea is that to end sexism you must change the
> mind of the sexist. And she was beginning to think, no, you don't change
> their minds, you change their behavior.
>
> —Amanda Bankier *Janus 6* (1976)

> It's always been possible for a woman to succeed in science fiction. All
> you have to do is accept the rules of the boys' club.
>
> —Lisa Tuttle

In 1974 fanzine editor Jeffrey D. Smith brought together a group of writers
(plus one fan and one agent) to discuss the issue of "Women in Science Fiction." The participants were Suzy Charnas, Samuel Delany, Virginia Kidd,
Ursula K. Le Guin, Vonda N. McIntyre, Raylyn Moore, Joanna Russ, "James
Tiptree Jr.," Luise White, and Kate Wilhelm. The material would be published in Smith's fanzine, *Khatru*.[1] The discussion swiftly left the confines of
genre (a move proposed by "James Tiptree"),[2] and the symposium became,
according to Helen Merrick, "a unique document of social history" as the

panel "debated, raged and agonised over sex roles, gender roles, literature, violence and rape."[3]

I asked writer and critic Lisa Tuttle,[4] closely involved in the scene at the time, if she had found the *Khatru* idea extraordinary:

> You asked if the symposium seemed "an extraordinary thing to do" . . . not at all, quite the opposite, really. Women (and some supportive/interested men) had been organizing for years, on the same issues that affected us in our "mundane" life. . . . *Khatru* or something like it at that time seems to me almost inevitable, as were the panels that began to turn up at conventions dealing with the issue of female representation in sf. Possibly the popularity of the consciousness-raising groups, in which women were encouraged to gather together and discuss their personal issues from a political perspective (remember "the personal is political"?) was another influence.[5]

Sarah LeFanu (author of *In The Chinks of the World Machine: Science Fiction and Feminism*) was astonished to be reminded of the early date but remembered Joanna Russ and "James Tiptree's" part in the debate vividly: "Which goes to show, again, how cutting-edge women (and some men) writers of SF were in terms of sexual politics and the politics of representation."[6]

Luise White, one of the youngest participants in 1974, made an important distinction when I asked her how it had felt: no, she did not feel "empowered" by the symposium. She felt powerful. "There was something about being able to say things for the first time, and how powerful and right—as opposed to empowered—that made one, or me, or whoever feel."[7]

## WOMEN IN SCIENCE FICTION: A REDISCOVERED HISTORY

"Seventies Feminism" was a contentious issue for fandom, and conversion to the cause could be painful, as Susan Wood, the Canadian academic, editor, fan writer, and feminist reports: "Friends who liked me when I laughed with them at anti-women jokes now dismiss me as 'bitter' and 'crazy.' . . . Other ex-friends urge me to 'stop knocking fandom' or stop trying to 'destroy' fandom by 'erecting barriers' (which are already there)."[8] But there was no going back. The recovery of women's rights in sf—as something other than decorative, compliant helpmates—was celebrated in Pamela Sargent's first *Women of Wonder* anthology (New York: Vintage, 1975).[9] In 1979 Charlotte

Perkins Gilman's 1915 serial *Herland* (see chapter 3) appeared in book form.[10] Jane Donawerth (1990) found an unexpected trove of female writers in the pulps, including Leslie Stone's "The Conquest of Gola" (1931), an early, provocative account of a (human) male invasion, vanquished by the insouciant, female-ordered Golans.[11] Lisa Yaszek's recovery of domestic revival writers, *Galactic Suburbia*, appeared in 2008.[12] The ancestor hunt still continues: Yaszek and Sharp's *Sisters of Tomorrow* (2016) brought to light an unsuspected crowd of female writers, editors, fans, cover artists, journalists and poets not only working in science fiction in the twenties and thirties but even creating the definitive look of the pulps and shaping the development of the genre.[13]

Some critics have not been convinced. Farah Mendlesohn commented, of the Yaszek and Sharp collection, "If this is what women wrote, thank god they left the field."[14] (A mass recovery of male names from the same era might fare no better.) Jeanne Gomoll was disappointed by the mixed politics in "Women of Wonder."[15] But quality and politics are not the the issues here. The issue is that the women in sf were somehow, repeatedly, erased.

Minorities tend to disappear from the records of any field and make a disproportionate impression when rediscovered because they weren't supposed to exist at all. Marginal groups tend to protect themselves by reinforcing the authority of the majority. In an oft-quoted fan letter to *Amazing Stories*, we see a member of "the weaker sex" taking care to be diffident:

> I am only a comparatively uneducated young (is twenty-six young? Thank you!), wife and mother of two babies, so about the only chance I get to travel beyond the four walls of my home is when I pick up your magazine. Ah, but then I travel indeed! For I journey to Mars and Venus, with side trips to the Moon, and down into the heart of the earth, yea, even into the Fourth Dimension. And *who* could do more? (De Hart, *Amazing Stories*, June 1928)[16]

But if the "women sf doesn't see"[17] were always there, wave after wave of them, all filled with the "sense of wonder" that has been, arguably, their gift to science fiction,[18] what was it about the seventies that created a *community* of women in sf and finally made their presence undeniable? There's little doubt that "feminism" is the answer: the radical feminism of the Second Wave, forged by the pressures of Cold War domestic politics, that was inescapable in seventies sf (for a while!) and changed, enduringly, the status of women in the genre. But another answer to that question might well be, quite simply, "Joanna Russ."

Joanna's credentials, as a politically aware lesbian feminist, a critic, an academic theorist, and a teacher, were exceptional, if not unique. Her ideas on gender, raw and personal, outspoken and specifically not "essentialist," were inspirational and uncompromising.[19] Her contribution to the *Khatru* Symposium is a summation of her formative, grownup influence, through the many writers and fans she reached, on the future not only of women in sf but of the genre itself.

## ESSAYS, 1973–1975

Two closely related critical essays from this period, on topics raised briefly in "The Image of Women in Science Fiction," are collected in *To Write Like a Woman* (1995). Joanna reversed their order of publication, and I respect her decision here. She also published an incisive review of the movie version of Harlan Ellison's Nebula-winning story "A Boy and His Dog."

In "Towards an Aesthetic of Science Fiction" (*Science Fiction Studies* (July 1975); collected in *To Write Like a Woman*) Joanna confesses that the essay is a response to the frank revulsion she (and Samuel Delany) have met with when revealing their interest in sf to academic colleagues. Instead of taking the usual approach and promising critics that if they choose very carefully, they will find conventional aesthetic beauty, character development, and fine writing in exceptional genre works, she explains *why* science fiction can seem so rebarbative and provides a corrective, fruitful deconstruction of the "disgust" reaction.

Any good story must be believable. In literary fiction plausibility relies on the writer's powers of "observation of life as it is lived." In science fiction, as Stanislaw Lem and Darko Suvin have noted, "observations of science" are equally important. Science fiction is *didactic*, just as medieval fiction was didactic, with the same relative indifference to "characterization" and the same assumption of a higher purpose. A pure science fiction story (Joanna's examples are H. G. Wells's *The Time Machine*, Ursula K. Le Guin's "The Masters," and Hal Clement's *Close to Critical*) will illustrate the received truths of science as reverently and impersonally as a medieval *conte*, or epic poem, illustrates the truths of Heaven or the spiritual state of Everyman. To see the famous H. G. Wells novella as a colorful fable about simpering, feckless Eloi and hardworking, cannibal Morlocks is not enough. The lesson Wells wants to teach is about "the Three Laws of Thermodynamics, especially the second." To read "The Masters," enjoying Le Guin's "fine writing" without understanding what the duodecimal system[20] means to science, is a travesty of appreciation. *Close to Critical* may seem nightmarish, but nightmare is not the point, nor is the antiliterary style a failure. Excellent science fiction stories can be almost as naked as a scientist's "thought experiment":[21] the Clement story is not about the adventure but the task (a godless act of worship) of "realizing" in fiction the conditions on the surface of a Jovian planet in the system of Altair.

Science fiction could be the bridge that crosses the gap between C. P. Snow's "two cultures"[22]—except that the core literary topic is not the sciences but epistemology: stories about knowledge itself. Perhaps the bridge leads not from the humanities to the sciences but from conventional fiction[23] (Joanna uses the term *naturalistic*) to the modernists: Nabokov, Borges, Brecht, and George Bernard Shaw (in his late plays), artists whose desire is to teach and to use experiment, in prose fiction or drama, "as a means of dealing with some drastic change in the conditions of human life."[24] After defining science fiction again as the only art form immediately engaged with *work*, with knowledge and "finding things out," and some speculation (referencing existing sf) on future directions for experimental fiction, Joanna exhorts her fellow academics to take the *differences* between conventional fiction and science fiction seriously and to teach these differences, in the growing field of academic sf courses, rather than seeking out sf texts that offer no challenge to literary prejudice.

In "Speculations: The Subjunctivity of Science Fiction" (*Extrapolation* (December 1973); collected in *To Write Like a Woman*), Joanna revisits a talk given by Samuel Delany at an MLA convention in 1968.[25] The subjunctive mood in English indicates an uncertain outcome: "I insist that she be here" or "I intend that she be there" making no promises about what will actually happen, one way or the other. Delany proposed that science fiction's uncertain (or subjunctive) relationship with reality stands at the end point of a sequence that leads through fantasy, about "things that can't ever happen"; "naturalistic" fiction, about "things that could have happened" (but didn't); to science fiction, about "things that haven't happened" (but are not absolutely impossible)—and went on to explore the ramifications of this idea in detail. Escaping from this grammatical and ontological maze, Joanna lists the more familiar nonrealist (or subjunctive) literary modes with which science fiction is mistakenly identified. Science fiction is not necessarily real-world predictive: the futuristic developments proposed are primarily *fictional*; they create the conditions in the story. Science fiction is not allegory: characters and events do not "stand for" figures in a moral lesson (the way Aslan the Lion, in C. S. Lewis's Narnia stories is a figure of Christ: both sacrificial victim and redeemer). Sf novels that "become known outside the field" tend to be dystopian, (*Brave New World*; *1984*), but the utopian/dystopian mode does not define the genre. Satire comes closest, but Joanna does not examine satirical science fictions. Instead, pursuing the theme of Delany's paper, she focuses on the relationship with reality the satirist creates. An exaggerated, grotesque situation is presented, which the audience or reader finds first unbelievable, then believable, because it is rooted in reality; finally, this leads to questions about the real world.

"[Science fiction] is very close to Brecht's *verfremdungseffekt* [distancing effect]. What is familiar is made strange—one disbelieves; however, it is rooted in the familiar—one believes (or rather stops disbelieving); yet it is absurd or comic—one begins to question the piece of actuality that has been used as a model for the satire."[26]

Reiterating that bizarre events in a science fiction story have to be taken as *what actually happened*, not as nightmare or psychosis (citing Hal Clement's *Close to Critical*, as in the later essay), Joanna describes fantasy as "a loop with two ends," moving out of the real and returning to the real—"but sometimes one loop is cut." In Sheridan LeFanu's "Green Tea" our confidence in reality is disrupted by the eerie persecution the scholar-protagonist suffers, and it's never reaffirmed. Tolkien's *Lord of the Rings* begins and ends in the real—with the author positing that the events of the epic are chapters from an enormously distant, forever-out-of-reach prehistory of our present world. Science fiction typically plunges the reader straight into the world of strange conditions, with no bridge either to or from our own reality. Instead of limits preset by the writer, the movement in and out of actuality is managed by the reader. This resembles the situation in "what has been called post-realist fiction": works that pull you in, demanding a suspension of disbelief, then force another and then another suspension of disbelief, until there is no hierarchy of meaning and there are no reliable witnesses, not even (or least of all) the author as narrator. Thus Nabokov in *Lolita* can "beguile the reader with overinterpretation and then, so to speak, hit him across the nose with facts."[27] Joanna's examples, besides *Lolita*, are Nabokov's *Pale Fire* and Genet's *Our Lady of the Flowers*. The techniques described, "the daydreamlikeness of the events, the obviousness of the book-as-artifact, as a record of the psychological processes of its creator"[28] are the techniques Joanna uses extensively in *The Female Man* (written but unpublished at this date); thus, she claims for avant-garde sf writers like herself the same status as the avant-garde mainstream.

Finally, dislocation has its limits. A postrealist novel must strike a balance between unreliable narrative and the reader's comprehension. A science fiction story must strike a commensurate balance between the strange and the familiar: "science fiction must be neither impossible nor possible." Occupying a paradoxical or dialectical relationship with reality, "the term 'science fiction' belongs in the same class as 'black comedy' and 'post-realism.'"[29]

In her foreword for "Speculations" in *To Write Like a Woman*, Joanna confesses that the technicalities of Delany's "Subjunctivity" no longer seem as important as they did. But as a closely observed account of "the intellectual athleticism good s.f. insists on in the reader," this earlier essay is as important as "Towards an Aesthetic".

"*A Boy and His Dog*: The Final Solution" (*Frontiers* [Fall 1975]; collected in *To Write Like a Woman*): Harlan Ellison's 1969 Nebula-winning novella, a "fellow traveler's" crudely woman-hating story was a shock for sf's feminists and antisexists. Joanna's review of the cult movie version pulls no punches. Urged to see the movie by unnamed "male feminist" friends, she reports: "Sending a woman to see *A Boy and His Dog* is like sending a Jew to a movie that glorifies Dachau."[30] The assignment of guilt in the battle of the sexes is "comparable to the theories that maintained that the only flaw in antebellum southern slavery was the wretched character and corrupting influence of the slaves themselves."[31] She does not condemn either the story or the movie outright. The movie has "considerable" technical and science-fictional virtues. Blood the telepathic dog (voiced by Tim McIntyre) is a genuine charmer, and the script, the scene-setting, and properties are compelling.[32] Problems arise with the young hero's imperative need to "get laid." Since the only fate available to women in this scenario is to be raped to death, quickly or slowly, fresh females are naturally rare. When Blood sniffs out a young, pretty woman (with clean underwear and shampooed hair!), naturally she turns out to be bait in a trap set up by an evil, remnant culture lurking in a subterranean enclave—where citizens in garish clown makeup maintain the standards of the domestic revival[33] and subsist (it is implied) by "farming" their malcontents as "Soylent Green."[34] But Quilla June is no innocent victim. She's depicted as corrupt, manipulative, and finally only fit for dog meat. Joanna's analysis of the sexual politics of this post-apocalypse, with a close reading of "Quilla June's" role, is a model of joined-up feminist movie criticism, very interesting to feminists at the time, far from out of date today. She concludes that she will now recommend a wonderful picture called *The Triumph of the Will*[35] to her friend Harlan and other male, Jewish fans. References to the *Khatru* fanzine symposium and to an expected volume publication (of *Khatru*) in 1976 appear in the notes.

## STORIES, 1971–1975

None of the unrelated stories from this period gained the reprint recognition of the *Female Man* titles. The most substantial are revisions of early works or continue her fictionalized, nongenre autobiography. There were also the "magazine" stories every sf writer of her time relied on to keep their names in view, plus "delightful, sharp-edged sf flash pieces,"[36] including "Innocence," "Risk," and "Passages," all first published in the *Cornell Writer* and reprinted in SF magazines in the seventies.

"Poor Man, Beggar Man" (*Universe 1*, edited by Terry Carr [1971]; nominated for the Nebula Award for novelette in 1972) is the only published survival of young Joanna's fantasies of "being Alexander the Great." Cleitus the Black— one of Alexander's generals, murdered for resisting the conqueror's demand for Asiatic-style (literal) crawling from his staff—appears as a black-cloaked ghost. A coarsened Alexander, at another turning point, "when he decided to turn back, and penetrate no further into India," is haunted by this dead friend who personifies his past; "Cleitus" is also visible to Alexander's young Sogdian wife, Roxane. It's a subtle ghost story set in fashionable inner space and all the spookier for it. An afterword from Joanna lists the grave historical inaccuracies that won't bother many readers.

"Foul Fowl" (*Little Magazine* [Spring 1971]; collected in *The Hidden Side of the Moon*)—"They shouldnta come down on Park Avenue . . ."—is a short short about a big, mean, clichéd alien invasion, brilliantly defeated by allergist Myron Goldfarb with banquets of delectable Terran allergens, administered *twice* (that's important), with the kicker of an unusual "antidote."

"The Zanzibar Cat" (*Quark 3*, edited by Samuel Delany and Marilyn Hacker [1971]; collected in Joanna's 1983 *The Zanzibar Cat*) is closely related to the English fantasy classic *Lud-in-the-Mist*, by Hope Mirrlees (1926). The good citizens of Appleton plain fear that wicked Duke Humphrey is about to return with his familiar the Zanzibar cat perched on his hump, bringing a glut of forbidden "fairy fruit"[37]—irresistibly enticing, dangerous to peace and quiet. The militia set off to repel the invasion, with the Miller's daughter (caught up in the excitement) as a kindly and useful *fille du régiment*. Across perilous mountains and into magical and uncertain terrain they march, until the duke's lofty castle appears from the mists. The duke terrifies the citizen army but cannot outface the Milleress (formerly the "Miller's daughter")—no longer a girl of twenty, but "a woman twice that age, and a spinster too." She conquers the Oz-like duke with a kiss, confessing that she "wanted so much for him to be true," with all his masterful miracles. But sadly (or not) he isn't, and we are on our own. Having delivered this lesson the Milleress reveals her true identity: "I'm the author." A lovely, slippery metafiction, full of allusions to the earlier fantasy. The Zanzibar cat itself is sweet but doesn't have much of a part.

"Useful Phrases for the Tourist" (*Universe 2*, edited by Terry Carr [1972]; collected in *The Zanzibar Cat*) is an ice-breaker from Joanna's time at Clarion Workshop West in 1971. In her note for *The Zanzibar Cat* Joanna says, "Since I was not getting paid much (there was a financial emergency) Robin Scott Wilson suggested that I edit, polish and add to this project, and sell the result." Phrases the interstellar visitor to the Locrine Peninsula might need include: "That is my companion. It is not intended as a tip." "Are you edible? I am not edible." "My eating orifice is not at that end of my body." "If you uncover your feet, I shall faint." There is a brooding, anxious, and paranoid tone to the handbook that many tourists may recognize.

In "The Soul of a Servant" (*Showcase*, edited by Roger Elwood [1973]; collected in *The Zanzibar Cat*), a governor's steward in a huge, obsolete border fort in the mountains, long ago fled the southern land where his dark skin was normal after an undisclosed crime. He's a desperately lonely outsider, waiting for the barbarians, freezing every endless winter, enduring the saltfish and the stink of his yellow-haired, white-faced (Russian?) idiot superiors, who never bathe, and occasionally managing to ease the lot of the lower orders. The governor's daughter tries to make a pet of him, imperiling them both. When the barbarians finally appear—hauled back to the fort by a hunting party—they are dark skinned and black haired like our narrator. He loses his knife, remembers where he lost it, and knows he's finished. The infuriating young lady invades his quarters again: it's implied that, now having nothing to lose, he rapes her as an act of revenge. When he's waiting to die for this crime, the barbarians turn up at the door of his cell—with his stolen knife, which they have put to good use. In dread and hope he departs with them into the wilds. In her note for *The Zanzibar Cat*, Joanna apologizes for her young self's use of a "justified rape." There are echoes of this accomplished early work in the 1983 "probability mechanics" story "What Did You Do During the Revolution, Grandma?" (see chapter 7).

"Reasonable People" (*Orbit 14*, edited by Damon Knight [New York: Harper and Row, 1974]; collected in *The Hidden Side of the Moon*) is another "probability mechanics" story (but here the science of the problem is shrouded), related to *The Female Man* and to "What Did You Do During the Revolution, Grandma?" A hopeful entrepreneur, from a city in the zone where human crowds reduce the uncertainty burden of this planet, has no idea how to cope in the backcountry, where landscape and other conditions can change utterly, from one hour to the next. Fatalities are common: only "reasonable people" (those who don't expect a rational universe) survive.

"The Experimenter" (*Galaxy*, edited by James Baen [October 1975]; collected in *The Hidden Side of the Moon*) is a tale of adventure on the high seas, nominally set in "twenty-two something-something," but opening, like an Alyx story without Alyx, "when the barbarian and the boy and I were riding on the Southern coast of—never mind." Our antihero doesn't use swordplay or Alyx-style wit and daring to make trouble; he plays the markets. It's an inventive, fast-paced, and ever-topical fable about the mayhem one rogue trader can create by messing with peoples' money-heads—a deception here, a few fake facts there—and all without a shot fired or a drop of blood spilled (by the perpetrator, that is). This was the second Joanna Russ story I read, after "When It Changed." I loved it. Original, sharp, and funny.

"The Clichés from Outer Space" (*Women's Studies International Forum* [1984]: first published, in a shorter form, in *The Witch and the Chameleon*, edited by Amanda Bankier [April 1975]; collected in *The Hidden Side of the Moon*): It's the seventies! You circulate a call for stories, for a feminist science fiction collection. What could possibly go wrong? Very funny—as long as you are not a rejected, would-be sf feminist contributor.

"Existence" (*Epoch*, edited by Roger Elwood and Robert Silverberg [November 1975]; collected in *The Hidden Side of the Moon*) is dedicated to James Blish, as a learned and affectionate riposte to the *Black Easter* books. When summoning the dark powers, Blish forgot to factor in the Great Mother; of course he did. Effective in its own right (or rite) as a feminist reading of the Great Art.

Three significant autobiographical short works date from this period.

In "Old Pictures" (*Little Magazine* [Winter 1973]; collected in *The Hidden Side of the Moon*) the author's mother is portrayed through a collage of old photographs: innocent, "arty" 1920s images of a girl dangling grapes above her open mouth; a volume of Shelley's poetry on show, memorializing Bertha's socially superior passion for the poet. Bertha on a hike, Bertha in a dress with no waist and a scalloped hem—and a daughter who sentimentally longs to enter the frame: to be somehow in the presence of this girl with the straight black hair and black "nymph's brows," who used to climb trees like a squirrel and disappear into a veil of leaves.

"The Autobiography of My Mother" (*Epoch* [Fall 1975]; collected in *The Hidden Side of the Moon*) is a story wherein Joanna imagines Bertha as a willful two-year-old; as an eighteen-month-old baby discovering her power to reject what she doesn't like; as a pretty nineteen-year-old whom the grown-up (and not so pretty) Joanna can overawe by taking her out to eat in a restaurant, wearing smarter clothes, and handling impressive sums of money ($45!). Did Joanna somehow steal, or borrow, the life this other woman dreamed of—Bertha, who never grew up to be a poet but lived instead in the cramped apartment of a marriage that didn't turn out too well? Could they be squabbling sisters? "In the first place I never borrowed it. In the second place it hasn't got a hole in it now, and in the third place it already had a hole in it when I borrowed it." Joanna tries possibilities: Might she be Bertha's parent? Might Joanna and her mother elope, or have sex together in dreams? Could Joanna rock Bertha in her arms, a fifty-year-old baby? It's stylish, psychoanalytical, very much of its era, and related to the better-known, very different "The Little Dirty Girl" (1984). During the *Khatru* symposium Joanna told other members, "My mother has also become a friend of mine, for the first time in my life." "The Autobiography of My Mother," reprinted in *Ms.*, January 1976, was one of the 1977 O. Henry Award winners.

"Daddy's Little Girl" (*Epoch* [Spring 1975]; collected in *The Hidden Side of the Moon*) is a stream of consciousness piece full of over-interpreted notions of fatherland, the father, the male dominance that permeates "our" culture, and the hypersexualized response that ideas about fathers (or all adult males) demand or incite. In contrast to the other story in this diptych, Joanna's father—as a figure in her life, a real person, an intimate friend or enemy—appears very little. Portentous, packed with literary images, "Daddy's Little Girl" could be a patriarchy-haunted, modernist gothic novel, "summarized." This story and "The Autobiography of My Mother," published separately, are united under the title "Old Thoughts, Old Presences" in *The Hidden Side of the Moon*.

## THE *KHATRU* SYMPOSIUM ON WOMEN IN SCIENCE FICTION 1974–1975

Jeff Smith "drew up the prospectus" for his symposium in May 1974. "With a lot of help" from agent and writer Virginia Kidd, he had a panel by September. Samuel Delany, Ursula K. Le Guin, Vonda N. McIntyre, Joanna Russ, and "James Tiptree" were all writers involved in sf feminism, as were Kate Wilhelm and Chelsea Quinn Yarbro, who also published in other genres. Suzy McKee Charnas had recently published her feminist, first sf novel. Raylyn Moore, a college instructor who taught some sf, wrote borderline fantasy stories and had just published what would be a very successful book about *The Wizard of Oz*. Luise White, the token "fan" with as yet no publications to her name (currently Professor White, who teaches history at the University of Florida, has published more than forty articles and books) came recommended by Samuel Delany and proved a provocative, interesting choice. The schedule, given the laborious process of copying and circulating packets of letters, was tight. The exchange ran from October 1974 to August 1975. Smith edited the responses into a work of sixteen chapters, taking his text from the panelists' letters. Preset questions were soon dispensed with, but each chapter had a distinct character and a heading chosen by Smith. After processing and revision, "Women in Science Fiction" was published as a double edition (*Khatru* 3 and 4) in November 1975.

Smith's first question (defining Golden Age sf as male territory and asking the panel to explain why women would be attracted to the genre) was not well received. The heading "SF is suited to the needs of *any* group that feels itself to be oppressed" is from Charnas's response.[38] Panelists took issue with the expression "Golden Age"—an "Age" established after the fact, by a very few, very select texts (Yarbro); criticized this "Golden Age" for its "vapid, stereotyped characters of *both* sexes" (Le Guin); and rebuked Jeff for "perpetuating the myth that [sf] is a man's field" (Wilhelm). Raylyn Moore explained that she didn't really see herself as an sf writer. Suzy Charnas (whose essay-length response seems to appear in full) gave her sf résumé: how she came to science fiction via a childhood fantasy epic, shared with a friend, with horses for characters. Influenced more by "comics" like *Weird Tales* than sf novels, she became a writer because, as she said, "I grew up and sf did not." She suggests that her experience is a common factor in the recent influx of feminist/female sf writers. Girls who loved the strangeness of pulp sf have grown up and seen that strangeness as a tool for inventing futures where women are free (or become free). Vonda McIntyre had the challenging, feminist reply:

> I start writing sf long before I realized what sf was doing to me and other young women. . . . The changes in my own personal philosophy, and ambitions, are due to the women's movement in general and Joanna Russ in particular.[39]

Joanna simply recycled her interview answers to the question: citing Mary Shelley, but not directly challenging Smith's sexist assumptions. She was attracted to sf "because it was wondrous"; she started *writing* sf because "if I wrote about Mars, nobody could tell me it was (1) trivial, or (2) inaccurate."

The heading, "*That's* a girl?" is from Smith's second question: "Science fiction used to be written by men, for men, about men, and there were no complaints. Now there are female sf characters, created by men, and greeted with [female] derision. How difficult is it to create a character 'of the opposite sex'? Are the female panelists [Smith directs this question at Le Guin, citing her male protagonist, Shevek, in *The Dispossessed*] worried about being 'called down' for not writing convincing men?"

Le Guin isn't worried at all. She can't get Shevek wrong because, she says, "I am Shevek" (she's also "every other character I ever wrote"). She dismisses the idea that men cannot write convincing female characters as "plain silly": What about Flaubert's Emma Bovary? Tolstoy's Anna Karenina or Natasha Rostov?[40] But having stated the obvious on her ownership of "Shevek," she backpedals, invoking Jungian dualism (a concept troubling to feminism). When writing male characters, of course she's guided by her *masculine* "Creator Spirit."

McIntyre, Wilhelm, Charnas, and Yarbro all take the view that women are better at writing male characters than men are at writing women because, as Suzy puts it, most strongly "the slave knows her master through and through." Joanna's response is more nuanced: a refinement of the argument in her landmark, nongenre essay "Why Women Can't Write." Readers accept stereotypical male characters more easily because they're familiar. Women's knowledge of men "may also be sharper out of necessity," but it's the *shared culture* that observes men more closely and creates many more—and more de-tailed—male models to be copied. Famous female fictional characters (Emma Bovary, Anna Karenina), unless created by women like "George Eliot" (Marian, or Mary Ann, Evans), are inadequate, which puts "men writing women" at a disadvantage. But characterization in sf is minimal, anyway. The real problem is that men use women's "societal role" as the whole woman.

In the same chapter, apparently in dialogue with her agent, Virginia Kidd (who says she "fell in love" with Machine, the male heroine of *Picnic on Paradise*), Joanna dismisses the fantasy that Machine is "wonderfully real." He was drawn from Joanna's "training in stereotypy" plus "projections of myself" and "wishful thinking." Now that she's a feminist and no longer shares the stereotypes of the sf audience, she expects her male characters to incite "howls of rage from here to Timbuktu."[41]

Raylyn Moore "damn well" does worry about being unqualified, as a woman, to create convincing men.

The next two chapters are single-author essays from "James Tiptree" and Samuel Delany. "With Tiptree through the Great Sex Muddle" freed the symposium from the limits of genre, but "Tiptree's" sentimental, scientifically questionable hymn to motherhood caused offense. Delany's "Letter to the Symposium on 'Women in Science Fiction,' under the Control, for Some Deeply Suspicious Reason, of One Jeff Smith" is more than twice as long as any published contribution from a woman. Borrowing from the experiences of his wife, the poet Marilyn Hacker, he tackles the problems women face in the workplace, as writers, even in terms of issues with women's clothing. He confesses (unwisely!) to casual lapses in his care of their baby daughter, and he berates Smith, mysteriously, for the "neuter" address "Dear People" in his circular letter.[42]

### *Khatru* 5: Feminist Anthologies

A brief item on feminist original anthologies follows. McIntyre's collaboration with Susan Anderson (*Aurora: Beyond Equality*) was on the whole a positive experience,[43] despite a rejection rate of 95 percent. "One surprise was that female participant [or female only] societies were almost invariably portrayed as more ecologically aware." Yarbro would rather not talk about her collaboration with Tom Scortia on *Two Views of Wonder*.

### *Khatru* 6: "There Actually Are Women in Science Fiction"

A single-author essay from Luise White (without a byline) defiantly celebrates the exciting, male-authored female characters in classic sf: brilliant Kathy Niven in Kornbluth and Pohl's *The Space Merchants*; Lady Olivia, the blind, beautiful millionaire in Bester's *Tiger! Tiger!* (titled *The Stars My Destination* in the United States), taking vengeance on the world; Jezabella McQueen, fabulous archcriminal in the same novel. Even Harlan Ellison's murderous "Pretty Maggie Moneyeyes" deserves a mention. These classic sf action-heroines can't marry and usually die instead. They're either criminals or state agents, armed and licensed to kill. But "getting on in the seventies," White asks, how much has really changed? "In the tradition of science fiction, if you're holding a gun or a ray gun or whatever, they call you 'Sir,' whether you're a man or a woman."[44]

"Perhaps We Should All Back Up and Start Over" (title from Raylyn Moore) is a digest. Joanna apologies for her "brief answer" (probably to the first question) and notes that Chip (Delany) can reply at length because "he does not have to live the problem." Joanna must defend her self-esteem "so constantly and in such petty situations. . . . Sometimes it's genuinely, personally ravaging." She endorses the essays from Suzy Charnas, Luise White, and Delany, but tells Delany: "Don't respond to accusations of sexism with feelings of guilt. You will only get angry afterwards, for having been made to feel so bad. . . . THINK. And try to understand that sexism is almost always enforced in petty ways." She speaks hopefully of science fiction as a refuge where "the Eternal Feminine and the Eternal Masculine become the poetic fancies of a weakly dimorphic species" and provides a nongenre feminist reading list.[45] The last entry in this long chapter—which includes Yarbro's despairing account of sexual harassment at conventions (bottom-pinching male "pros")[46] and signs that Moore is out of sympathy with the whole project—is "Tiptree's" defense of "his" motherhood essay, and "his" question for the panel: "If men did not exist, would women have invented them?"

## *Khatru* 8: Trashing Jeff Smith

"Trashing" (title from Vonda McIntyre) is Jeff Smith's confession: "To me the idea of Women in Science Fiction was an intellectual concept. . . . I was interested in the subject, but it didn't apply to me directly." He now realizes he's directly concerned: his part in feminism is "helping to turn a mass of Catholic guilt and supposed inadequacies [he means his wife] into a person."[47] In the derision that greets this boast, Joanna's is the gentlest voice: "Every time you open your mouth your foot goes in further. Stop it, man!" But Smith won't let go, until McIntyre floors him with a direct criticism of his and Delany's "male feminist" crimes against the women they safely assume will pick up their chores and who are absolutely forced to take over the childcare responsibilities their partners abandon. "How can you do that to people you care about?" (All credit to the young editor—Jeff Smith was twenty-three when the symposium began—for leaving this unflattering exchange on the record.)

Another short item. Suzy McKee would like to write fantasy, because it interests women, but "the writer who makes use of the echoes of ancientry (Kurtz, Chant, McCaffery—myself if I can solve my problems) can't help raising those other, sexist echoes too." Only Delany takes her up and encourages her: "Is the answer perhaps to get heroines out into the world, with less illusions about it, ready to see just how nasty it is in sexist terms? . . . Many . . . books are written in which the women have simply vanished from the society."

*Khatru* 10: "Gimmicks Are Not Enough"

Smith compares the reversal of expected genders in two recently published stories: Joan Vinge's 1974 novella *Tin Soldier* (a female hero spacewoman roams the galaxy, returning after long absences, to her male heroine, Earthman lover) and Joanna's "An Old-Fashioned Girl" (an extract from the novel *The Female Man*, unpublished at this time), featuring the "Jael and Davy" sex scene. He's sure "only a woman" could have written Joanna's story, which "burns with an inner truth." Vinge's story could have been written by a man, the genders switched just before publication as a gimmick. But Smith, try as he might, is still "foot-munching." McIntyre takes issue with his assumption that there *is* a natural order that compels women stay at home while men go adventuring. Joanna rather sneakily appears to agree with him: of course it matters whether the viewpoint is male or female, but she then explains, referencing Jean-Paul Sartre, that this is how prejudice operates. Are Jews really "different" from other people? They certainly are: *because the rest of the community has agreed that they are different.*[48]

*Khatru* 11: "This Is Your Life"

Joanna's late entry into the "single author" club is an extended, gender-reversed version of the alienating catalogue of male professionals in the last chapter of *The Female Man* (203–4) plus an appendix, "On the Nature of Concrete Phenomena and Rhetorical Sleight of Hand"—subverting "universal" assertions and terms about humanity to nail the point home: "Men have permanently enlarged breasts, with which they suckle their young. In this way, men are unique among mammals.[49]

Joanna's implicit challenge—How would men survive, if this was the way they saw themselves represented (or *not* represented): expunged and negated, in every context, every day?—is followed by a second single-author piece from Samuel Delany (not necessarily meant as a riposte). The response from the female, feminist writers on the panel is tight lipped. They don't need to be reminded that their position is as precarious as ever and that the gender pay gap (Virginia Kidd had provided some hard facts on this) is almost impossible to bridge in a genre so weighted toward male readers. Joanna (who seems to have woken up) is the only woman who takes Delany on. With his categorical "women writers don't sell" he's ignoring all the women whose sf *does* sell—and sells very well. She cites Anne McCaffery, Andre Norton, and Ursula K. Le Guin but refrains from pointing out that it's *feminism* that doesn't sell.[50]

## *Khatru* 13: "If Only One Could Get Away . . ."

"If Only One Could Get Away from the Whole World, but That Would Be Lonely" is another digest. Joanna, who addresses several panelists on different issues, supplied the heading. A response directed at Raylyn Moore (disingenuous, since Moore by this time obviously wanted nothing to do with feminism or feminist organizations) sympathizes with Raylyn's disillusion with feminism as a classroom subject and suggests she joins the MLA female caucus. Joanna also reveals, "Having written a good deal about my power-situation as a woman, I find I'm now writing about death. Which is hardly sex-segregated. Maybe this means something."[51] In reply to a query from Delany (the query is unseen; the reply is interesting for *The Female Man*) she speaks of "the extraordinary difficulty of describing experience as it is": "Autobiography is absolutely the hardest thing in the world to write." On the strong distaste Yarbro and others have expressed, for Luise White's praise of women with guns[52] she asks, "But seriously, are you and I going to *get the chance* to kill anyone?" She also recounts her bitter experience at Cornell: encouraged into graduate studies by a department that had never employed a woman; finding out that her university had a policy of warning young women that "their marriages and personal lives would be imperiled by careers."

In the same digest McIntyre notes Delany's denunciation of sf with no female characters as "a good refutation" of Poul Anderson's sexist attack on the recent reprint of "The Image of Women" in the sf journal *Vertex* (casting light on an issue that must have been preoccupying Joanna during the symposium).[53]

## *Khatru* 14: "Female Equals Nature Equals Death"

Suzy Charnas, in a chapter titled "Female Equals Nature Equals Death" (actually the rationale of the brutal, male remnant society, in her novel *Walk to the End of the World*), pondered on the dreadful roots of sexism and made the panel uneasy: "Tiptree" (p. 92) feared Charnas was flirting with clinical depression.

## *Khatru* 15: "If Men Did Not Exist, Would Women Have Invented Them?"

In this, the most ragged of Smith's "chapters," Moore covers a variety of issues, on the whole reserving the right to find women as much of a pain as men. Joanna confesses that she's the one who convinced Smith to invite Tiptree and Delany, but she thinks their time is up: "Both have contributed a good deal, but it's true that they are time-hoggers and they—and Jeff—keep drawing our attention away from what (to me) is truly interesting: what *we* think." Demolishing the three men (not undeservedly!) while expressing effusive solidarity with each of the women, she adds her apologies: she's probably also guilty—"Having to answer Poul Anderson's article in *Vertex* would make anyone pugnacious." After examining the feminist Heroic Quest possibility and recalling how strongly she was influenced by the fate of her mother, the "Squashed Woman" (this response is a biographical source), she concludes, "Men *have* invented women, the whole nightmare / ecstatic dream / fantasy projection." But "women, alone, might well have invented something like . . . women . . . that servant-cum-goddess on whom you can project all sorts of useful things, including all sorts of shit-work, and the myth that she loves doing it."[54]

The sf legend that "James Tiptree" (really a woman, Alice Sheldon) "got kicked out of the symposium for his sexist views"—confirmed, with reservations, by "Tiptree's" biographer[55]—is hard to substantiate in the text. Delany falls silent after "Women Science Fiction Writers Don't Sell," but "Tiptree" seems to participate to the last page. But as Suzy Charnas reveals in her commentary for the 1993 reprint, the published version of "Khatru" is not chronological.[56] Jeff Smith had simply edited all the content into a striking whole. Meanwhile the panelists—especially Joanna and "Tiptree," whose friendship was a stormy, intense meeting of minds—were writing to each other privately all along, doing deals and picking fights behind the moderator's back. The original *Khatru* letters are lost, but if they'd survived, a "reliable" or "complete" version of this complex artifact would still be out of reach.

Were Delany and "Tiptree" to blame for their "hogging"? It was the editor's decision to print the men's essays early, with bylines and in full, while using only short extracts from the women—and perhaps Smith was right, on his own terms and ours too. If two major, popular male writers (or one major male writer, and a woman in disguise) hadn't been highly visible, we'd have missed some fine, biting ripostes, and the symposium would inevitably have attracted less interest.

*Khatru* 16: Any Freedom That Is Granted Can Be Rescinded

In the final discussion Joanna, responding to "Deliberately Irritating Comments" from Le Guin (in chapter 14), definitively takes the lead at last, presenting, in effect, her radical feminist political manifesto. She defends the term "power struggle" (which Le Guin had criticized as absurdly male), insisting that women must come to terms with possessing power, and seeking power, and reiterates her belief in the value of female anger—even female rage. "People do not give up their privileges by persuasion alone." There's a difference between "John Wayne wet dreams" (Le Guin's expression) and the "struggle" of the trade-union movement, for instance. And as for the fantasies of killing:

> I find it astonishing that so many of us are worried about women's anger, when a cursory watching of TV indicates who is indulging rage, and against whom . . . anger is an entirely human, entirely predictable emotion . . . it is honorable and we ought to accept women's anger against men as a potential in every situation . . . until the power struggle is won.[57]

But power (and equality) come from legislation, not from the barrel of a gun: "I indeed hate Men and would like to abolish them forever, in the same sense that George Bernard Shaw wished to abolish the poor, 'and make their restoration forever impossible.' While Men exist, male people cannot exist; while Women exist, I cannot exist as a female person."[58]

Finally (invoking *The Left Hand of Darkness*, by way of mending fences), she dares to imagine the human race without sexual polarity. Kate Wilhelm, with an essay on the radical agenda of socialism, ends the debate.

The symposium is a difficult resource to summarize, even when concentrating primarily on just one voice. I recommend the entire, rambunctious, and energizing work to any student of sexual politics (in sf or elsewhere). In 1993 the symposium was republished with updates from Jeff Smith and all the panel members who could be reached, including Joanna—plus a commentary from Suzy Charnas. The third and latest printing was in 2009.

If Joanna's voice becomes the strongest in the ensemble, it's because she has clearly thought hardest and longest on the issues, and she speaks with authority. But if she often seems distracted, she had good reason, and the symposium marks, ironically, the high point of her engagement with sf feminism. "When It Changed," her 1972 Nebula Award–winning story, had attracted crude and vitriolic criticism from science fiction's male supremacists. "The Image of Women in Science Fiction," reprinted in *Vertex* in February 1974, drew letters of open contempt from Philip K. Dick and Poul Anderson. "The context in which critiques of science fiction's androcentrism or sexism was received"[59] had changed before *Khatru* began.

To many women, and men, sf feminism still felt wonderfully positive, but Joanna was feeling the weight of that change. The role of "first among equals" had become a back-breaking responsibility.

# CHAPTER 5

# THE SPOOK BY SCIENCE FICTION'S DOOR
## Joanna Russ, Violence, and *We Who Are About To . . .*

> The hatred, the destructiveness that comes out in the story makes me
> sick for humanity. . . . I've just come from the West Indies, where I spent
> three years being hated merely because my skin was white—and for *no
> other reason*. Now I pick up A, DV [*Again, Dangerous Visions*] and find that I
> am hated for another reason—because Joanna Russ hasn't got a prick.
>
> —Michael G. Coney in *The Alien Critic*, reviewing
>    "When It Changed," 1973

> Lady militants are always like Joanna, hitting you with their umbrella,
> smashing your bottle of whiskey—they are angry because if they are not,
> WE WILL NOT LISTEN . . ."
>
> —An open letter from Philip K. Dick, in *Vertex*, responding to the
>    publication of "The Image of Women in Science Fiction," 1974

Joanna's anger is part of her legend. "I think I will not trust anyone who isn't
angry," she told Susan Koppelman in a much-quoted letter from 1984.[1] In the
*Khatru* symposium she defended women's anger as an "honorable response,"

justified by the abuse that women suffer, continually, from violent and oppressive men. Yet violence plays a surprisingly modest role in her novels. Male-authored, classic sf's active female characters may be few, but they tend to be (as Luise White noted with enthusiasm) extremely murderous. From Joanna we have a young Alyx defending herself boldly, but only by accident fatally, against much bigger and stronger men; an older Alyx who will only kill to save her life; and the Alyx of *Picnic on Paradise*, who avenges her murdered lover in a passion of grief. In *The Female Man* Janet Evason, law officer from utopian Whileaway, accidentally injures an aggressive man at a Manhattan party, and she is obliged to shoot, to her great distress and after due warning, a woman caught in the act of a capital crime. The Womanland secret agent "Jael," powered by bio-chemically induced super-powered rage, assassinates a Manland boss—with her teeth and claws alone (no coded-male weapons!). But the sole act of real-world, "revolutionary violence" in that "angry" book consists of "Joanna" deliberately shutting a door on a man's thumb.[2]

The superhumans in *And Chaos Died* scheme to annihilate the vile and dangerous government of Old Earth. The Trans-Temp secretariat has a bloody falling out in a small town American kitchen: Joanna is not *squeamish* about sf lethal violence, but her forays are rare and at a remove from her viewpoint. Then we come to *We Who Are About To . . .*, a short novel, like *Picnic on Paradise*, again involving stranded survivors on an alien planet, and there's slaughter—a realistically treated "pocket genocide,"[3] as the perpetrator's own conscience calls it. What's going on?

In Sam Greenlee's 1969 novel, *The Spook Who Sat by the Door*,[4] Dan Freeman, the CIA's first black agent, is the "poster boy" for their integration program. (A spook is a ghost, but spooks can also be secret agents; or ghettoized Black Americans, scary *because* they are oppressed.) Dan becomes a high flyer, rising rapidly on talent and work ethic, but eventually things turn sour. A "spook who sits by the door" is a "black employee positioned prominently"—hired and displayed to make the firm (in this case Uncle Sam Inc.) look good. There are congruencies between Greenlee's antiracist fiction and Joanna's career in an "organization" that routinely treated women as inferiors. Talent-spotted by sf's literary elite, she'd swiftly become a notable writer, an entertaining speaker, an influential critic and essayist, and a pioneer of sf scholarship. She was a desirable asset, and for a while (like "Dan Freeman") she seems to have believed in her career path. But perhaps to science fiction's Civil Improvement Agency (the fictional institution with the suggestive initials, responsible for policing radicalism in *We Who Are About To*) she had always been a spook who sat by the door.

Unlike Judith Merril, who "seemed to assume a postfeminist argument (in which commentary on gender roles and limitations is no longer necessary)"[5] or Ursula K. Le Guin, voluntarily assigning to female characters the womanly roles men preferred, Joanna was an "exceptional woman" who resisted assimilation. Public flash points had escalated with Michael G. Coney's letter to the fanzine *Alien Critic* (quoted at the head of this chapter) and the battle of letters that followed, maliciously curated by the zine's editor, Richard Geis.[6] Poul Anderson's response to the February 1974 reprint of "The Image of Women in Science Fiction" in the sf magazine *Vertex* made the more reputable male establishment's position equally clear. His "Reply to a Lady" (*Vertex*, June 1974) describes Joanna as "one of the perhaps half a dozen science fiction critics worth anybody's attention" but also as "a biased female who has let the fervour of her cause run away with her." She ought to know that "women" are irrelevant to most sf, useful only as "love interest."[7] Philip K. Dick's "Open Letter" (*Vertex*, October 1974) purporting to "defend" "Lady militants" like Joanna (also quoted) must have almost driven her to despair.

Joanna's perfect storm of crude and contemptuous male criticism, running at exactly the same time as the *Khatru* symposium, seems to have made her only more determined to work with the men she could reach, in order to achieve reform by peaceful means (her principled, gentle responses to male sexism in that forum are remarkable, given the grief she was getting in the sf press). But even her friend and mentor, James Blish, had published an antifeminism novel. Even her comrade in sf theory, Samuel Delany, had not been able to conceal his unease in his introduction for the hardcover collection of the Alyx stories, calling Joanna's warm and witty style "cold" and barring the way to his appreciation with a howling, jeering mob of teenage boys, screaming angry derision at a Bond-movie heroine—a woman unwisely trespassing in a man's world.[8] Maybe she recognized that the violence was not one sided (although one "side" certainly had all the heavy artillery). Helen Merrick suggests there'd been combative private exchanges, before Anderson's and

Dick's strong responses in print (see also Jason Vest's report on Philip K. Dick and Joanna, in Mendlesohn's study). But perhaps Joanna was also coming to recognise that no appeasement would make her demand for equality palatable. The fear of women and the insistence on women only in sexualised, womanly roles (should they gain entry to sf at all) was far more deeply rooted in genre than the seventies feminists, including Joanna, had understood—until they put it to the test.

Joanna was teaching at a prestigious university and established in her lesbian feminist identity. She'd published acclaimed and controversial novels and fine stories; she was revered by many fans. But sixties radicalism had failed to change the world. Her job was insecure, and in the science fiction community she faced (in a nonlethal form) the same implacable violence that threatens the protagonist of *We Who Are About To*, whose only crime is telling the truth to people who don't want to hear it—and refusing to back down.

Dan Freeman, in Greenlee's novel, quits the CIA to work on social projects among "his own people." When that path fails and he's lost all hope, he becomes an organizer of violent revolution, turning his buried CIA expertise against the State. There's something of the same story in the career of the narrator of Joanna's fourth novel.

REVIEWS, 1976–1977

In November 1976 Joanna contributed her first "Books" column in eighteen months for the *Magazine of Fantasy and Science Fiction*, where Algis Budrys was now her editor. Her lead novel was Kate Wilhelm's *The Clewiston Test*. Faced again with an excellent novel (like *The Dispossessed*) by a woman of worth and talent, her admiration was again clouded by frustration and, in this case, possibly a feeling of personal offence. In Wilhelm's riveting lab-science thriller, Anne Clewiston Symons, a brilliant scientist who has made a breakthrough in pain relief,[9] is confined to a wheelchair after a car accident. When the drug runs into problems just as it's been passed for clinical trials, the fates conspire to make Anne's restricted life descend into hell by excruciating turns of the screw. There are clear feminist issues in *The Clewiston Test*, but the only "feminist" character is a half-crazy closet lesbian, and other women in Anne's life are singularly unsupportive. Joanna admires Wilhelm's constant, "cross-lighting" change of viewpoint (keeping the reader off balance, not sure whom to trust) and the book's "real, difficult subject matter," but once more the genre's great feminist critic couldn't praise an outstanding female sf writer as she deserved.

This is the column with the "rabbit" motif. Joanna decided to apply (to almost every book) George Bernard Shaw's distinction between a "mechanical rabbit"—a commercial play, good for an hour or so's entertainment, but basically just a toy—and a "live rabbit," a real, organic, dramatic work. Kate Wilhelm's novel (some amends for the lukewarm review) is the only rabbit alive and kicking. Ben Bova's *Millennium*, a "slick, optimistic" replay of the American War of Independence, involving a mixed Russian and U.S. colony on the Moon, is a toy: "My copy tried to eat grass in the back yard and died." *Star Mother* (Sydney Van Scyoc) is a "science-fiction-cum-gothic" combination, "as horrid as it sounds." A frail, courageous heroine, a dark, arrogant mysterious hero who lives in a castle, and a couple of spooky murders enhance the heroic liberation (led by the heroine) of mutant children. It's a derivative, artificial rabbit with purple pom-poms, "but only those who try to eat it or breed from it will be disappointed." Jane White's *Comet*, "a dreadfully pretentious replay of the Birth of Christ and early Christianity," is set in a post-Holocaust society created by the complete exhaustion of raw materials—yet the ruling classes dress in plastic and defend themselves with tanks and planes. This one's a "wind-up rabbit that doesn't even go." Pamela Sargent (the *Women of Wonder* anthologist) is spared the rabbit test. Her *Cloned Lives* is "sketchily and badly put together" from episodes that have appeared elsewhere, but it's "an interesting and promising first novel" that comes to life when the clones of a genius grow up: six *different* people, Joanna notes with approval, struggling with the notoriety of their creation. *Star Trek: The New Voyages* was the first *Star Trek* fan-fic collection. Joanna, a major fan, regretfully pans these stories—not for poor content, but because they're full of a bewildering variety of technical creative writing errors, resulting in "a ten-year-old child's toy rabbit, made very carefully with love and effort, but a lot of little wheels and things got left on the kitchen table." (A footnote reports she's since been told the writers were not responsible, the faults were somehow added in the production process).

Joanna recommends "James Tiptree's" "Beam Us Home" as a model, if amateur writers want to do "Star Trek" stories, and adds an interesting note (in the light of her later K/S Slashfic publications) on the (mainly female) writers' obsession with Spock, their curious form of sexism, and the "sociological phenomenon" of fan fiction, a fascinating area that "deserves study."

No other reviews are collected for this period.

## ESSAYS RELEVANT TO 1975–1977

"Amor Vincit Foeminam: The Battle of the Sexes in Science Fiction" (*Science Fiction Studies* 7 [1980]; collected in *To Write Like a Woman*) is more modest in scope than Justine Larbalestier's later study, which shares the same title, but digs deep into sf history, fanzine archives, and textual analysis.[10] In Joanna's essay, three novels and seven stories—in which women have seized power, or attempted to seize power, and men have either fled into the wilds or been forced into feminized roles (including four stories from Sam Moskowitz's timely anthology *When Women Rule* [1972]) are examined, dating from 1926 to the early seventies. A topic long prepared (the content was summarized in "The Image of Women in Science Fiction") but not published until 1980, the essay must have been completed no later than 1976.[11] Only one of the stories is intentionally funny ("War against the Yukks," by Keith Laumer). Most of them are, by Joanna's report, laughably crude and makeshift in construction, and the more accomplished (like Edmund Cooper's *Gender Genocide*) are the least forgivable. Eight of the ten are unashamedly stories about rape as a weapon of war and about the violent subjugation of human beings by other human beings who are gender supremacists. In three of them, Joanna notes, "women are not actively engaged in fighting men, they have merely withdrawn from men's company, but the challenge to male domination is seen as identical."[12] Typically the penis, simply displayed (in *The Feminists*, by Parley J. Cooper)[13] is enough to ensure instant victory so that (as Joanna noted in "The Image of Women in Science Fiction" but without the supporting detail) it's difficult to imagine how a female rebellion ever got started. Women are overwhelmed simply by the pleasure of being raped. Men are never reported as experiencing sexual pleasure, and reproduction is not an issue: the purpose of rape is subjugation.

Despite the spectacularly sexist content of these texts, the really interesting revelation for Joanna is the congruence between this penis exposure motif, which Joanna calls "flasher fiction" (for obvious reasons), and Joan

Bamberger's "The Myth of Matriarchy: Why Men Rule In Primitive Societies," an article that "arrived in the same post" as Cooper's *The Feminists*. Bamberger examines three instances, in tribal society in South America, where men tell stories of a time when women held power by pretending to be spirits or taking unlawful possession of ritual instruments. Because they ruled by deceit, women were evil, so men took control by force, typically using gang rape as a punishment. This is exactly the sequence of events in the "flasher" stories, and in the tribal myths, just as in the "flasher fiction," the issue is not reproduction, it's the justification of men's rule by force.[14] The implication for Joanna's fourth novel is interesting. The tenth story examined is "Mama Come Home" by "James Tiptree Jr," published in *Galaxy* in 1968. Joanna didn't know that "James" was Alice Sheldon when she drafted her essay,[15] but she noticed an important variation. In other stories only the penis, or a penis-shaped dildo, can rape. The giant women of Capella, who see earth humans as inferior mutations, can and do rape human males, who find the experience terrifying and horribly painful.

"On the Fascination of Horror Stories, Including Lovecraft's" (*Science Fiction Studies* 7 [1980]), noted here with the shorter work on Lovecraft that follows (both collected in *To Write Like a Woman*), and in association with the short story "My Boat" [1976]), is a free-ranging discussion, touching on R. D. Laing's treatise on schizophrenia, *The Divided Self*; cryptic social criticism in Shirley Jackson's *The Haunting of Hill House*; and the feminist content of Charlotte Perkins Gilman's "The Yellow Wallpaper" (which Joanna, as a teenager, had simply read as a very scary story). Ostensibly addressing her friend, Croatian academic and critic Darko Suvin, who has asked for an explanation of the attraction of horror fiction, Joanna explains that young people, and perhaps particularly young sf fans, find in "horror" a relief from and a validation of their worst and strangest fears about the world, about their relation to others, about their own state of being. It's good to know, in the grip of a waking nightmare, that "someone has been here before." Joanna's own adolescence illustrates the point. At fifteen she became obsessed by "The Colour Out of Space"[16]—one of Lovecraft's greatest stories, in which a tract of New England is weirdly poisoned, or *possessed*, after a demonic meteor strike. She couldn't stop (re)reading the story; she was scared for months, but it was "infinitely preferable to the repressions of the nineteen fifties, and the suburban future I was supposedly heading for." Looking back, she suspects (the italics at the close of this anecdote are a Lovecraftian touch) that Lovecraft's foul, mysterious wasteland was for her *the 1950s, and that imaginary future, in fictional form.*[17] After a tour of Lovecraftian images, relating his very personal visions to Laing's theory of the diseased self, Joanna returns to the ground covered in her "Daydream Literature" essay, citing Edgar Allan Poe as proof that "the best of pure horror" can only be second-class literature, since horror's necessarily coarse and crude visceral shocks "cannot tell the whole truth about anybody's situation." "Avoiding thought is not a good recipe for art." Thus the fascination inspired by Lovecraft becomes simply a hunger for another of those compelling shock moments—and another, until the only remedy is (fittingly!) a kind of madness: with obsessed readers seeking more "HPL," and ever more "HPL."[18]

"H. P. Lovecraft" (Introduction to the author, for *Twentieth Century Science Fiction Writers*)[19] is shorter and more polished. Joanna positions Lovecraft as an sf writer, citing his insistence on "creating a non-fantastic and materialistic fictional world" and his "cosmic" fear of displacement in space and time. His motifs of physical incoherence and appalling bodily *engulfment* set him apart from the sex and aggression of conventional horror writers, and the quality of his best stories is unique. An appreciation of specific works follows: the "charming," but "unfortunately never revised" *Dream Quest of Unknown Khadath*; "The Strange High House in the Mist"; "The Call of Cthulhu"; "The Dunwich Horror"; "The Colour Out of Space." Cannibalism, or "engulfment by the other," psychic or actual, was eventually replaced as a theme by an understanding (expressed in the monster ancestry of the hero of *The Shadow over Innsmouth*) that the menace the narrator feels comes from inside himself. Lovecraft's originality and talent, plus the "very rarity of literary treatments of his main theme" ensure that his work will survive: "narrow . . . and even considerably flawed . . . but securely loved."[20]

## STORIES, 1976–1977

There are three published short stories from this period. "My Boat" (*Magazine of Fantasy and Science Fiction* [January 1976]; enshrined in the "Cthulhu Mythos";[21] collected in *The Zanzibar Cat*) is the most striking. Two seniors at a Long Island Public High School, in the early days of integration, fall under the spell of Cissie Jackson, a timid little black girl, disobeying her dragon of a Christian Fundamentalist mother to study drama. On stage Cissie can do anything, become anyone, with absolute conviction. In a bid for Cissie's attentions, Straight-As, college-of-my-choice, successful Jim loses out to his best friend Al, who is crazy about Lovecraft's weird tales and "pretty much of a fruitcake." Maybe Cissie can hear the embarrassing "good racist" thoughts that keep running through Jim's head: her funny hair, her pitiful clothes, her meager chances. One day Al and Cissie get Jim to drive them to the marina at Silverhampton. He sees a rotten, old rowboat, which Cissie names "My Boat," wonderfully transformed: Cissie becomes a Caribbean princess with a ruby-and-sapphire-studded knife in her belt, and "fruitcake" Al metamorphoses into someone like Sir Francis Drake, in a silver and black doublet. The princess and her captain are off on an impossible voyage, across the Spanish Main and up into the stars: to Ooth-Nargai, Celephais the fair, Kadath in the Cold Waste, the city of Ulphar (destinations from Lovecraft's *Dream Quest of Unknown Khadath*). Maybe they meant to take Jim along. Maybe not. But anyway, his nerve failed. He couldn't face the strange dreamlands of "Beauty, Despair, Mortality, Compassion, Pain." Jim, our Lovecraftian narrator,[22] now a "disappointed adult" screenwriter, pitches this true story to his agent: claiming that Al has come back—in fact Al is here right now, in another booth of the lunchroom, *and he still looks seventeen*—but whether Jim is really given a second chance at the dreamlands is left untold. "My Boat," a fan tribute to the actor Cicely Tyson[23] and to Lovecraft's gentlest weird worlds, is heavily laden (there's a section about Cissie meeting her savior, a man with wounds in his hands and feet, in a mental hospital) and a little too long, but its charm is undeniable.

"Corruption" (in Susan Anderson and Vonda N. McIntyre, *Aurora: Beyond Equality* [1976]; collected in *The Zanzibar Cat*) features Alpha, a long-haul infiltrator, who rises slowly through the enemy ranks in the single installation on a poison-swamp of a planet: the "Outpost on Outpost." At last two old comrades turn up, one of them the blind woman who was once his lover. The problems that made direct attack impossible have been solved. Alpha is free: but it's too late, he's changed sides. A convert to the Outpost's dreary regime, he attacks the invaders. The Outpost gets blown up anyway, and to the new colonists all three saboteurs will be heroes. A dreary response to the call for stories set in societies "beyond equality," as Joanna, in her foreword for *The Zanzibar Cat*, seems to agree.[24]

In "How Dorothy Kept Away the Spring" (*Magazine of Fantasy and Science Fiction* [February 1977]; collected in *The Hidden Side of the Moon*) Dorothy fears the spring because her cough will get better. Her father will force her to go back to school, and she'll be behind in everything. In daydreams she escapes into the snow that falls endlessly outside their castle to meet magical friends: the silver Hunter who can make roses out of frost; the Clown, and Little. They're adventurers together, off to dethrone a tyrant. Her father finds her leaning out of a window in her cotton nightdress and sends her to bed, but Dorothy joins her magic friends again, in the freezing cold. She has discovered her mother's secret and succeeds in keeping away the spring; the tyrant, roaring in vain, "Put on your glasses, Dorothy," dissolves into a puddle of tears: it's a fragile, pretty "Wizard of Oz" variant featuring a girl-child's suicide.[25]

## WE WHO ARE ABOUT TO . . .

The year is 2040. A starship (not a luxury vessel like the Big One in *And Chaos Died*, perhaps more on the scale of the cruiser/freighter *Nostromo*[26]) suffers a "mechanical dysfunction." The ship's computer locates the nearest planet "tagged" as marginally habitable and dispatches the noncrew humans, in their life-support compartment, to this landfall. The "intensely brilliant flash" of their ship's demise reaches the eight survivors on the planetary surface. After a long, grey "day" of twenty-five hours (our narrator guesses they've landed fairly close to one of the planet's poles) the cloudless night sky is a black, disturbing void, almost starless, confirming their worst-case scenario. They are nowhere, on no route; nobody will drop by and find them. They have limited supplies, a few personal possessions, a chemical toilet, and a drinking-water still, but no way to send a distress signal and no hope of rescue. They're all going to die, probably within months. Seven of the eight castaways immediately start planning to colonize.

On closer acquaintance—details provided by our narrator, who is recording a secret audio diary on her vocoder—the group seems neither as random nor as natural as the "affluent technology junkie" tourists in *Picnic on Paradise*. Businesswoman Valeria, with her trophy husband Victor and her trophy daughter Lori[27] (an adopted street kid whose health problems cost a fortune to fix), is genuinely rich and has the makings of a Bitch Goddess. Cassie, whose shipboard costume was silver nipple stars and cache sex, is genuinely poor. Both these women have a vested interest in traditional female roles: Valeria treats Victor, her aging toy-boy husband, like a servant, but she insists on being called "Mrs." Graham. Cassie frankly makes a living out of being female. The other men—Alan-Bobby Whitehouse, hugely muscular with a tiny head, who dresses in scarlet with "gold braid and epaulettes,"[28] and John Ude, a "historian of ideas" who sports a "pipe" and a "sporran," not to be taken too seriously, and is excited about the "new lease on life given capitalism by the unlimited power of hydrogen fusion"[29] (but our narrator knows he's never been "behind the crew panels," where real technocrats travel), represent male supremacy: Alan as the pernicious "he-man" of Joanna's essay "Alien Monsters"; Ude proving that sexism is just as rampant in university common-rooms (or in the sf community). Lori is the "female child," presumably here to get rescued some way or other. The other adult woman, young Nathalie, in her all-black skin-tights, wears the uniform of the "Trans-Temporal Military Authority," symbol of the seductive power of science fiction. (The narrator, who also favors black bodysuits, will call her "my mirror sister.") She's a high-flyer, hoping to escape from the girl role.

All the costumed figures in this "ship of fools"[30] dramatis personae are of the same class, "the people who do nothing real"—traveling on the cheap or taking an adventurous trip off the luxury circuit, perhaps, in the case of Valeria's family. Even Valeria does nothing but make money. The eighth cast-away, our narrator, is a musicologist but seems to have been stranded on the starship-cruise circuit for quite a while, lecturing tiresome passengers on po-lyphony. Her ancestors were Jews who fled persecution, their wealth in jewels sewn into their robes: "X"[31] has taken the same precaution. Her treasure is a "pharmacopoeia" of stolen and hoarded drugs.

On the second day, exasperated and abrasive, X tells the others what's wrong with their colonizing plan, starting with Lori, who could die of some-thing as commonplace as impacted wisdom teeth. A "tagged" planet only means breathable air, liquid water, and bearable temperature. They don't even know if there's anything they can eat when their meager supplies run out. X has no intention of bearing her first child at forty-two, but it would be insane for anyone to get pregnant deliberately—what if there's a problem birth? Her list of negatives is relentless: her fellow castaways are infuriated. Life must go on, and *obviously* step 1 is to get the child-bearing-age women pregnant.[32]

That night, trying to sleep in the cramped compartment, X contemplates "survival," if it was even possible—without culture, without literature, without music or history—on this stranger-world, and she mentally embraces her preferred alternative, a chance to practice the lost art of *ars moriendi*, of dying well.[33]

Joanna's fourth novel was serialized in *Galaxy* in January and February 1976 (the two-part text is identical to the version later published by Dell in July 1977). Brit Mandelo, in a webseries on Joanna Russ's work for Tor.com, suggests that the novel missed award consideration because of this confused "first publication" status.[34] But there were complex reasons why *We Who Are About To* was poorly received. Conservative male critics were almost duty-bound to punish Joanna's next book, after *The Female Man* and the controversial reprint of her essay "The Image of Women in Science Fiction." The fact that *We Who Are About To* features a recalcitrant "heroine" and the demolition of American sf's most treasured scenario was perhaps a bonus as much as a provocation. Algis Budrys derided the story as boring and indelicate (the narrator, living in the wild, defecates in running water and includes this detail in her audio diary), declaring, "I cannot imagine why Dell published this book."[35]

The popular "lowbrow" female sf/fantasy writer Marion Zimmer Bradley was another problem. In 1972 "MZB" had published *Darkover Landfall*, an origin story for her neopatriarchal planetary romance series. When a damaged colony ship lands on the wrong planet, loses its communications systems, and has no chance of returning to Earth, the male authorities strip female officers of their rights and force them to join the colonial breeding program "to ensure the continuance of the race."[36] Resistance is classed as pathological, and the uppity, over-qualified feminists, at first outraged, are soon content in their captivity as "protected child bearers." Vonda N. McIntyre wrote a scathing review, for the short-lived, legendary Canadian feminist fanzine *The Witch and the Chameleon*. Bradley responded indignantly, and Joanna took her to task:

The question, to put it bluntly, of whether a woman's uterus belongs to her or to the community she happens to find herself in (or rather its male authorities) has been a very hot political issue in the U.S. and some parts of Europe for at least a decade; I am surprised that Bradley didn't expect vehement reactions to a novel in which just this question is the central issue of the plot.[37]

*We Who Are About To . . .*,[38] published three years later, mocking the "romance" of sf colonization and denouncing pregnancy by rape, soon attracted Bradley's attention. In her next "Darkover Newsletter" she provided a weighted synopsis: "A group of colonists makes landfall on an uninhabited planet, and most of them wish to reproduce and carry on their race. But one determined character stands out against this distinction and murders all the rest so that they cannot."[39] Readers were invited to read the offending book and pass judgement. Some respondents (their letters were printed in a later newsletter) admired the book and sympathized with Joanna's narrator, but none of them questioned Bradley's outline of the story. *Darkover* fans were not Joanna's natural audience. To many of them planetary romance was the same kind of comfort food as the modern gothic, the home-making displaced to an even more exotic locale—but this was still bad publicity. Bradley and her admirers were an inescapable presence in seventies feminist fandom, and Bradley, a problematic[40] "lesbian feminist" at this time (in the eighties she decided she was not a feminist), demanded respect.

Though Bradley's summary misrepresents Joanna's novel, it highlights a real difficulty. *We Who Are About To* is two books.[41] One is about a woman stranded on an alien planet; she has an intense back story in radical politics, refuses to be raped, and rationally rejects the claim that "the continuance of the race" is at stake. The other is a demolition of science fiction's "fantasies of an impossibly generous universe"[42] and the insatiable American expansionism that sf represents. Joanna may have seen these issues as two sides of the same coin, but once the powerful narrative of pregnancy by rape emerges (almost immediately), the other story—about embracing mortality and abandoning "fantasies of immortality"[43]—almost vanishes. The book "about death"[44] that Joanna seems to have intended is lost, and the innocent reader is left unprepared for our heroine's extended, solo finale. This imbalance, as much as the hostility of the critics—plus the machinations of a highly organized rival—has obscured the value of *We Who Are About To*, the only Joanna Russ novel that *isn't* about feminism. Recently, it has won new readers and greater appreciation.

The castaways, schematic roles apart, are an odd bunch. It's difficult to imagine them coming together naturally. But a critique of endless expansion seems to place the germ of the story in frontier America, home (in the 1840s) of the original Manifest Destiny "doctrine." I found it fun and helpful to think of Alan and Cassie, Ude and Nathalie, and the Grahams as stagecoach passengers—dumped out of their hospitable nineteenth-century world and stranded in hostile Indian country. Beset by peril, these mismatched strangers need a common cause. They don't realize that the puny outlaw hidden in their midst, who swiftly becomes their scapegoat, is also their nemesis.

She's been on the run for a long time, and she's very tired.

On day 3, Alan-Bobby finds a "Neo-Christian" or "Trembler" symbol among X's belongings. She is baited for her faith (apparently a fusion of Taoist and Quaker beliefs) and responds (typically) by telling everyone she also used to be a Communist, "in the twenties riots." On day 4 Nathalie takes a trip on their single-person flying stick—a strange-sounding gadget.[45] When she returns, announcing there's a small river nearby, Alan-Bobby, who has just taken a bath in the water distillation tank, immediately throws his water away. Nathalie is furious: this is insanely wasteful—yes, she's found raw water, but every drop will still have to be treated! They trade insults; Alan socks Nathalie in the jaw, then hits the slight young woman again, savagely, amazed and delighted with himself. It's a moment X has been dreading. Patriarchy is back.[46]

More days pass. X tells her diary she's everybody's punching bag yet also everybody's confidant. (Condemned as a refusenik, her public word isn't trusted, so she can't reveal secrets.) She gives Cassie, who suffers from migraines, painkillers from her secret stash. She handles Alan-Bobby, who needs someone to forgive him for hitting a woman, fearlessly but carefully. She listens to Valeria's complaints about Victor—who has been appointed the first prospective father, whereas Valeria, too old for childbearing, has been demoted. She plays cards with Lori, often left alone by everybody else. Ironically, X is warmly interested in her companions, despite their willful insanity: she is sharp but kindly in her judgements, amused and tender with the self-absorbed, fragile child. She's an asset to this tiny society. But her rejection of the colonizing project and her resistance to compulsory childbearing are unforgiveable crimes, and the women are as vengeful as the men.

Cassie, who never had a chance at reproduction before, is convinced the babies she'll have will "love *me*, not their daddies." To gain favor with the patriarchy she tells Ude and Graham about X's drugs (considerately warning X what to expect before punishment descends). X is set upon, and the treasure is ripped out of her clothes. Luckily she's hidden most of her stash more securely, anticipating this situation—but it's an evil scene and a warning that her luck is running out. Ude taunts her about her part in a failed revolution (revealing he's not a "historian of ideas" at all: he's a government spook who's recognized her as a fugitive from justice), and X starts planning her grim escape.

> They won't be able to leave me alone. I know. Not because of the child-bearing, because of the disagreement. The disagreement is what matters. How far will I push them? To where? All the way?[47]

Nobody has even begun to test the local vegetation for edibility, they have at best five months of emergency supplies, but still "the great womb robbery" is going ahead. At an absurd but sinister formal "meeting" chaired by Ude, Cassie announces that she wants to be called by her full name, "Cassandra," now that she's going to be a mother to the world. When X recovers from her choking fit (Cassandra was a Trojan princess whose (accurate) prophecies of doom were ignored), she manages to fast-talk herself a respite. But she will soon be raped. They'll rape her until she's pregnant and keep her shackled until she gives birth.

On day 9 it begins: Nathalie and Victor Graham "disappear dutifully" together. But Victor, the best of the men, has a bad heart. Three days later, X follows him when he leaves the camp to die alone. When he declines her vial of "instant exit" nerve poison and embarks on his own, modest *ars moriendi*, she hears his last confession. The shallow life he's lived, trading on his masculine beauty; his simple belief that Valeria and Lori will live happily ever after on this virgin world. She stays with him, alone, until the end. But though X's services are appreciated on this occasion, the would-be colonists don't feel they need a celibate, female priest. There's a plan to tie her up at night.

Her last hope is her "mirror sister": "You won a lot of scholarships, didn't you?" X comments, when she tries to gain Nathalie's sympathy.[48] But Nathalie (X sees her as the real Spirit of Death around here, in her insane determination to keep going when she's lost everything she ever valued) has settled for the only chance of upward mobility left to her and has suffered a gross humiliation. She's not going to let X escape unscathed.

There's no way out.

In the next vocoder entry everything has changed. "By writ and tort, by hullabaloo and brouhaha, I declare this tapedeck locked to all voice-prints but mine, locked *re* playback, locked *re* printout, and may God have mercy on your soul."[49] With the traditional words of a judge condemning a murderer, X seals a detailed confession nobody will read.

She made her escape, aided by the rather miraculous drug hoard (including a lethal gas gun) she'd recovered from its hiding place. She sprayed the sleeping colonists with "hypnotic nerve gas" to keep them under, bundled up a share of supplies, took the "broomstick," and rode it to a cave at the head of the river. She drank raw water and it didn't kill her; the stranger-world's rocky river valley seemed "altogether beautiful." But just as she'd predicted, the others couldn't let her alone. She saw them coming: Alan, Ude, Nathalie, and Cassie, and she didn't mean to kill them, but that's what happened. Alan bashed his head in the dark cave. When he was down, X smacked him on the head again, with a rock—a little too hard. Ude and Nathalie she shot with the gas gun, in self-defense, and Cassie, in despair (both the potential fathers of her babies were dead), chose suicide. So X gave her the right pills, and when she'd dumped Ude and Nathalie's bodies into the river (Alan was too heavy to drag), she headed down the valley, to deal with Valeria Graham—and Lori.

The extended "Wild West" showdown makes exciting reading and may leave sympathetic readers convinced that X meant no harm. But though she can call four deaths self-defence (Valeria met her with a loaded gun at the castaways' base) and one death suicide, why did she go back down the river, if not to complete her slaughter? She returns to the cave, straps Alan-Bobby to the broomstick, points it over the drop, and off he goes. Cassie lies on the hillside, "on her back, limbs a little sprawled, staring at the sun." The bodies will rot; X is alone, but how can she make her peace now? The second great challenge of her life is over and she's failed, catastrophically, just like the first time.[50]

But *ars moriendi* is a powerful rite, and gradually it absorbs her. There are periods of fugue, and lucid intervals. There's a pebble calendar she creates and destroys, and a castaway's diary that almost sounds like fun. She makes exoplanet nature notes; she reveals a name, Elaine, we have never heard before. She dreams of singing "with immense power and élan, alone on an empty stage," begins to starve, and recalls the advice of the old monks: "Sit in thy cell, and thy cell will teach thee all things."

Eventually she attempts to explain her beliefs and to describe what happened to the "Neo Christians," a movement founded by her boyfriend, a giant of a musician called L. B. Hook (Elbee), who played the tuba. All they wanted was spiritual worth and meaningful work for everyone; in a world where the masses just weren't needed anymore. She was drunk the day they had their Neo-Christian "cross in a circle" symbols made; she remembers trying, drunk, to play the tuba. In disjointed fragments, wiping the record and starting again, she recalls a failed revolution. A crowd of protesters locked in a carousel shed overnight; a friend walking as if casually past a significant building, checking for signs of CIA action . . . Elaine/X was only arrested once. She spoke at events that were respectably funded. But one day she lost her nerve, an experience as terrifying as "the silhouette of a chickenhawk to a chicken" or like hearing a "fascinating, ominous growing roar" from the audience at a speaking event. Or possibly the way a controversial feminist sf writer feels, frightened by the violence of the male anger she has provoked.

Joanna's fiction always, deliberately, drew on autobiography. Her experiences in the science fiction world, before and during the writing of *We Who Are About To*, certainly contributed to this work "about death." But she also tells the story of the collapse of sixties radicalism: how some walked away, some became outright terrorists, and some took their radical ideals with them into conventional life. Elaine/X ran and never stopped running. She'd been living "outside history": enduring for years the fate that she furiously rejects as a castaway (a life without culture, tradition, or a future) when she ended up stranded with the seven figures in her alien-planet morality play.[51]

When she starts to hallucinate, she sees Cassie ("the only one I liked") spread-eagle, as if on the hillside, but upright; a welcome visitor, even if she's rotting. As her lucid intervals become more lyrical (with piercing memories of music, "grief without bodily pain, joy without bodily pleasure, emotion without flesh," and of Elbee's wonderful mind), the others assemble, Elaine/X's Six Lasting Things: Valeria, Nathalie, Cassandra, John, Alan, and Lori. Luminously detailed (Lori is reading a big fairytale book), they stand around the walls of the cave to accuse the woman who judged them. Alan the he-man, stupid and timid: she could easily have deceived him. Valeria was half-crazy, rich and old: is that an excuse for murder? John Ude, who opposed her world view, was a reasonable man who could have been persuaded: a despairing man whose despair she never saw. Nathalie, the mirror-sister, says "Look in my face and you'll see your own rage and your own deprivation. I know you. Do you think I don't?" Cassie just sobs. At last, Victor Graham, spruce in a blue dress suit, comes to lead Lori away. The child (as they disappear into a brilliancy Elaine/X can't see[52]), says *thank you*. Thank you for killing me.

Elaine is still prevaricating. Killing Lori was her only outright murder, and now she's making the child say "thank you"![53] Perhaps that's why her lover, Elbee, appears next and gives her such ferocious dressing-down, she's forced to realize she's talking to herself. Lucid again, she admits that yes, she murdered them; yes, she hated them; and yes, she "rather enjoyed killing them off." The next lesson is the parable of the sparrows. There was a sparrows' nest under the air conditioner, on the outside wall of Elaine's apartment. The nestlings screamed their dawn demand *feed me, feed me*, right by the head of Elaine and Elbee's bed. It was intolerable. *Feed me, feed me*, the world screams, helpless and hungry. Start hearing this cry and you'll never stop. You may flee all contact with your fellows because their needs are so unassuageable; but you won't escape, because *you* are screaming too.

Feed me, feed me, feed me. Read me, read me, read me.

And that's it. Elaine/X, against all the odds, has completed her task.

Accepting mortality, acknowledging all your failures and forgiving yourself, is difficult, painstaking work; it's a project that won't appeal to all sf fans, but it deserves a little space (though perhaps not the whole seventy pages.)

In the envoi "Marilyn," a daughter or daughter figure from the Neo-Christian days, pays a graceful, silent visit, and Elbee returns, in such a happy dream that Elaine/X wakes up laughing. She creeps out, by now too weak to walk, to sit above the water, and she hears Handel's Messiah ringing around the lovely, alien river valley. The last visitation is a five-year-old child, Kennedy, Marilyn's daughter, who died in a car crash: a marvelously comforting apparition. "A gateway. A sign. A messenger. Though nothing's settled."

Forgetting that the vocoder is sealed and will never be found, she plays a joke on her future listeners: pretending—Oh, look, a rescue party! Coming up the valley! Then she claims she's putting a printout (where did the paper come from?) in a box under a rock: another tease. Harrowed and blessed, light as a feather, light as Ebenezer Scrooge on Christmas morning, yet aware of all the horrors of existence, Elaine / X decides *its time*, and she breaks open the vial of nerve poison. It's been a virtuoso performance, and more a medieval / modernist allegory or an atheist spiritual fable in sf imagery than a critique of science fiction's crazily "hospitable universe." Many questions are left unanswered, but that's realistic. The one thing the living can be sure about, when somebody dies, is the unanswered questions.

# CHAPTER 6

# JOINING THE CULTURAL MINORITY
## *The Two of Them* Puts the Female Man on Trial

This fantasy of rescuing the self (usually disguised as another character) may not be exclusive to women, who do not have a monopoly on miserable childhoods. But for women who grew up before the advent of feminist teaching (which still includes most adult women) the desire to go back and undo those deforming lessons, to unbind the feet, so to speak, of our own younger selves, is a particularly compelling dream.

—Kathleen Spencer, "Rescuing the Female Child:
    The Fiction of Joanna Russ," 1990

They gave her a spot in the tiniest room at the end of a winding corridor that was almost impossible to find. I got there a little late, and by then it was standing room only. It was packed; I couldn't even get into the room. I had to stand on my tiptoes to see over the heads of the people in the doorway. I could barely hear what was going on."

—Jeanne Gomoll, describing the response to the first ever "women in science fiction" program, organized by Susan Wood

Vladimir Nabokov, the great modernist[1] who had a formative influence on Joanna's writing, wrote "novels" as deceptive, equivocal, and multilayered as real human experience. In an interview with Larry McCaffery in 1987, Joanna described her interpretation of his approach:

> I don't do what Borges or Barth (perhaps) does—that is, call into question any-thing about the reality of real life—and I don't really think Nabokov has done that either. His themes are exile, loneliness, and isolation, from which art is an escape and to which he usually returns the reader at the end of the book, as in *Pale Fire*. I'm certain—often painfully certain—that real experiences *are* real. They're far too refractory not to be. The reality I call into question is not that of life but that of fiction, and I do it (as Nabokov sometimes does) to emphasize that fiction is fictive, artifactual, a communication between persons. . . . Emphasizing a story's status as fiction doesn't render reality unreal; rather, it emphasizes that life / actuality *is* real and that stories aren't.[2]

Modernist and "post-realist" sensibility enabled the dual project of Joanna's feminist novels: both a fictional autobiography of her own evolving feminism and an interrogation of the sexism in "science fiction." She was not alone, as Kathleen Spencer reminds us in the quote above. Feminist science fiction writ-ers in the 1960s and 1970s, reclaiming a stolen future, enjoyed a comradeship of shared danger and daring. Writers and fan writers who belonged to this club explored the same themes and responded directly to each others' stories with elaborations or rebuttals (a phenomenon very much in the tradition of genre). "This incredible bounceback"[3] could be treacherous, as Joanna had discovered with *We Who Are About To* and the "MZB" connection, but she still found sf's "*re-visioning, and re-perceiving* of other people's fictions"[4] (the process she describes in "The Wearing Out of Genre Materials") irresistible.

"Re-visioning" was central to the creation of her fifth novel, *The Two of Them*—dedicated to Suzette Haden Elgin, "who generously allowed me to use the characters and setting of her short story 'For The Sake of Grace' as a springboard."[5] In Elgin's story a young woman strives for high honor as a State poet (an extremely important role in her Islamic-style "medieval" society). The title is homage to the protagonist's aunt Grace, punished atrociously for trying and failing to win the same prize. In *The Two of Them* a similar scenario is embedded in a new "Trans-Temp" adventure. This time the all-powerful agency, ruler of worlds—that entered the life of a teenager in 1925 small-town America in "The Second Inquisition" and scooped Alyx from the ancient Mediterranean in *Picnic on Paradise*—is initially known as "The Gang" but easily identified by Russ readers by the familiar black uniform.[6]

Agents Irene Waskiewicz, a young Polish American woman of Joanna's own time (but from a slightly different probability world), and Ernst Neumann, her older, more experienced sponsor, are partners and lovers, isolated in the intense private world they share. Irene is the active agent on their routine mission to Ka'abah, an Islamic-style asteroid colony; Ernst is her "Conscience." On the next assignment they'll swop roles. When Ka'abah society starts to expose, like a distorting mirror, the flaws in her relationship with Ernst and the truth about the nature and purpose of their organization, Irene is at first confused, then devastated. How can she have been so deceived in her striving for high honor? How can she bear to break with Ernst, whose body is so exciting, who understands her so perfectly?

Joanna had been in love with science fiction for a long time. She'd fallen for the genre as a child. As a young woman longing for escape, she'd found refuge in sf without noticing, perhaps without caring, that women *as agents* were usually excluded from the game. She'd been faithful for years: explaining science fiction to itself; excusing its faults and trying to transform it, even as an "out" lesbian feminist. Maybe she still wanted the relationship to work, as the seventies drew to a close. But her belief in the mission was shaken, and her unease was growing. Was this increasingly difficult position, as an exceptional woman in a male-ordered organization, even morally tenable?

REVIEWS, 1978–1981

Joanna's critical acuity and her entertaining style are intact in her last reviews for the *Magazine of Fantasy and Science Fiction*, but her editor's disgusted treatment of *We Who Are About To* (Algis Budrys, *Magazine of Fantasy and Science Fiction* [February 1978]) can't have helped their relationship. A proliferation of footnotes—correcting her errors and adding afterthought asides—suggests carelessness or weariness. Occasionally, as if tired of being anything but a teacher, she slips into workshop mode.

There were also sf reviews in the *Washington Post*'s "Book World" and reviews of nongenre feminist works elsewhere.

In the fall 1978 issue of *Frontiers* she found Marge Piercy's gritty urban novel *The High Cost of Living*, featuring a lesbian protagonist and an unusual love-triangle on the margins of society, less attractive than *Woman on the Edge of Time* but nevertheless impressive: "Books that are truly alive and individual don't fit easily into preconceptions" (a riposte that could serve as a defense of Joanna's own recent work).

In the *Magazine of Fantasy and Science Fiction* (February 1979) *Khatru* panelist Raylyn Moore's only full-length fiction did not impress: *What Happened to Emily Goode after the Great Exhibition* was a time-displacement story with an excessively ladylike, thoroughly dishonest heroine. *Rime Isle*, a double from Fritz Leiber, Joanna found to be tired old stuff—without noticing both stories were recent reprints. In *The Year's Finest Fantasy*, edited by Terry Carr, the only outright failure, "The Cat From Hell," a "clumsy piece of grue" would at least get Stephen King's name onto the jacket. A "youthfully energetic and rather appealing" pastiche from Steve Utley and Howard Waldrop won a special mention, and "The Kugelmass Episode" was "perfect Woody Allen." Harlan Ellison's "Jefty Is Five" gets line-by-line, classroom attention, for the curious reason that Ellison "ought not to be writing 'the best of the year' but something much better."

The rest of this column is devoted to her legendary denunciation of sub-Tolkien "heroic fantasy." The works reviewed—Stephen Donaldson's *Lord Foul's Bane* (a "daydream of Byronic suffering and self-importance . . . that could easily have been cut by three-quarters") and Joy Chant's *Grey Mane of Morning* (a smoothly crafted "daydream of primitive, idyllic nomad life")—are treated fairly gently—though it's a shame Joy Chant spends her skill on the "supreme worthiness" of the male characters, leaving nothing for the women. The (sub)genre gets a pummeling. Without real change, which "heroic fantasy" must avoid at all costs, these "guided daydreams" are just a parade of scenery, absurdly fixed characters, and a "dreadful predictability" that only Tolkien and possibly C. S. Lewis knew how to disguise. Her final paragraph gets to the heart of the problem and is worth all the rest:

> The desire for escape is understandable. It's the supply that's spurious. Unfortunately, after Tolkien had wrung the last drop of meaning-freighted landscape out of an extremely tiny genre, the cry went up "Now we know how to do it!" and another, "There's money in it!" and the flood began.[7]

There are multiple footnotes, including a discursion on the failures of *Star Wars* versus the success of Ursula K. Le Guin's *Earthsea Trilogy*, a proper fantasy that uses the invented world to confront real issues.

In the *Washington Post*'s "Book World," April 1979 (a new venue), Joanna recommended *In Memory Yet Green: The Autobiography of Isaac Asimov* to Asimov fans, but only for his charming memories of childhood as an Eastern European, New York Jewish kid in the 1930s. The rest is a dry list of facts, "a mine of information for some secondary biographer." A new Asimov collection, *Opus 200*, is notable for excerpts from his recent novel *The Gods Themselves* (1972), but most of the material can be found elsewhere. In the same venue, in May, she reviewed an Adrienne Rich collection, *On Lies, Secrets, and Silence: Selected Prose 1966–1978*. "Inevitably the book is uneven," but special mention goes to a fine study of Emily Dickinson, "Vesuvius in the Home," and another on Charlotte Brontë's *Jane Eyre*. "The attack of 'man-hater' will most likely be made," but Rich, citing institutional and domestic sadism toward women, will have the right "to point to the evidence and ask simply [compare *Khatru*, 102] 'Who hates whom?'"[8]

In the *Magazine of Fantasy and Science Fiction*, June 1979, Joanna took a skeptical view of *Immortal: Short Novels of the Transhuman Future*, edited by Jack Dann. Only religious mystics, who use the subject as "a metaphor for transcendence," have anything useful to say about immortality, "one of the great unrealizables." (The collection, however, seems to be about perfectly "realizable" extended lifespan.) Dismissing R. C. W. Ettinger's enthusiastic introduction—If we are so radically imperfect, won't the improvements we devise for ourselves be radically imperfect too?—she finds George Zebrowski's "Transfigured Night" a clumsy cautionary tale and Gene Wolfe's "Doctor of Death Island" a chilling study of long life as a commodity. Pamela Sargent's "The Renewal," is at least real science fiction: teaching the lesson that "evasiveness, ordinariness and fear are high-survival traits." "Chanson Perpetuelle," one of many separately published pieces from Thomas Disch's *The Pressure of Time*, suggests the novel might be better off without its sf elements.[9] In his original anthology *Anticipation*, editor Christopher Priest tries too hard to prove his theory that "all good science fiction hovers on the edge of being something other than science fiction." The best stories are Ian Watson's "The Very Slow Time Machine" and Brian Aldiss's "sprightly and optimistic" "A

Chinese Perspective." Reviewing *Ursula K. Le Guin's Science Fiction Workshop: The Altered I*, by Lee Harding, "a student at the first Australian Science Fiction Workshop of 1975," Joanna the teacher takes over, with some feminist notes for sf students addicted to the male pronoun.

> Bite your tongue and write *she*. . . . What the normative male usage does is to insist, usually below the level of conscious awareness, that all of us shes are *special* people, confined to *special* (not broadly human) functions—or that we, like Gethenians, are (sort-of) male ninety percent of the time except when we revert to being (truly) female for the purpose of that special chapter of the human story called Sex and Reproduction—[10]

In the *Feminist Review* (July 1979) Joanna celebrated, under the title "When We Were Everybody: A Lost Feminist Utopia," the volume publication of Charlotte Perkins Gilman's *Herland* (serialized in 1915). She finds that the all-female enclave, discovered by three rich young male explorers in 1917, "bears a striking resemblance to the feminist utopias written in the United States during the last ten years": with the same emphasis on a classless, cooperative, peaceful society; on living in harmony with nature; and on reclaiming the public world for women. Joanna is doubtful on the sublimation of the sex drive into motherhood but makes a joke of Gilman's racism (all the women the explorers meet will look just like the blonde "Gibson Girls" at home!). A letter to the editors, published with the review in *The Country You Have Never Seen*, corrects this solecism.[11]

In *Frontiers* 4, no. 1 (1979) Joanna reviewed *Gyn/Ecology: The Metaethics of Radical Feminism*, by Catholic feminist theologian Mary Daly: "a wild, whirling, terrifying, ecstatic, *haggard* book" (haggard is rescued, in a footnote, as meaning not disheveled or worn out, but "intractable, willful, wanton"). The book "has two faces": one "a description and celebration of the feminist journey into authenticity," the other "a condemnation, through a multitude of examples, from foot-binding and *suttee* to Female Genital Mutilation, of the primary patriarchal project."[12] Another feminist work, *The Mermaid and the Minotaur*, by Dorothy Dinnerstein, reviewed in *Frontiers* 4, no. 2, excited Joanna tremendously. She later decided Dinnerstein's revelation (that fathers should pay attention to their infant children) was relevant mainly to her own middle-class, American, mid-twentieth-century parentage.[13]

In November 1979 the *Magazine of Fantasy and Science Fiction* gave Joanna the opportunity to respond to dozens of letters received "vehemently disagreeing" with her trashing of heroic fantasy—some of which had been published in the July issue. "Joanna Replies" is an entertaining exercise in explaining what critics do (and what they can't help doing), immediately reprinted in a *Best of Fantasy and Science Fiction* collection. A few quotes may give the flavor:

1. *Don't shove your politics into your reviews. Just review the books.*

I will—when the authors keep politics out of their stories. But they never do. In fact it seems absolutely impossible to write anything without immediately making all sorts of assumptions about what human nature is, what good and bad behavior consists of, what men ought to be.

2. *You don't prove what you say, you just assert it.*

This statement is, I think, based on a cognitive error inculcated by American high school education. Proofs need not be cut and dried and presented in a syllogism; a surprising amount of "scientific" proof is not this kind.

. . .

7. *Never mind all that stuff. Just tell me what I'd enjoy reading.*

Bless you, what makes you think I know?[14]

In January 1980 Joanna reviewed science fiction in the *Washington Post*'s "Book World" again. Ursula K. Le Guin's *The Beginning Place*, an intelligent, touching fantasy in the classic style, in which two young people meet, fall in love, and achieve a quest in a fantastic realm, is let down by the excessively dreary "real world" to which the lovers must return. Vonda N. McIntyre's' collection, *Fireflood and Other Stories*, including the famous "Of Mist Grass and Sand," was excellent. David Gerrold's *Yesterday's Children*, a war novel set on a cramped, deteriorating space ship, had many faults, somehow adding up to a "tiring, ultimately worthwhile metaphor." Poul Anderson and Mildred Downey Broxon's *The Demon of Scattery* is a publisher's package: medieval atrocities served up as fun, in big print with lavish illustrations.

In February 1980 she returned to the *Magazine of Fantasy and Science Fiction*, covering several titles. In Thomas Disch's *On Wings of Song*, set in a deeply divided near-future America, a young man, Daniel, escapes the conservative farm belt to find freedom and fame practicing a new artform (a kind of psychedelic astral projection). Joanna found Daniel's sexuality difficult to track, and she objects mildly to the suggestion that the liberal cities are "seething with corruption"—and the grotesquely restrictive farm states aren't?—but finds Disch's blend of sf and mainstream admirable. *On Wings of Song* won the John W Campbell Award in 1980 and was nominated for a Nebula and a Hugo. *The Painted Devils*, by Robert Aickman, was a mystifying collection. Aickman's horror stories are superior but best enjoyed one at a time in anthologies, where the absence of any rationale for what's happening won't start to jar. Octavia Butler's *Kindred* retains the author's "stubborn, idiosyncratic gift for realism," as she makes new and eloquent use of a familiar (sf) idea—protecting one's own past via time travel—to express the tangled interdependence of black and white history in the United States: Dana, the heroine, *has to* keep Rufus, the appalling and perversely reckless slave owner, alive—at least until he's impregnated one of his slaves, who is Dana's great-grandmother. The present-day world gets crowded out, but that's a minor flaw, justified by the gripping strangeness of Dana's visits to the "past." *Kindred* won no sf awards or nominations but swiftly became Butler's runaway bestseller.

Terry Carr's *Universe 9* is "a good collection, generally optimistic-social in tone." Robert Silverberg's *New Dimensions 9* is a "strongly homogenous collection" devoted to white, male alienation. "It's as if the authors . . . had woken up one morning in David Bunch's *Moderan*, or a Barry Malzberg novel,"—but without Bunch's "loud ridicule" of the hypermale predicament or "Malzberg's agonized moral sense." Felix Gotschalk, in his machine adventure land, and Jeff Hecht, with his "old-fashioned *Analog* hero," seem to be having a good time. The rest (of the anthology, or the authors) are in a miserable condition and need to be sent to Ursula K. Le Guin's "dazzler," "The Pathways of Desire," a maverick in this collection, to be psychoanalyzed.[15] Finally, Le Guin's "novelistically graceful" essays, collected in *The Language of the Night*, are best when she's writing spontaneously for fanzines and display a delicious sense of comedy (plus a little too much interest in morality). Susan Wood deserves the thanks of all lovers of Le Guin's work for initiating and editing this volume. This was Joanna's last column for the *Magazine of Fantasy and Science Fiction*.

For *Sinister Wisdom* 12 (Winter 1980) Joanna wrote about feminist sf under the title "Listen, There's a Story for You." *Retreat As It Was*, by Donna Young, the lesbian feminist utopian novel she'd been asked to review, wasn't up to much. The only use of technology is lamentable, the "science fiction" seems to have been gleaned from bad TV; the plot is indiscernible and erotic content mainly absent: "What *is* the book about? Hugging, I think." But Joanna uses this "limp and thin" story as an introduction first to wild-woman Sally Gearhart and her idiosyncratic *Wanderground* (not short of hugs itself, as I recall), and then to a "Titan at the forge" of the future, representing either Suzy McKee Charnas or her new novel, *Motherlines*, or both. *Motherlines* is an ideal of what lesbian feminist sf should be: scientifically and politically literate, rich in detail, and populated by strongly individual, sexy characters, good and bad, strange and simple, who all happen to be women.

In *Frontiers 3* (1981) Joanna reviewed *Woman's Creation: Sexual Evolution and the Shaping of Society*, by Elizabeth Fisher (founder of the feminist journal *Aphra*)—a study dating the emergence of "patriarchy" to a change in human social organization, in the Middle East, around 2000 BC. This change, variously dated, is common currency in ancient history now, but in 1981 it validated (possibly) the legendary existence of prepatriarchal, female-ordered civilizations. The thrill Joanna felt electrifies her review.

In the *Washington Post*'s Book World" of May 10, 1981, Joanna praises, in depth and detail, Lilian Faderman's rich study, *Surpassing the Love of Men: Romantic Friendship between Women from the Renaissance to the Present*. Faderman has restored the normalcy of "intense emotional relations" between women, dispelling the myth of a few "sick" women who have lesbian feelings. This is the last of the Joanna's collected reviews.

## ESSAYS RELEVANT TO 1978–1980

Joanna published two science fiction essays between 1977 and 1981. One was her important "Recent Feminist Utopias." The other, and earlier, is a foray into political science, with reference to the successful mass-market sf that had emerged in movies and on TV (*Star Wars* and *Star Trek*). An autobiographical essay and two interesting letters of comment are also noted.

In "SF and Technology as Mystification" (*Science Fiction Studies* [November 1978]; collected in *To Write Like a Woman*) Joanna investigates a topic that has become wildly popular with both humanities academics and science fiction professionals: generating endless conferences, symposia, and informal discussions. The issue is "Technology," but what exactly *is* "Technology"? Nobody seems to know. She compares this empty fascination with America's addiction to refined sugar and detects the same phenomenon in the popularity of the spectacular, fascistic *Star Wars* movie narrative: purpose-built to turn the kids into sugar-junkies. The *Star Trek* TV series, with its utopian aspirations and more modest, fan-driven success, has similar characteristics, but almost rises above "Technology" addiction. The effect can be seen again in the relationship between the modern gothic genre, popular literature for the female market, exploiting for excitement (and profit) the perils that women face in a sexist society, and the original, serious works of nineteenth-century female authors (Charlotte Brontë, George Eliot), who used the same material to confront and analyze those problems.

"Technology" addicts, Joanna suggests, suffer from Rebecca West's "male defect" of Lunacy (seeing only the outlines of all structure, none of the detail).[16] West's "female defect" of Idiocy, "a refusal to go beyond the specific details to any larger pattern," won't qualify you for academia or futuristic triumphs (there's only one woman in the *Star Wars* universe by the time we reach the finale), but it defines you as one of the people who "clean up after themselves": markedly absent from the *Star Wars* model; essential to the *Star Trek* ideal. The question remains: What do all these people *mean* when they talk about "Technology" so importantly? Feeling her way, she discerns that it's something *modern, ubiquitous, autonomous, uncontrollable,* which enthusiasts would rather not call by its proper name. "Technology," in fact, is a mask for advanced, industrial capitalism, and the "Mystification" in the essay title is used in the Marxist sense: a deliberate obfuscation of capitalist and social dynamics, as an impediment to critical consciousness. For humanities academics, calling capitalism "technology" is a means of avoiding social and political realities (such as their endemic financial insecurity). Advanced industrial capitalism is also a sore subject for the science fiction community[17]—a party to which they and their dazzling technophilic inventions haven't been invited. What's the solution? Tackle the technology craving like an addiction to sugar, suggests Joanna. Are you feeling shaky? Reaching for that sweet technology hit? "Eat a little economics; eat a little political analysis. You'll think better."

"Recent Feminist Utopias" (*Future Females: A Critical Anthology,* edited by Marleen Barr [Bowling Green, Ohio: Bowling Green University Popular Press, 1981]; collected in *To Write Like a Woman*) draws on and consolidates earlier material for an overview and a (flexible) definition of seventies feminist utopias.

The works considered are Monique Wittig's *Les Guérillères* (1969), published in English translation by Viking in 1971; Ursula K. Le Guin's *The Dispossessed* (1974); *The Female Man* (1975); and several works from 1976: Marion Zimmer Bradley's *The Shattered Chain*; Samuel Delany's *Triton (Trouble on Triton);* Marge Piercy's *Woman on the Edge of Time*; Sally Gearhart's *The Wanderground*; Catherine Masden's "Commodore Bork and the Compost;"[18] two stories by Alice Sheldon ("Tiptree" had been unmasked) from the *Aurora, beyond Equality* anthology, "Houston, Houston, Do You Read?" (as "James Tiptree Jr") and "Your Faces, O My Sisters! Your Faces Filled of Light," (as Racoona Sheldon); and Suzy McKee Charnas's *Motherlines* (1978).

A feminist utopia is "a society better than our own in explicitly feminist ways, for explicitly feminist reasons"—a definition that allows Joanna to include *The Shattered Chain*, though the Free Amazons Guild is an enclave in the far from feminist society of *Darkover*, and *The Dispossessed*, though feminism takes second place in that novel to Le Guin's communitarian anarchism. (I would add Delany's "ambiguous heterotopia" *Triton* to the variant class, since it's an exception to almost every rule Joanna defines.) All the writers except Wittig[19] could have had knowledge of each other's works, but the "numerous areas of consensus," as Carol Pearson noted in her 1977 essay,[20] are still striking. Previously, science fictions have proposed changes in innate biology to solve the sex problem, as in Theodore Sturgeon's *Venus Plus X*[21] but goodwill attempts to change the facts, without understanding how those "facts" are maintained, achieve nothing. Currently, the popular fiction version of sexual equality amounts to placing men and women together in a workplace, the women still performing feminine, supportive roles and women's gendered work (childcare, domestic chores) off scene. The utopias featured in this essay are something more: based on a shared political analysis, identifying the same abuses, and providing similar solutions and remedies. Societies are communal, tribal, or quasi-tribal. Decision making is by consensus. Social units are small even if the society is global, and government hardly exists (except for Triton). The ethos is ecology minded except for Triton, an urban "heterotopia" under the surface of a moon of Neptune, and classless except for the stratified society of Triton. Gender stereotypes are not discussed (except for Triton[22]): "We merely see that they are not true, and do not apply." Armed conflict is minor, absent, or experienced the way women usually experience war (as in the systems-sabotage war that causes overwhelming civilian casualties, in *Triton*)[23]—as disaster and social collapse, not as adventure or sport.

Sexual permissiveness is the norm, "not to break taboos, but to separate sexuality from questions of ownership, reproduction and social structure." *Woman on the Edge of Time* is the most sexually innovative, with homosexuality unremarkable and not even named, exogenetic pregnancy, and both sexes suckling infants. *Triton* may go too far, divorcing sex from affection and validating extreme sexual practices. The six all-female societies are "not subtle" about the rationale for separatism: "men are dangerous, and they hog the good things of life." Alice Sheldon's stories, "Houston, Houston" and "Your Faces, Oh My Sisters," feature graphic evidence of men's sexual brutality. In *Motherlines*, the male enclave "Holdfast" keeps "fems" as chattel slaves.

Physical freedom and freedom to travel are emphasized, an indication of how little real freedom from intimidation women enjoy in the present, especially in the urban environment. In *The Female Man* the women of Whileaway travel alone, in perfect safety. In *Les Guérillères* "bands of strong women roam freely everywhere." In Sally Gearhart's *Wanderground* the Hill Women use psi powers to travel great distances but avoid the cities, where men still rule. Yet some men may be "invited in":[24] In *Les Guérillères* young men are recruited to the war against the fathers.

Several texts feature the (symbolic) rescue of the female child,[25] a project made explicit in *The Shattered Chain*, *Woman on the Edge of Time*, and *Motherlines*. In Vonda N. McIntyre's *Dreamsnake* and in Joanna's *The Two of Them* a female protagonist rescues a pubertal girl from an abusive fate.[26] For girls under patriarchy, puberty is a closing down of horizons. In feminist utopias, "what is crucial is that she be free."

A brief note covers "Battle of the Sexes"[27] stories, typically written by men: emphasizing the sexual violence and the depiction of the "battle" as private, between one man and one woman, with the man as victor, as opposed to the "curious gentleness" of the public war against patriarchy. Joanna also notes (with personal resentment) the tendency of male readers to perceive minor, feminist violence as extremely shocking. Finally, "utopias are not embodiments of universal human values, but are *reactive*, that is, they supply in fiction what their authors believe society and/or women lack in the here and now."[28] Hence these feminist utopias, instead of providing the usual sf wish fulfillment, have to rectify "the grossest and simplest forms of injustice"; but this does not detract from their value. The essay concludes with a strong invitation for sf readers to seek out titles they may not have encountered; the Alice Sheldon short stories, and *Woman on the Edge of Time*.

"Is 'Smashing' Erotic?" (*Chrysalis* [Fall 1979]; collected in *To Write Like a Woman*): in the previous issue of *Chrysalis*, a short-lived Feminist journal,[29] Nancy Sahli[30] had written about passionate relationships between American women, on the cusp of a destructive cultural change in the late nineteenth century. Her special reference was to the intense college-girl romances, compared with amusement rather than disapproval to heterosexual courtship, known as "smashing," a term that seems to have originated at Vassar. The suitor, or "aggressor," in a "smash" would pursue her prey with bouquets, candies, and compliments. Once paired, a couple would sleep together, "spoon continually," and stay up rapturously talking all night.[31] But around 1875, everything changed. Attachments between women and girls were suddenly a threat to the system: pathologized, policed, and proscribed: this is the "Fall" Sahli references. The term "Lesbian" became a stick to beat women with, no matter what kind of relationships they shared. It was a high price to pay for the privilege of being *named* in a male-ordered world. In her letter of comment Joanna accuses Sahli of separating "same sex attachments" from "lesbianism," as if one is innocent and the other guilty, and using the prurient "genital activity" as a restrictive dividing line. But in fact Sahli's article defines lesbian attachments inclusively, citing Blanche Cooke: "Women who love women, who choose women to nurture and support and to create a living environment in which to work creatively and independently, are lesbians."[32] Seventies feminism was a tangled coil. "Smashing" surely is, or was, erotic; yet perhaps Joanna's defense of visibility was timely. Sahli's article (available online) and this letter should be compared with Joanna's essay-review of Lilian Faderman's *Surpassing the Love of Men* (in *The Country You Have Never Seen*, 190).

"Not for Years but for Decades" (*The Coming Out Stories*, edited by Julia Penelope Stanley and Susan J. Wolfe [Watertown, Mass.: Persephone, 1980]; collected in *Magic Mommas* [1985])[33] is not a "coming out story" in the usual sense. Whenever Joanna realizes she's a lesbian, tells people she's a lesbian, or tries to behave like a lesbian, in this account of a young woman's sexual awakenings she's invariably ignored or misunderstood—even by herself. The first part, titled "Fact," traces issues of sexual identity through the adolescence and young adulthood of a "tall, overly bright, overly self-assertive girl, too much so to fit into anybody's notion of femininity (and too bookish and odd to fit other children's ideas of an acceptable human being)"[34] There's the "necking and petting" at summer camp with her first love, Carol-Ellen, and Joanna's bewilderment when, next year, all the other girls (including Carol-Ellen) seemed to have forgotten this behavior. There are excruciating teenage experiments in heterosexuality; attempts to seduce (a repeating pattern, apparently) gay male friends; the school psychiatrist who told her she had "penis envy." In her teens she developed a passion for "Love Comics," wrote "Lesbian" stories "to shock my teacher," and asked her friends to *pretend* she was a lesbian. At college, where she'd hoped to be treated as an equal, the serious indoctrination in "how to be a woman" began. After college she married, in desperation (for the shameful, secret reason that she couldn't make her own living), spent time in group therapy, persevered with sexual relations she loathed, and had terrifying, desolating nightmares.[35] But then says Joanna, without further elaboration, she got out.

Part 2, the "Fantasy" section, details a sexual inner life, from childhood to adulthood, that she regarded as "both crucially important and totally trivial." Dreams about saving gentle Danny Kaye from peril were superseded by male-on-male erotic fantasies: a solution to the problem of "not knowing what lesbians do," and the other problem that as she didn't want to "be a girl" in sex, she didn't want her imaginary partner to "be the girl" either, "knowing what a rotten deal that was."[36] A vividly told story, deceptively frank and determinedly reticent, with an emphasis on the importance of fantasy, this essay provides rare biographical detail and insights into many of Joanna's fictions.

"On 'The Yellow Wallpaper'" (NWSA journal [Autumn 1988]; collected in *To Write Like a Woman*) is noted here for its relevance to *The Two of Them*. Again, as in "Smashing," responding to a published article, Joanna finds that Diana Price Herndl, when reviewing Charlotte Perkins Gilman's "The Yellow Wallpaper," reveals her culpable ignorance of "paraliterary tradition"—forms of literary expression, that is, historically most accessible to female writers and readers. The large house, so cheap to rent, so long untenanted; the big strange upper room with its grim furnishings; the complacent husband who insists that he and his sensitive wife take this scary den as their bedroom—all these markers signal "ghost story" to genre readers, by established convention. The artful-naïve description in Gilman's opening passages, designed to heighten the reader's dread, certainly does invoke domestic oppression as a woman's "hereditary estate,"[37] but the unnamed protagonist isn't being driven mad. She is haunted or possessed. The project of diagnosing a literary character's psychosis in genre fiction of this kind is doomed and absurd. The story is a feminist *fable*, and the heroine's madness (which doesn't resemble, coherently, any recognizable mental disorder) is a vivid metaphor for the desperation Gilman felt, under the regime of *invalidization* her doctor prescribed as a cure for her "grinding depression"—an affliction that women "whose perceptions are at odds with societally imposed familial truths" often feel is akin to madness. But in fact Herndl devotes only a few pages to Gilman. Her real topic, and maybe the real source of Joanna's ire, is the Lacanian psychoanalysis of "female hysteria."[38] Joanna questions eighties feminism's project of "assimilation" with powerful male-ordered disciplines like psychoanalysis. "Once a radical politics (or literary criticism) is limited and diluted to the point where it can safely become part of the establishment," she warns, *"it can also be dispensed with."*[39]

## STORIES, 1978–1980

Joanna published three short stories in this period, and two longer fictions: *Kittatinny*, her only children's (or teenage) book, and *On Strike against God*, her only nongenre novel (see chapter 7).

"The Extraordinary Voyages of Amélie Bertrand" (*Magazine of Fantasy and Science Fiction* [September 1979]; Nebula nominee; collected in *The Zanzibar Cat*) is a tribute to Jules Verne, hence the title.[40] A male business traveler (not otherwise identified) encounters Amélie "the true type of our *bonne bourgeoise*" on a provincial railway station, where a mysterious portal, opening on other worlds and locations, coincides, at certain times, with the covered passage that crosses over the tracks. He visits Uganda with her (they see an elephant), and she recounts other "voyages," including an unexpected visit to Tierra del

Fuego that initiated a two-year romance with a sailor, and a trip to the Moon, two thousand years in the future. When the traveler returns to make a serious investigation, Amélie is on the platform again. She tells him the station is to be demolished and hurriedly departs with her friend (another woman)—to catch a train that doesn't feature on the timetable. An aerodrome is to be built on the site. Our narrator plans to go up in a small plane, hoping the portal is still open, above the former railway tracks, and so the story ends. A hit with the public.

"Dragons and Dimwits" (*Magazine of Fantasy and Science Fiction* [December 1979]; reprinted in *The Zanzibar Cat*), as the full title indicates ("Dragons and Dimwits: or, There and Back Again: A Publishers' Holiday; or, Why Did I Do It?; or, Much Ado about Magic or Lord of the Royalties or . . . or . . . or . . ."), is further persecution, after Joanna's February review column, for fans of *Lord Foul's Bane* and sub-Tolkien "heroic fantasy" in general. Thomas Covenant, thinly disguised as "Thomas of Cornwall" and afflicted with TB instead of leprosy, suffers spiritual agony in the tents of The People, and helps Joanna to mock the subgenre's blurry inconveniences for a few pages before returning to his own world and a comfy sanatorium, leaving the maiden, "May the Unpregnant," to puzzle over a great mystery: "What is '*Food*'"? Readers are invited to follow May's adventures through interminable subsequent volumes. Nobody gets raped. Mildly amusing and not entirely pointless.

"It's Important to Believe" (*Sinister Wisdom* 14 [1980]; collected in *The Hidden Side of the Moon*) is a short piece, barely 150 words. Virginia Woolf, certain she was descending into madness again and unable to face another bout of torment, died by suicide at the end of March 1941. Her body was later recovered from the River Ouse, which runs close by Rodmell, where she and Leonard were living in their weekend cottage, having been bombed out of London. Here Joanna imagines her gently rescued "by friendly aliens" and taken to a good place. It's dedicated to Jessica Amanda Salmonson, "who had the idea," and to Allie Sheldon, "who wrote 'Beam Us Home'."[41]

*Kittatinny* (New York: Daughters, 1978)

Kittatinny Blue-Eyes, a Valley girl whose life is a round of chores, relieved by rough games (that her pretty friend Rose isn't allowed to join), exploring, and "learning to read and write with the Parsons," storms off into the woods one day—sore at being told she can't grow up to be a Miller, she can only marry a Miller. She loses herself in the Ridges: follows a wolf,[42] unafraid until he vanishes, leaving her in the midst of a dark wood—and embarks on the spirit journey that will lead her to adulthood. Many adventures ensue, but the first—when she stumbles upon a band of wispily draped nymphs and hairy-legged satyrs (very incongruous in this old-time rural American setting) and is obliged to adopt a baby they leave behind—may be the most significant. She knows the baby is male: she sees the "hangar and bag"[43] between his little furry satyr legs. And he can already talk. She calls him BB (Baby Brother). He's light as paper to carry and doesn't need to eat or drink: he feeds on human heartbeats. As they travel on—squabbling and bonding; meeting a golden dragon who gives Kit a sword; encountering monster Slonches who attack BB until Kit slashes their legs off; finding a lost city by the seashore, and a great book where Kit reads a much-told tragic fairytale (more comic than tragic here)—[44] BB starts becoming human and seems to have an affinity with the myths and stories that weave themselves into this quest. In the high country they meet Woman Warrior, a female hero from China, and her many relatives—legendary female heroes from all the ages, who turn up to put out a raging forest fire. In the soft, voluptuous land beyond the mountains they find Sleeping Beauty's castle (which BB refuses to enter). Kit learns that Beauty is a beautiful little girl, locked up in the prison of femininity, who became a vampire long ago. . . . But all stories end in ordinariness. BB, now as tall as Kit, vanishes, and Kit returns to the Valley with the taste of tears in her mouth. Back at home, it's as if she never went anywhere, and she realizes a part of her must have stayed behind while she was off questing, for six or seven years. She kisses Ondry Miller, the miller's son, and feels excitement in her body: but when he gets serious, proposing marriage, she "suddenly finds herself on the other end of the bench." She kisses her friend Rose, now engaged to a rich merchant, and feels something very different. When Ondry and then Rose have left for the harvest dance, the strangest meeting is with BB, who reappears *looking out of a mirror.*[45] This is the lesson of the spirit journey. Knowledge, art, and writing are not male preserves. The satyr baby she found in the wood and carried on her back, whom she rescued and fought with, was her own talent, which she saw as "male," because that's what she'd been taught: it was her own talent that kept giving her good advice. The good advice from the mirror now is

*Go with the one who goes with you.* Kit sets out on her adventures again and sees someone following her, dressed in boy's clothes, same as she's wearing herself. Is it Ondry, or is it Rose? A coming-of-age story for young girls, full of references to Joanna's own *bildungsroman* and to stories she has loved (the female dragon's cave bears a strong resemblance to Smaug's gold-flooded cavern under the Lonely Mountain, in Tolkien's own illustration; Maxine Hong Kingston's *The Woman Warrior* gets a credit). Illustrated with naïve line drawings by Loretta Li; sadly, it was never reprinted. Quirky, gentle, and charming—and with a happy ending!

## THE TWO OF THEM

The connection between the novel *The Two of Them* and Suzette Haden Elgin's story "For the Sake of Grace" is well known to Joanna Russ fans. It's less well known that Elgin's story (1969), about the female writer incarcerated and forbidden to write (like the protagonist of "The Yellow Wallpaper") and the "exceptional" young girl who escapes this fate, became the prologue to a novel, *At the Seventh Level* (1972), best described as sharing the values of "evolved pulp" on the *Star Trek* model. Jacinth, heroine of "For the Sake of Grace," now holding the vital post of chief poet (and war leader) but still appallingly isolated in her patriarchal society, needs protection from unknown forces. Elgin's serial male character, Coyote Jones, undercover agent of the Tri-Galactic Intelligence Service, is dispatched to the Islamic-style civilization of the planet Abba to tackle the problem. His motives are impure—he's protecting Tri-Galactic commercial interests, and his methods are crudely patriarchal: he fools the natives with his superior "magic" and overwhelms the virgin poet with his phallic prowess. Yet he is not a bad man. He's a *good* man, respectful of the prime directive[46] and trying to do no harm. Effectively, Joanna interrogates and updates this entire scenario in her feminist tale of a male state agent with conventional liberal views who tries to nurture and care for his women, and of two young women, neither particularly exceptional or admirable, who, when it comes to the crunch, would rather be free.

Joanna's other main source is, as usual, autobiographical. Irene Waskiewicz, the Polish American Trans-Temp agent from a 1950s United States much like our own, invokes another past or possible Joanna—brash and sexually aggressive (and politically naïve), to add to the four Js in *The Female Man*. Irene was an overly assertive middle-class teenager, age sixteen, just like Joanna in her version of 1953—but no high-flyer, and facing a far more limited future. She liked pretending to be Irene Adler, "*the* woman"—the only woman the great Sherlock Holmes regarded as his equal, a classy game she could share with her opera-loving best girlfriend.[47] She also enjoyed heavy-petting sessions, after dark in the local park with her beautiful Jewish boyfriend; acceptable (covert) behavior in the prim but highly sexualized 1950s. But David expects Irene to be a docile wife once they're married. On one of their hectic nights, when she's had to forgo orgasm, "being careful" for both of them, he parrots at her the entire official catalog of restrictions to which well-adjusted women must conform. Enraged, she calls him a filthy Jew and hits him with a rock.

Ernst[48] Neumann, a friend of her mother's, oddly dressed and intriguing, entered her life with an astonishing gesture. He called her *Ireenee*, the "British" pronunciation of her name, marking her as exceptional, like "Irene Adler." His friendship with her very ordinary mother is unaccountable; he once said Rose Waskiewicz had "inherited" him. Irene has been fascinated by Ernst, forgotten about him, and then become fascinated again (the replication of the circumstances in "The Second Inquisition" is eerie). One night, desperate to escape from a choice between the local junior college and "State for Domestic Economics," with only David and marriage beyond, she decides to throw herself at this older man, and she traces him (using considerable ingenuity) to his hotel room. He tells her it's part of his job to "collect little boys and little girls." She tells him she needs "to get right out of this world"—and wonders why he laughs. The sex they share that night, with Irene very much the initiator, seals an enduring contract.

The planet Abba, in *At the Seventh Level*, had a population based on the classic sf Theory of Convergent Humanoid Evolution and boasted thirty centuries of vaguely Islamic civilization. The "Islamic civilization" of Ka'abah, a hollowed-out asteroid, is just three generations old. The inhabitants are Earth-human in origin: genetically engineered for a world of low passages and nested chambers. Joanna lifts names and flowery language from *The Thousand and One Nights*, but there's no serious attempt to replicate a Muslim society. The bourgeois wives of Ka'abah, kept in seclusion for the honor of their families, are transparently 1950s American housewives in fancy dress, medicated into passivity and obsessed with consumerism—endlessly buying and selling each other's embroidery and purchasing off-world fripperies with their profits. Female servants and prostitutes (the latter alluded to but never seen) are not enclosed; girl children of respectable families are spoiled by adoring fathers. Zumurrud, the wife of Wezeer 'Alee, who will play host to the Trans-Temp agents, tends to look at her husband with "mad dislike." He can't imagine why but reveals that she "conceived her last two children while medicated"—a refinement on similar tactics in Suzette Haden Elgin's story. The Khadilah Althea, the poet Jacinth's mother in *At the Seventh Level* had to be "tied to four bedposts at her last impregnation"; her husband rated this regrettable, but perfectly normal.

Ernst and Irene, "honor guards" to a Diplomatic Mission, tall, exotically pale, and identically dressed "entirely in black, with belted tabards over what looks like long underwear"—the familiar Trans-Temp uniform—are easily taken for two males by their local host, but Irene insists on being recognized as female and thus gains access to the hareem. She meets Zumurrud, the invalidized wife, and the shrewd maid (a fairly kindly prison guard), whose chief function is to stop the lady from procuring abortions and to administer the drugs that keep her subdued. When Zumurrud's tiny twelve-year-old daughter appears, announcing she's taken her mother's "old medicine," panic ensues until the maid has induced the little girl to vomit. Zubeydeh's father has forbidden her to "enter the poetry contest," even though she's as good as her brother Jaafar and "knows all the forms": hence the suicidal gesture. Reminded that only men can be poets, she appeals to the foreigner for support, which Irene provides without a thought: of course Zubeydeh could be a poet on Irene's world. Zumurrud's reaction of utter horror impresses Irene, but she does not connect the mother's panic with a story about "Aunt Dunya," who also wanted to be a poet and is dead now.

Irene, the active agent, sneaks into Ka'abah's computer systems and extracts information, under cover of her role as "Honor Guard." Indifferent to the politics behind these assignments, she's more concerned about whether her tampon will last the day than about the espionage.[49] She's one of the Gang: playing with the boys, not the girls, that's what matters. But Ka'abah and the young girl Zubeydeh will gradually get under her skin.

As Zubeydeh, precocious and charming, keeps insisting she wants to be a poet, and the awful example of aunt Dunya, who wanted to be a poet and came to a mysterious bad end, keeps coming up, an unprecedented tension builds between Irene and her partner. Ka'abah's public society is entirely male; even female parts on daytime TV are played by beautiful female impersonators. Ernst thinks nothing of it: Irene begins to take the subjection of Ka'abah women personally. Then Zumurrud, to protect her daughter, shows Zubeydeh what *really* happened to Aunt Dunya—and the girl, hysterical, drags Irene to the tiny cell where her aunt has been kept in solitary confinement for decades. Through "one small shuttered window," by the light of a naked bulb, Irene sees a heap of old clothes stir, as Dunya resumes a constant obsessive behavior: creeping bestially around the cell, her shoulder fitting into a smudged groove around the walls "some sixteen inches high."[50] "We kept taking her papers away," says Zumurrud, who has followed her daughter and the foreigner. "And then she went mad, so we knew we'd done the right thing."

Trans-Temp agents "collect" special children, but Irene is "over her quota," and Zubedyeh isn't special. Her poems, everyone agrees, are what you'd expect from any bright twelve-year-old. But she's in danger of sharing Dunya's horrible fate, and that should be enough. Ernst, acting as "Conscience" finally agrees to Irene's plan. Extracting Zubeydeh from her loving family does not go smoothly: Irene bullies the Wezeer into signing the visa, but they fail to rescue Dunya, and Zubeydeh's mother only wants to be left alone. At the Port of Entry, when they are nearly prevented from leaving, Irene furiously strong-arms her way through, and Irene, Ernst, Zubeydeh, and her squirrel Yasemeen are free, out of Ka'abah's artificial gravity and on their way.

*The Two of Them* is, ironically, the most approachable and most conventionally fictional (most of the time!) of Joanna's sf novels. Secondary characters on Ka'abah have life and individuality well beyond their roles in the plot: bothered little 'Alee the Wezeer; Zumurrud, with her flashes of bitter intelligence, clinging to the lovely cats in her drugged dreams; El-Ward fi-il-Akmam, the loyal, unscrupulous maid; even Jaafar, Zubeydeh's "stuck-up but kind" brother, and Ala-ed-Deen, the insouciant female impersonator. Zubeydeh, the hareem child, with her shrieking tantrums and naïve commonsense, her startling self-knowledge, and her wise young eyes, unblinded by Irene's delusions of equality, is the most vivid of all. To meet this family and then find out what they did to Zumurrud's inconvenient sister is a shock and a reminder: ordinary people do terrible things.

Ernst Neumann is another appealing character. He's older, Irene is his protégée, but to both of them Trans-Temp has been a refuge from unbelonging—his recurring dream image of himself, a Jewish refugee with a small suitcase, standing on a submerging desert island, waiting to drown,[51] is very touching. She's sexually aggressive; he's sensual and gentle. She's daring and he's cautious. He loves submitting to her; he loves guiding her. She depends on him and bullies him. He calls her Ada Lovelace; Marie Skłodowska; Kopernik; flattering pet-names; female geniuses; or Polish, or both. But he sees only "cultural difference" in the subjection of Ka'abah women, and though he's agreed, reluctantly, to let Irene have her way over the little girl, something strange happens when the two of them are in their cabin on the ship. For once, Irene isn't ready for sex. But Ernst takes her anyway.

Irene starts brooding. She wonders why the Trans-Temp Authority is enabling the horribly unequal society of Ka'abah. Could it be that Trans-Temp isn't all that *different* from Ka'abah? She decides it's about time she found out whom she's working for: what is the *purpose* of the Trans Temp Authority? She shares these thoughts with Ernst, and his response is disquieting: he tells her not to meddle. Just do your job. Many years too late, it dawns on her that at the Center, where she and Ernst are debriefed between missions, other women have desk jobs, or they're support staff, or they're "jolly girls" (there are no "jolly boys"). Irene has been unique, and never worried about it. She keeps working on Ernst, and the more she insists, the more he reveals opinions that shock her, and a version of their relationship that she never knew existed.

Ernst *orders* Zubeydeh to obey Irene (a bad slip, demoting her from authority). He belittles her ("Are you going to cry?") when she's arguing her case.[52] When she asks him to help her get into Trans-Temp's secret files, he tells her that he would "never allow her" to get into such bad trouble. This is "conventional" space travel. The unraveling plays out over shipboard "days and nights" in cramped accommodations and low gravity that makes getting about difficult. Irene hides in the puzzled greenery of the hydroponic gardens to deal with her discovery that Ernst, the friendly Goliath, is actually no different from David, her junior-patriarch boyfriend of long ago.

> To come so far. Like Elf Hill. And all for nothing. To spend your adolescence dreaming of the days when you would be strong and famous. To make such a big loop—even into the stars—and all for nothing.[53]

The parallel between Irene's experience with Trans-Temp, the organization that made her special and took her to the stars, and Joanna's experience with the genre and community of science fiction is very close.

She tells Ernst she wants a female partner in the future. Impossible, says Ernst: there's no other female agent—and he warns her against further strange behavior. The next time she needs to use an ID, it's rejected. She finds that Ernst has wiped her Trans-Temp identity. Irene's been the "active agent" often, but she's never had such power over Ernst. She's distraught and heartbroken for several minutes, but she still has her skills (did Ernst think they would vanish?), and the ship's systems aren't sophisticated. She soon creates a new identity for herself, as "Iren*ee*," and a new ID for Zubeydeh. An alignment has been shifting since the escape from Ka'abah; now the change is complete. *The Two of Them* means Irene and Zubeydeh, not the exceptional woman and the enabling man but a woman and a girl, bound together by their female, subaltern status. The next challenge is getting off the ship without being stopped by Ernst.

And here the author intervenes, warning readers that the comedy is over: what happens next won't be *nice*. Joanna tells us she contemplated having Ernst get stomach flu, so the women can run while he's retching, but she's decided on something more drastic. She has Ernst and Irene meet in a corridor when Ernst has just found out that Irene intends to make a break for it with the little girl. He bars her way—and he is *still* a sympathetic character, afraid Trans-Temp will use this upset as an excuse not to hire women if he doesn't put a stop to it. Neither will back down, so they fight, physically and clumsily, in the low gravity that equalizes their weight and muscle, until Irene, weary of the impasse, takes out a gun and shoots Ernst dead.

In my review of the Wesleyan edition of *The Two of Them*, I pointed out that it's Joanna, with her authorial intervention, who directs us "to see the death of Ernst as a shocking transgression," not the logic of the plot.[54] She's just uncovered an evil conspiracy that goes right to the top of her organization: it's tragic that she has to shoot her partner, but she has to save herself and the little girl . . . not terribly culpable, in thriller movie terms! Why then, does Joanna step out of the fiction, agonizing and accusing herself?

Jeanne Cortiel finds that "the killing of a male"[55] is central to Joanna's stories of agency. Escaping from patriarchy, "women cannot get away without murder"—without, that is, acts that *feel like* murder. In "The Second Inquisition" a fantasy laced with murderous violence ended with the loss of an escape route; "no more stories." In *We Who Are About To* a failed activist went on a killing spree to gain her freedom. In *The Two of Them*, another violent gesture signals a new beginning, as Joanna's avatar rejects, after years of willful blindness, the role of "honorary male." Ernst's death may be symbolic rather than actual, even in the fiction (close reading suggests that Irene's anger "may have fooled her" into *imagining* that she actually killed her partner),[56] but it must be read as genuinely final and painful for both character and author. Fantasies about killing are a palliative, deadening anger. Real renunciation hurts.

There is no disposal of a dead body or of a guilty weapon. Irene just hurries to get herself, Zubeydeh, and the squirrel off the ship without arousing suspicion—a feat complicated by the unappealing little boy Zubeydeh has adopted. She bullies him sexually, but she loves him: he's different from all other men, who are hateful. So the cycle is set to repeat—but the little dirty boy vanishes (like the androcide), and Irene and Zubeydeh are deposited, alone and secretly, on a world very like the place Irene started from. They'll have to get rid of even the clothes they stand up in, but Trans-Temp has provided a severance package. A thirty-year-old woman with a child and a pocket full of unset diamonds, hitching a ride to Albuquerque on a desert roadside at night: Irene is starting again in what she hopes is the right direction, at last.

In the final scene of the novel Irene, asleep and dreaming, sees Zubeydeh watching over a vast cavern or an endless dry valley. The floor of this hollow space is heaped with the bones of countless women: dry bones, sterile and silenced, like mad Dunya. A voice whispers as she gazes into this haunting image of patient desolation . . . *Shall these bones live?* The answer to this question, in the book of Ezekiel, is supposed to be *yes*;[57] and this is Joanna's answer too. It's going to take longer. It won't be easy. But women will rise.

Joanna was still, if not the queen, then the First Minister of feminist science fiction, but she was tired of fighting a battle she couldn't win, and though it was a cruel wrench (like some kind of murder), it was time to walk away and concentrate on feminist politics. But the breakup would not be as complete, or as final, as that sounds.

# CHAPTER 7

# BEYOND GENDER?
*Extra(Ordinary)People* Imagines a World without Feminism

> From 1953 through 1967 there had not been one single woman to win a Hugo Award for fiction. Between 1968 and 1984 there were eleven, and the increase of popular SF writers who were women was the exciting event of the 1970s. Anthologies of SF by women were published not only for the novelty of their authorship, but for the significantly different way that women were writing SF. Their emphasis on character development and human interaction completely changed our expectations of the genre.
>
> —Jeanne Gomoll, "Open Letter to Joanna Russ," 1987

> The importance of clearly articulating experience that is not mirrored in available, conventional myths cannot be exaggerated.
>
> —Keridwen N. Luis, "Les Human Beans?" In Mendlesohn, *On Joanna Russ*, 2009

> *Soyez réalistes, demandez l'impossible.*
>
> —"May 1968 Graffitti," Bureau of Public Secrets

In 1977 Joanna moved to Seattle to join the faculty of the University of Washington, where she would teach, having finally found a tenure-track post, until she retired as a full professor. In 1978, the year *The Two of Them* was published (and also *Kittatinny*), she had a back operation for the "chronic disease" that had troubled her for many years.[1] The procedure was not an unqualified success. She'd been prepared for after effects, she told Larry McCaffery in their 1987 interview. The reality was worse. She could not sit at a desk. She had to read and write standing, and relearn how to write by hand, "which wasn't as easy as you'd think."[2] She couldn't concentrate: her medication (for chronic pain and fatigue) made her sick; she took electroshock treatment (to the horror of some of her friends) for the depression.[3] Illness can become a full time job: she might have five different medical appointments in a week, and it went on for years.[4] Helpless and constrained, like a fifties housewife drugged into compliance; like Zumurrud, the harem wife in *The Two of Them*, Joanna had joined the "cultural minority of women"[5] with a vengeance.

Despite her health problems she managed to pack a lot of writing, commentary, academic work, and lesbian feminist activism into her restricted life. It was in 1978 that she put together *How to Suppress Women's Writing*, a scholarly, outspoken, and funny classic of feminist literary criticism that draws on science fiction tropes and cites material from the *Khatru* symposium (not published until 1983). She withdrew from fandom and never accepted a standing invitation to be guest of honor at Wiscon, the "feminist" convention in Madison, Wisconsin,[6] but she was an inspirational teacher of sf at the University of Washington, where editor and writer Kathryn Cramer was one of her students,[7] and she shared the social life of feminist writers and fans in Seattle.[8] In 1980 she published her only nongenre novel (*On Strike against God*). Five "interlocking stories," *Extra(Ordinary)People*, a project she'd planned before her operation, eventually became her last major sf work. It's a sequence that starts with the story of a female hero—the isolated, lonely "exceptional woman"—and progresses through playful male masquerade, a gender-blind utopia, and a re-visioning of the tortured "Manland vs. Womanland" world of *The Female Man*, before (like Nabokov) returning the reader to the "artifactuality" of fiction.

There were also unrelated stories, an essay collection (*Magic Mommas*), and the preparation of her story collections: *The Zanzibar Cat* in 1984, *The*

*Hidden Side of the Moon* in 1989. In 1985 she "came out," in the fanzine *Nome*, as an eager consumer and producer of K/S (Kirk/Spock) pornographic fan fiction. In 1988 she was presented, rather awkwardly, with the Pilgrim Award for lifetime achievement in sf and fantasy scholarship. At the ceremony she was called the first woman to receive the award (described as "redressing an imbalance" rather than recognition of her stellar work). In fact, Marjorie Hope Nicolson was the first woman to receive a Pilgrim Award, in 1971.[9]

## LETTERS, 1970–1995

The letters published in various journals, chosen by Joanna for the collection *The Country You Have Never Seen* (2007), are snapshots of an activist writer's life. Here we find lively commentary on books and articles; dispatches from storms in teacups; personal glimpses available nowhere else; and incisive observations on the feminist, and sf feminist, contentions and conversations of the times.

In the selection from the seventies, Joanna steps in to soothe warring lesbian feminists (*Sinister Wisdom* 11 [1970]); takes issue with a blatant "all she needs is a good ****" review of Phyllis Chesler's *Women and Madness* (*Village Voice*, October 1972); is intrigued by the sexy secret world of Victorian tight-lacing; and unjustly attacks a mediaeval scholar, who took it well (*Signs* [1977]). She defends lesbian lust (*Frontiers* [1979]), delivers a lecture on the realities of feminist (book) publishing (*New Women's Times* [1980]), and sends up the (gay male) issue of vital communication via clothing quirks and moustache trimming—have you guys ever tried this new thing called "talking"? (*Gay Community Newsletter* [1980]).[10]

The eighties and nineties selection is more substantial. In "Women and SF: Three Letters," a correspondence triggered by feminist literary critic Susan Gubar's fine essay "C. L. Moore and the Conventions of Women's Science Fiction,"[11] Joanna offers minor corrections (rockets are generally held to be phallic, not womblike, by the sf community; female sf writers probably did not collaborate before the sixties) and responds to Linda Leith, who'd called Susan Gubar and Joanna "female chauvinists." A scathing review of Ed Bryant's "Dark Angel" for *Venom: The Magazine of Killer Reviews* was never printed, as *Venom* had ceased publication.[12] She sees Ruth Hubbard's "The Social Construction of Sexuality" (1985) as a threat to lesbian identity; scolds *The Women's Review of Books* for allowing notice of Joyce Carol Oates's "Loathsome Lez" novel (*Solstice* [1985]) to sully its pages, and sorts out the difference between segregation and separatism for a gay newsletter (*Seattle Source* [1986]). In a reprise of her 1978 essay (see chapter 6) she attacks the "mystification of money and power" in *Gender Justice*, by David Kirp et al. (1986): Liberty, a key concept in this right-wing study of gender, is a fake—"it doesn't exist today except for a very small minority of the rich and powerful."[13] Commenting on Janice Raymond's *A Passion for Friends*, she asserts that "it's hard to be heterosexual and a feminist"—an opinion softened in a footnote for *The Country You Have Never Seen*.[14] In November 1989, writing to the SFRA newsletter, she defended Sarah LeFanu's *Science Fiction and Feminism* against Rob Latham's narrow views, questioning his call for a "clear definition" of the genre—"genres always have clear, point-at-able centers, and fuzzy boundaries"—and supporting LeFanu's "particular readings" of unknown texts: expanding the genre's focus is vital to the creation of a canon of women's sf.[15] In spring 1990 she sent letters written to her by James Tiptree / Alice Sheldon to the Lesbian Herstory Archives in New York and wrote to the journal *Extrapolation*, affirming Sheldon's lesbian identity; in March 1992 she reminded the MLA that there may be practical reasons (such as staying out of Reading Gaol) for artistic-exquisite mystification in the writings of Wilde, Huysmans, and Sacher-Masoch.[16]

Two letters are personally and biographically revealing. In *Lesbian Ethics* (Summer 1987) Joanna "untangles" "butch/femme, masculine/feminine talk." As a "masculine-identifying lesbian," she was troubled for years because she didn't fit the butch profile. Now she understands: it's because Ashkenazy men are not supposed to fix the car! In Jewish culture masculine superiority is intellectual (see also chapter 1 herewith). Joanna's need to "belong" as a lesbian, her painful unease if she felt herself out of step with her community, is an insight into her sf career, too.[17] In another letter, inspired by a New Age belief handbook (*Ecstasy Is a New Frequency: Teachings of a Life*, by Chris Griscom) she recalls "many experiences of what I can only call mysticism, in my teens and twenties: a feeling of unity with the natural world, and even moments in which I 'knew' . . . that space and time were illusions."[18]

But the world had been changing. In the year that Bruce Sterling wiped the revolutionary feminist seventies out of sf history (in his introduction for new star William Gibson's first story collection)[19] Joan Wallach Scott had published "Gender: A Useful Category of Historical Analysis" in the *American*

*Historical Review.* Initially poorly received, the paper was soon acclaimed and recognized as a game-changer. By the time Joanna commented bitterly on Wallach's *Gender and the Politics of History* (*The Women's Review of Books* [April 1989]),[20] "gender studies" was supplanting academic feminism everywhere. The new discipline, or definition, had practical advantages. It covered the same rich material; it wasn't exclusive to women or controlled by a radical elite; and it didn't require commitment to moral and political goals. Gender studies could go mainstream, and it did. Meanwhile, young lesbians, enjoying the freedoms won by older activists, dismissed "feminism" as "a conspiracy of evil witches" taking the fun out of sex. Joanna's response to this irony, based on Lyndall MacCowan's essay in *The Persistent Desire*,[21] is more nuanced than her treatment of Wallach Scott, but both works carried the same message. Joanna might still have hopes for her great feminist project, long in preparation, but her battles had become history.

## ESSAYS, 1981–1989

Two literary essays (one of them for a journal feature) were published in this period. There was also her feminist collection, *Magic Mommas* (1985), responding to crises in the women's movement but including science fiction related material.

"To Write 'Like a Woman': Transformations of Identity in the Work of Willa Cather" (*Journal of Homosexuality* 12, no. 4 [1986]; collected in *To Write Like a Woman*) is an essay Joanna first sent to feminist journals, believing that Cather's lesbian identity was an open secret, and was astounded when editors and readers rejected the suggestion that Cather was a lesbian. One reader was outraged at the "accusation." There was also (it seems) galling criticism of Joanna's lack of academic polish.[22] The essay finally found a home in the *Journal of Homosexuality*, but the exclusion from feminist scholarly discourse clearly stung.

Joanna had been introduced to Cather's novels by Michele Barale, a friend and colleague at the University of Colorado (where Joanna taught from 1975 to 1977). Cather—Pulitzer Prize winner, author of beloved U.S. classics, including her Nebraska trilogy, *O Pioneers!* (1913), *The Song of the Lark* (1915), and *My Ántonia* (1918)—is a famous creator of strong, attractive, and independent fictional women, notably Alexandra Bergson, protagonist of *O Pioneers!*, but she preferred male-viewpoint characters. As a young woman she favored masculine dress. All her important relationships were with women, and she lived with Edith Lewis in a pair-bond relationship for thirty-nine years before she died in 1947. But she never identified herself as a lesbian. Joanna argues that Cather *could not* be open about her sexuality when lesbianism was still stigmatized as a morbid perversion. But to feminist Cather scholars in the seventies, it seems the author's silence either proved she was not a lesbian or—equally effectively—that she preferred to keep her sexuality private.

Joanna's focus is on significant male characters who can be "read" as self-portraits of the author in masquerade: Jim Burden, the narrator of *My Ántonia*, who shares many aspects of Willa Cather's own life story; Emil Bergson, Alexandra's younger brother, in love with a married woman, who chastely accepts the situation (as does she) without overt frustration, and, more persuasively, the unfortunate Claude Wheeler in *The Professor's House*, denied access to his wife's bed even on their wedding night. To Joanna these "males" are types of lesbian women in love with heterosexual women in a world of enforced gender roles: allowed free access to the objects of desire, *because they are women*, yet with no hope of consummation. But she also discerns that for Cather the real focus seems to be the masquerade itself. Fictional adoption of male clothes and manners offers the vicarious luxury of solitary, independent travel, public invisibility, and all the other (nonsexual) freedoms of American manhood—the same luxuries that Joanna and her female readers enjoy in the character of Janet Evason, the law officer of Whileaway. I think it's not unreasonable to suggest that Cather, whatever her sexual preferences, felt the same delight.

The Nebraska novels, for me, are haunted by the absence of the Plains Indians and the overpowering presence of American expansionism, concerns that Cather chose not to foreground[23] and on which Joanna does not comment. Male masquerade features elsewhere, in various guises, in Joanna's writing in the 1980s, in the stories that make up *Extra(Ordinary)People* and in "Sword Blades and Poppy Seeds" (1983).

"Writers Comment on Their Own Work" (*Women's Review of Books* [July 1989]; collected in *The Country You Have Never Seen*) is Joanna's response to a questionnaire (the questions are not included, but their presence punctuates the text). It repeats familiar details, describes the limitations of illness, and offers new insights, including a surprising rationale for the finale of *We Who Are About To* and an aside confirming her shift toward separatism. "Fiction is always a joy, always an obsession and always hard,"[24] but Joanna's delight in her work has to be fitted into the chinks between teaching, correspondence, friendships, household chores, business issues, and the inexorable demands of ill health. The gestation of *We Who Are About To* (probably Joanna is answering that favorite question, "Where do you get your ideas?") was triggered by "another writer's" colonization scenario[25] and a different book in which the message "there is nothing to be done, we must die gracefully" is delivered by a kindly patriarch (rather than a cranky female ex-activist). The perennial task of telling naïve students they can't end their story, with "And I died" inspired the ending: Joanna decided to see if she could make that impossible last line possible.

Getting published (and staying in print) is important, but the "vanity stuff" of payment and recognition is independent of the thrilling *sensation* of success: in nonfiction when the writer knows a statement is "true and good"; in fiction when "everything is the proper shape and alive." Efforts to define "women's writing" or invent a "female language"[26] shade into essentialism, recreating the ghetto that feminism has been trying to dismantle. Joanna tries instead to "create the female reader": to speak *as if* to a default female audience instead of to the default male.[27] When you want to say something that isn't part of the dominant cultural model, the last thing you should do is abandon established methods: you should be *adapting* and *deforming*—like Virginia Woolf, like Melville—the useful and important techniques already available. Joanna's own approach is "a kind of isometrics—pulling against tradition, *and* pillaging it" (an instantly recognizable description of her own science fiction, arguably setting the bar for all good sf writers). To a question about obstacles she's faced, she responds obliquely that women who've made "any sort of name for themselves" often claim they've encountered no obstacles—perhaps because women assume that they will not succeed at all. Success is measured, gratefully, against "nothing," instead of against "more success." But of course there are obstacles for women that men never have to face. "Networking with women only—which I try very hard to do—brings in little fame or money."

"Political obligation" is not a burden: the political *is* her aesthetic. She didn't deliberately contrive *Kittatinny* as a "lesbian feminist *bildungsroman*," she simply put together the most magical and exciting things that came to mind. But critics who get things wrong are a useful warning system: you learn from their mistakes. Feminist criticism and commentary will always "get into" her fiction, since that's how her life is spent, but her desire to apply "pressure on the process of writing" until the sparks fly will keep her on the experimental side of literature, and she will always write fantasy (Joanna does not cite science fiction) because "the visible surfaces of life are not enough. With fantasy, you can analyze a story as you write it, and do laboratory experiments on themes and people; imaginary experiments, of course."

*Magic Mommas, Trembling Sisters, Puritans and Perverts* (Trumansberg, N.Y.; Crossing, 1985) includes four feminist essays "previously published in either *Sinister Wisdom* or *13th Moon*"[28] and an introduction, dated November 1984 and serving as a corrective and a reflection on the earlier material, plus the autobiographical "Not for Years but for Decades" (noted in chapter 6) and "Pornography by Women, for Women, with Love," Joanna's enthusiastic report on the "K/S" or "Slash" fiction phenomenon.

The feminist essays engage, directly or indirectly, with a crisis that split and poisoned the women's movement in the eighties. On one side of the ideological divide, men were (probably) irredeemably evil, and feminism, including lesbian feminist sex, must be exclusively *womanly*. Sex outside a loving, committed relationship; vaginal penetration; consensual S&M; or any of the butch/femme role-play natural to lesbian culture before the seventies[29] were condemned. Masculine-coded "assertiveness" was suspicious. On the other side were women like Joanna, who believed that feminism is a class struggle, that it was absurd for feminists to revere male-ordered "womanly" rules of behavior, and that consent, safety, and goodwill were the only unbreakable rules in sexual practice.

"Power and Helplessness in the Women's Movement" (first published in *Sinister Wisdom* 18 [1981]) critiques the supposedly non-hierarchical "women's group" (or "consciousness-raising" group, the original social unit of the movement). "Magic Mommas" are women silently, unilaterally elected by their peers, on the grounds of visible achievement, and are expected to enable and support other group members without limit. "Trembling Sisters" are the women who demand this service, while resenting "Momma's" status. Joanna, whose reasoning suggests she sees herself in the "Magic Momma" hot seat, unpacks the consequences: "Put the MM and the TS together and you get the conventional female role. You also get trashing." She proposes that as long as both parties are basically good-willed, the way forward is to recognize that "the MM/TS polarity is an illusion." Both Mommas and Sisters are *afraid* of having power: both need to learn to be effective for their own sakes. Impeccable in its group-dynamics analysis, this essay can also be traced to Joanna's withering review (in *Sinister Wisdom* 12 [1980]) of Donna J. Young's prudish and uneventful feminist sf novel, *Retreat as It Was*,[30] and thus to the ideological divide. Criticism of Joanna's "cruelty" toward Young from Marion Zimmer Bradley (and others, but Bradley was the aggressive trasher) had previously appeared in *Sinister Wisdom* 14.

"Being against Pornography" (first published in the feminist literary journal *13th Moon* [1982]) examines, without citing the texts, the issues in Andrea Dworkin's *Pornography: Men Possessing Women* (1981) and Laura Lederer's *Reclaim the Night* (1980). The (radical) feminist dilemma was that though Dworkin had right on her side, her campaign played into the hands of the "Moral Majority"—a coalition (founded in 1979 by Jerry Falwell, dissolved in the late 1980s) between the Christian Right and the Republican Party, bent on banning abortion, outlawing homosexuality, and forcing women back into "traditional" feminine roles. Joanna vividly recalls the fifties, when heartless young men hustled her and her friends for sex, and they complied: forced to risk death by illegal abortion because they were desperate to be seen as "free, beautiful and spontaneous"[31]—but she concludes (I don't quite follow the logic) that she must support complete license, because she is a user of pornography herself, and not all of it self-generated.

"News from the Front" is a continuation of the discussion, recognizing and naming the divide between "Puritans" and "Perverts" (Joanna being a "Pervert"). Susanna Sturgis, reviewing the collection for the feminist newspaper *Off Our Backs*,[32] notes that this essay was written *after* the notorious Barnard Conference on Sexuality (Barnard Women's Center, April 24, 1982), held to mark the outbreak of the "feminist sex wars." Joanna points out that lesbian "Puritans" are professing beliefs about "womanly sex" that match the views of the Moral Majority and lead straight back to Krafft-Ebing's conclusion that homosexuality is a sickness. Her own position is that she joined feminism believing it to be a political movement, bent on fighting injustice, and now sees the "femininists" bizarrely insisting that the behaviors *enforced by patriarchy* will save the world. Politics has to be the right answer. Biological causation, which the Puritans cite as the basis of sexism, is the counsel of despair. "In the late sixties and early seventies, feminists didn't believe that the personal was political, but that the personal *led to* the political—a vital distinction. . . . If men are plain evil and always have been, and women have always been good, why on earth should anything change now?"[33]

"Pornography for Women, by Women, with Love" (an extended version of "Another Addict Raves about K/S"; first published in the fanzine *Nome* [May 1985]): when Joanna, a *Star Trek* fan with a secret history of male-on-male sexual fantasies,[34] discovered the K/S phenomenon, "My hair stood on end!" (she recounts, in an interview with fellow enthusiasts).[35] She sought out and devoured the stories and wrote her own (not seen). Here she gives her report. Writers, readers, illustrators, and editors of K/S are almost exclusively female. The model (as with the modern gothic) is strongly consistent. First Officer Spock and Captain Kirk are in love (or lust) but can't admit it: some contrived situation isolates them and releases their inhibitions. The material is graded from "G" to "R," in which the men suffer a lot, to "X," the explicit pornography. Often the sex is a first encounter. The coded-feminine situations where the men are "helplessly flung together," the *waiting*, each for the other to act, and the instability of "male" and "female" characteristics (passivity, initiative, aggression), plus practical details (frictionless anal intercourse with no lubrication)[36] led Joanna to conclude that this isn't women fantasizing about men having sex, as men would enjoy a lesbian sex video. One or both of these partners is cryptically female or (more accurately) tweaked to suit female sexual arousal. "Patricia Frazier Lamb and Diana Veith," Joanna reports, "have suggested, brilliantly, I think, that although Spock is not literally female, his alienness is a way of 'coding' into the K/S fantasies that their subject is not a homosexual love affair between two men, but love and sex as women want them, whether with a man or with another woman."[37] The first published K/S story, featuring Kirk and Spock in a twisted, emotional sexual encounter, was "A Fragment in Time," credited to Diane Marchant, in 1972. This Joanna Russ essay is now safely enshrined in the *mythos* of Slashfic.[38]

In the final essay, "Pornography, and the Doubleness of Sex for Women," Joanna returns, repentant, to the antipornography protests. Referring, as always, to her own experience, she recalls childhood and teenage incidents (some of them familiar from the "Joanna" passages of *The Female Man*), enduring memories of sexual shame, betrayal, and bewilderment of which every woman surely has a store: "Uncle Max" who insisted on grabbing and slobbering on your fourteen-year-old-self—*and your mother told you to put up with it.* The scary dentist, at another family party, who forced you to dance with him, held you disgustingly close . . . *and everyone laughed.* The boys who dragged a girl into the boys' bathroom, told her she had big breasts and therefore must enjoy sexual humiliation, and jeered at her when she cried.

The message was always the same. You had to endure it; you were supposed to *like* it; you were not entitled to have your own opinion. Nothing's changed. Boys and men still have all the entitlement, all the choices; and they are often cruel. Joanna previously saw the antipornography protest as an attack on sexual freedom. She now sees that to many women "sexual freedom" sounds like just more of those "bad and painful things . . . done to you, that you can't control." But that's not the whole story. The doubleness of sex for women is that "sex is ecstatic, autonomous and lovely for women. Sex is violent, dangerous and unpleasant for women"—not as a dichotomy (that is: some women hate sex, some love sex) but as a continuum. Even really horrendous sex training—even rape—may include positive sexual feeling. And how do you deal with that? Even X-rated pornographic images can be arousing. Even lesbians can be brutal in sex.

Joanna's proposal that violence, not sex, is the real enemy in all this sounds positive, but she finds an inspirational conclusion elusive. What about Wilhelm Reich's idea that things look worst when sexual repression is *partly* lifted and the preexisting violence becomes visible—but genuine progress is also being made?[39] Would more sex all round improve things? To end hopefully, it seems the only answer is: try again. Let's all the women in the movement talk about it and not fall out this time.

The irony that haunts these essays is that, inevitably, it's men who set the agenda for radical feminism. A girl's horizons close down at puberty; she will never be "treated as an equal" by her male peers. Women in a feminist group need to embrace men's ability to handle power. A mighty industry that fosters sexual violence and teaches men and boys to see women's bodies as commodities has the feminists at each other's throats. In K / S fiction (the topic that seems out of place in this company, but it is not) the "contrarieties"[40] are resolved in a sexually charged masquerade. Given that the all-female utopias of seventies feminist sf either survived as enclaves or proposed the annihilation of half the human race, perhaps masquerade; a masquerade that becomes reality and makes *women*, as subjugated inferiors, disappear isn't such a bad idea.

## STORIES, 1982–1983

Joanna published four stories in the early 1980s (three of them very significant) and also her short, nongenre novel, which appeared in 1980.

In "Elf Hill" (*Magazine of Fantasy and Science Fiction* [November 1982]; collected in *The Hidden Side of the Moon*) the pictures in a fairytale give a middle-aged woman, Mary Ellen, a fright, because she's just visited her mother at Sunset Estates. There's meager space for retirees in Mary Ellen's world, but at Sunset Estates all fully-paid-up residents have sole access to a single, large, beautiful apartment, a trick that works, essentially, by shaving reality into infinitesimal slivers. The residents also have to be "shaved fine," so the woman our narrator visited was only a surface—ethereal, contented, but shorn of human *depth*: she never touched her daughter and showed no pity for the "solid" retirees, huddled in Sunset Estates' dirty corridors, who resist (or can't afford) the treatment. Mary Ellen is a realist: we leave her coming to terms with the prospect of sharing her mother's eerie fate. A dystopian yet successful future (old age is dreaded, but there are developed settlements "beyond the rings") with echoes of Joanna's first sale, "The Forever House," this was her last story for *Magazine of Fantasy and Science Fiction*.

"The Little Dirty Girl" (*Elsewhere*, vol. 2, edited by Terri Windling and Mark Alan Arnold [New York: Ace, 1982]; collected in *The Hidden Side of the Moon*). On therapeutic walks around Seattle a middle-aged woman with back trouble meets cats, confiding little boys, and one dirty little girl who firmly, irresistibly, insinuates herself into an adult stranger's life. The little dirty girl refuses to name herself except by repeating, "A. R.," the initials embossed on the narrator's handbag. She's the picture of neglect and has insatiable appetites, but she's not intrusive. The narrator starts to care for her, affectionately and practically, providing hot baths and washing grubby clothes, flushing away offerings left in the toilet bowl, showing the child beautiful astronomy photos. She takes her out to eat in a real restaurant and allows her the delight of exploring an intellectual grownup's home, humble but *so swanky* to little dirty girl. Our narrator soon realizes she's dealing with some kind of ghost (the child is changeable in age and size; her visits leave no material traces). It takes her longer to guess the visitor's identity, but while learning to mother a child, she's also becoming reconciled (like Joanna herself, after long years) with her own mother. In the last lines of the story, presented as a letter to a friend, we learn that our narrator has enclosed a picture of the Little Dirty Girl: a photograph, that is, of herself. Published as fantasy, this story of mothers and daughters, and an adult woman rescuing her long-neglected child-self, is hardly genre but very appealing.

"Main Street: 1953" (*Sinister Wisdom* [Fall 1983]; collected in *The Hidden Side of the Moon*), a haunting fragment invoking the young Joanna's mystical experiences, is the story of Elaine Beach, who one night, as she was being driven home from a Christmas dance "by a boy she didn't like," jumped out of his car at a crossroads and ran away through the pelting snow in her organdy dress and her "dyed lavender pumps." She made it all the way to "Brocéliande," where the snow became May blossom, daisies, and fallen petals, and no time was passing. But she came back. She resigned herself to mundanity, and that's all—except for a strange rumor that she had a baby (or "gave birth to herself" perhaps) on that trip. Elaine is also the name of the death-devoted protagonist in *We Who Are About To*.[41]

In "Swordblades and Poppy Seed" (*Heroic Visions*, edited by Jessica Amanda Salmonson [1983]; collected in *The Hidden Side of the Moon*) a young woman, coming away alone from Victor Hugo's *Hernani* (possibly the play's notorious 1830 premiere[42]) and pleasingly disguised in her new, men's overcoat, is accosted by an old man. He takes her to his shop and offers her the "weapons of her trade"—edged blades on one side; dreams and visions on the other.[43] Generations of literary women have been served by this shopkeeper, including Mary Shelley, who chose a greenish, glowing substance (radium) and wrote *The Modern Prometheus* (or, *Frankenstein*), and Jane Austen, who picked "two inches square of ivory."[44] The woman in masquerade is Aurore Dupin (or "Dudevant," her husband's name), soon to be better known as George Sand[45] and omniscient for the purposes of this story. The president of Harvard's sister (the lesbian poet Amy Lowell) was wrong, Aurore decides: the "old man" is really an old woman. Derived from Lowell's narrative poem, "Sword Blades and Poppy Seed," with an epigraph from Ellen Moers's *Literary Women*, this visionary celebration of female authorship ends with an exhortation: "Are you truly curious? *Then read our books.*"[46]

### On Strike against God

Esther teaches English and lives in an intermittently lovely, isolated college town (possibly modeled on Ithaca, New York, home of Cornell University). Thirty-eight and recently divorced—the analysis and group-therapy sessions meant to rescue her marriage are much on her mind—she knows her time is running out but can't control a fatal habit of "having the last word" when a man engages her in conversation.[47] In the desert wastes of the long vacation she's much consoled by her friendship with Jean, the graduate-student daughter of a university academic and his faculty wife; Jean lives in a "co-op" apartment in town. Moments of magical sympathy with Jean alternate, in this first-person narrative, with derision for those therapy sessions (she sees her [deceased] analyst as a vampire) and collisions, notably at a hateful faculty party, with smug masculinity. But Esther is reticent or confused about what's really going on, as she "accidentally" gazes at the shape of Jean's breasts, beautifully outlined in sunlight, and wonders whether Jean, like herself, is a "something else." One day, in a little public garden, as they are sharing jokes about Lovecraft, she admits to herself that she's in love—but it's okay because she will never *do anything*. Renunciation is soon followed by a daring declaration, and miraculously, Jean feels the same! The two women share ice cream, in the intimacy of nakedness, and have awkward, funny, first-encounter sex.[48]

*On Strike against God*, a nongenre story with postrealist flourishes,[49] stylishly analyzed in Keridwen Luis's essay "Les Human Beans?"[50] has congruencies with Joanna's autobiography,[51] her autobiographical short fictions (Rose, the flatmate in "The Precious Object," makes a guest appearance), and with *The Female Man*. When the lovers part, after their first clumsy, ecstatic adventure, semi-autobiographical fiction fills the gap as Esther breaks her coming-out news to a (somewhat resentful) gay male friend and then visits a hospitable, hipster literary couple. "Ellen," the woman in this pair, is an obvious stand-in for Judith Merril and perhaps other sf *"femininists"*—expounding Merril's highly male-friendly feminism so that Esther can counterattack: Ellen claims she *enjoys* doing all the housework and childcare. She has to get up at four in the morning to write, and that's fine: "Everybody has to make sacrifices." She can't, however, come up with the sacrifices made by her male partner.[52] But point-scoring doesn't detract from a charming lesbian love story that borrows, slyly and delightfully, the prettiest tropes from antique heterosexual Romance fiction (Esther's study area), Jean's affection for her sewing projects (which she carries around with her like pets), and Esther's blindness to Jean's ulterior motive, as the younger woman keeps finding excuses to "come over." The loveliness of the world; of light on flowers, a rainbow after a storm, in the heightened emotional state of a new romance. The only element missing is the "happily ever after." Instead, there's a poignant moment when Esther realizes, after a lifetime of sexual starvation, that there are other desirable women in the world, besides Jean, (*What a field of ripe wheat!* thinks Emily, the new-made vampire[53]).

Esther's deceased analyst and her oddball company in group therapy reveal a lifelong relationship usually tacit in Joanna's fiction. Psychoanalysis may never have "cured" anyone of anything, but *On Strike against God* reminds us that for Joanna, "therapy" was ever present: a fertile source of concepts and a guide to her thinking; like a childhood religion, irreplaceable, though never deserving belief or even respect. A more disturbing reminder emerges when Jean decides to teach Esther how to shoot, and Esther discovers in herself a deep, heartfelt longing "to be able to kill a man."[54] But androcidal thoughts are inescapable in Joanna's fiction. (When one of those smug college males, in this story, asks her, "Tell me, what's it like to be a woman?" Esther "takes her rifle from behind her chair," and shoots him dead, saying: "It's like that"—neatly conveying the flash of murderous rage male chauvinism can provoke.) The shooting practice belongs here, as much as the group therapy does.

Genre authors tend to write the same stories over and over, with different details. Literary writers write different stories over and over, in their special signature style. Joanna preferred to write like an Impressionist painter in front of a favorite scene, forever re-visioning her dreamworlds and finding new effects, deeper resonances, in the inescapable bedrock material of her own life. *On Strike against God*, her last novel, is a fine, if minor, late treatment of her chosen subject.

## EXTRA(ORDINARY)PEOPLE

In her 1987 interview with Larry McCaffery, Joanna described *Extra(Ordinary) People* as a play on the classic sf model where stories published separately form a series and may be published as an episodic novel but remain malleable, so the writer can change the meaning (or the facts) of previous episodes, in the light of new ideas.[55] Three of the five stories had been published separately. "Souls" (*Magazine of Fantasy and Science Fiction* [January 1982]) won a Hugo in 1983. "The Mystery of the Young Gentleman" (*Speculations*, edited by Isaac Asimov and Alice Laurance [New York: Houghton Mifflin, 1982])[56] was nominated for a Nebula Award. "What Did You Do During the Revolution, Grandma?" appeared in the *Seattle Review* (Spring 1983). "Bodies" is original to the collection. "Everyday Depressions," also original, is very different from the others: Joanna proposes that it "functions more or less as a thematic summing-up."[57] In the ironic and minimal framing story, a "schoolkid" suggests, after each narrative has been delivered as a history lesson by an educational robot, "So *that's* how the world was saved?" The schoolkid is always wrong. Utopias appear and vanish, and no world is definitively saved in these stories, unless the rescue of any individual (not always a female child) counts as the same thing.

### "Souls"

The story of the Abbess Radegunde—a marvelously learned, wise, and gentle old lady—and what happened when the Norsemen came is recounted by Ranulf the Happy, a child when these events occurred; he was the pet and errand boy of the wonderful abbess. When the great beaked boats came up the river, fearless Radegunde went out to parley, identified the leader of the leaderless "Vikings" by subtle clues, spoke to him in his own language, and romanced him into striking a deal: the abbey's treasures handed over intact for the lives of her helpless people. The truce appeared a marvel but didn't last: rape and slaughter took their usual course, and the abbey was ransacked anyway. The abbess remained serene, bold, wise, and unexpected: comforting one young nun, guilty and confused after surviving rape, with a shameful story from her own past; tending another girl reduced to gibbering madness; giving equivocal comfort to the rapist,[58] whose wounds she heals just by sitting with him all night. She could do things like that, remarks Ranulf. She can also hear unspoken words and see things happening far away. But the raid changed her, and that's the real story. She was ready to abandon her people; she tried to get Thorvald, the Viking leader, to take her to Constantinople. She had started, she said, "forgetting how to be Abbess Radegunde." Little Ranulf saw the person who'd been able to survive, in this chamber-of-horrors world, only as long as the carapace of the saintly abbess endured, transformed—frantic, blasphemous, calling on invisible people: *Help me, find me. Oh, come, come, or I die.* And Ranulf saw them, too, clothed in white and held in shining light, in a glade in the trees: "Radegunde's people, come to take her home." Before leaving she gave Thorvald the cruel gift of making him "a good man," with eyes opened to the horrors, but told the little boy, "Remember me, and be content." Which is how Ranulf the Happy's been able to recount every detail of these far-off events (including speeches he really can't have heard).

Joanna seems to have fallen out with her Hugo-winning story,[59] and maybe I can see why. It's deftly crafted, historically evocative; the saintly, sharp-tongued, and worldly abbess is a delightful character, and every objection to the genre narrative tricks is so neatly swatted, it makes you grin in admiration. But "Radegunde's" exceptional, heroic powers are alien, not utopian, and her superiority over the miserable medieval world is too easy. It should be read alongside Alice Sheldon's "Beam Us Home."[60]

"The Mystery of the Young Gentleman"

"Joe Smith" of Colorado, a rich young man with flashy tastes (gold nuggets for shirt studs) is returning to America on the SS *President Hayes*. Maria-Dolores, a street child from Barcelona, is registered as his daughter but is later explained as an orphan who's been offered a home by one of Joe's female relatives. Foul-mouthed, dangerously intelligent, lacking in manners, Maria flirts with Joe, loves her pretty boots from the Rue de Rivoli (but hates wearing them), and devours juvenile adventure novels to improve her English. She passes for twelve, so she's still a child, in a pinch. Joe passes as a gilded youth, barely adult himself, so that a smooth face, a light voice, and noticeably small hands and feet won't arouse suspicion. The year is 1885. Life at this luxury level is all appalling clothes, rigid convention, stifling manners, and stultifying, huge meals. Krafft-Ebing is in fashion and the gender police are on the prowl. This lively, sexy story is all about *passing* and the perilous delights of masquerade. But performative gender and physical sexual difference are not the only difficulties: "One must be careful, speaking: it's too easy to answer questions that haven't been asked."[61] Joe and Maria-Dolores are telepaths and, perhaps inevitably, also gender-blind. (Maria-Dolores decides she'll travel as Joe's son next time. She bets there are no women "in the mountains," and Joe agrees, this is correct.) They're on their way to utopia, an enclave where there are no women, no men—just rather special human beings. The reader is left to imagine how Maria-Dolores made contact, or was detected, over thousands of miles. It doesn't matter: she's been found and they're going home—*if* they can survive the temptations of the crossing.

Joe piles up telepathy-enabled winnings at the poker table, relying on excellent reflexes and a throwing knife to deal with doubters (a young man can't afford to seem effete). Maria lusts after her guardian: she's hard to resist, but it won't do. Not here, not now. The retired doctor in the next berth is a different problem: he's inquisitive and interfering; disaster strikes. Exposure seems inevitable, but Doctor Bumble, cruelly tricked and lewdly handled, is no match for the utopians, who steal his best lines and scare him into burning his notes. The doctor is undone. *The Mystery of the Young Gentleman* (he's a not-so-young lady, we find out)[62] is the title of one of Maria's trashy novels, and this story is an indulgence, a trashy novel in its own right, playing with fantasies of outlawry and insisting the *performance* of gender isn't an aberration. It's what human beings do—all of us, even in utopia.

### "Bodies"

The supernatural/utopian humanoids never came back, after they rescued Radegunde, says the schoolkid's robotic teacher. The gender-queer, telepathic minority died out. But flash forward two thousand years or so, and there's another, much more ambitious utopian development (notionally global, effectively U.S. American). The third narrator isn't strictly a native. In 1970 she was living in the Pacific Northwest (in Washington, that is, where Joanna wrote this story; but the narrator lived in Portland),[63] making money out of real estate. Just before she died of cancer at age thirty-nine, the scientists of utopia reached back, having identified a "characteristic pattern," and lifted her DNA and her EEG (brainwaves). They grew her again in a vat, exactly as in life, and now she's transmitting an instant letter, long distance, because she needs to explain a few things to another returnee, who died in the 1930s: Jimmie Bunch, whose Dad and Mumsie had threatened to get him locked up if he wouldn't leave the nail polish and lipstick alone.[64] The pattern the scientists look for, she notes, is chronic misery.

All the stories in *Extra(Ordinary)People* are *performative*—recounted by characters, delivered as testimony[65] (Joe Smith writes to another utopian about that voyage on the *President Hayes*, intending to mail the letter in New York). Here the narrator's rueful, tender account of her relationship[66] with James Bunch doubles as the classic utopian tour of a possible future where gender polarity has vanished, and male or female *bodies* are equally acceptable: the giant solar power stations, the high tech solutions, the fairly shared physical work, companion animals, random ceremonies, colorful performances, tiny music consoles that look like flowers, and a social model that sounds like Whileaway on holiday or the postscarcity tribes of "Nobody's Home." Rescuing like minds from the cruel past was an experiment that didn't work out and has been discontinued. Returnees ought to stick together, and in ways our narrator *has* been sticking to James, following his famous misadventures (gossip is the life force of this society). But the romantic desert camp-out was probably a mistake. The sex was ill-conceived, they've both been looking for fantasies that no longer exist; basically, let's make up.

"What Did You Do During the Revolution, Grandma?"

The fourth story, seeming to abandon the narrative of serial utopias, returns to *The Female Man*'s "probability mechanics" and the covert-ops career of Jael, the Womanland secret agent and assassin (see chapter 3). The title is a comment on Ursula K. Le Guin's Nebula-winning story "The Day before the Revolution."[67] The narrator is Jael, writing to the woman she loves. She explains how "probability mechanics" works: it's vital information her busy lover has never tried to understand. There's a value called *Ru*, a measure of consistency, and cause and effect are only truly reliable at *Ru* 1.0. The further you shift away from there, the crazier things get.[68] Her own world, where Manland and Womanland are locked in horrible embrace, is held to be at *Ru* 1.0—which pleases a lot of people, as if it's some kind of achievement, but not Jael. With seeming irrelevance, she then embarks on a story that will be familiar to attentive readers of *The Female Man*: it's the mission Jael describes to impress the three "Js," in her "palace" in the Vermont woods, after she's slaughtered the brothel boss. Here the detail is richer; her adventures in "the sheer craziness of *Ru* .08" have room to breathe, and there are other, significant changes. Jael is still taking the place of a Manland diplomat, "in a primitive patriarchy on an alternate Earth," still wrapped up like a Kabuki actor in layers of elaborate padding.[69] But her surgical enhancements (the steel teeth, silver eyes, razor fingernails) are now part of her disguise as a "Demon Prince," not gruesome weapons, and her seven-day tour is interrupted by her control, Fairy Marvin, "six foot four and almost the color of egg-plant," a feminized male menial who works for the same secret organization (a revolutionary group within Womanland, it seems) as Jael herself. The Manland diplomat who couldn't make it has been assassinated. Jael's to stay where she is, but from now on she'll be taking her instructions from the United Front.

Stranded, far from exciting events back home, waiting for new orders that never come, Jael works on the king, serving Womanland's interests as planned. She amuses herself by teaching the insufferable jocks—sorry, "noble knights"—ballet, which they take for jujitsu. She "all but seduces" Count Sid, a latent homosexual, for fun; bitterly regrets causing the death of an innocent peasant and succumbs to the charms of little princess Charlene ("a barbarian woman fell in love with me," as she puts it in *The Female Man*). When jealous Count Sid finds out about the dalliance, Jael is forced into a duel with an ogreish nobleman she can't possibly beat on Ruritanian terms. She gets Marvin to unlock her access to a secret weapon—apparently a "dirty" instability ray? In the chaos that ensues, the mission collapses. Fairy Marvin appears as a rival Demon Prince, backed by "the typing pool," and Jael is rescued from delirium to wake at home. But it's a different world. Manland/Womanland is no longer *Ru* 1.0. The center of reality has moved somewhere else.

In the McCaffery interview Joanna describes her probability-shifted "Ruritania" as a thinly disguised, satirical view of modern America[70]—but what else is there to read in this "revision, self-criticism and change" of material from *The Female Man*? Most significantly, Jael seems a different person. She's licensed to kill, and she'll do it, but she's not the psychopath she was. She hated all men: now she trusts Fairy Marvin with her life. Manland and Womanland are still corruptly entangled, but there's a revolution brewing that involves both women and men. Whom is Jael writing to and calling *Beloved Woman*? Does the *Ru* shift—textual and metatextual, changing the story and announcing Joanna's own changes—mean that "Whileaway" (no longer exclusively female) has become "more probable" than "Manland versus Womanland's" mutually assured destruction? What's the significance of the giant solar collector? It's confusing. But for students of Joanna Russ, and for all those who either enjoy deciphering puzzles or can accept them as part of the décor, the last *"Female Man"* adventure is well worth revisiting.

### "Everyday Depressions"

The fifth story is presented as a one side of a discussion in letters of the "lesbian gothic" Joanna has been inspired to write—having spotted *Gaywyck*, the "first gay gothic novel,"[71] in her local bookstore. Her title will be *Lady Sappho*, in curly gold letters. The two heroes will become two heroines: otherwise, like *Gaywyck*'s author, she intends to follow the formula to the letter. The period is the classic, early nineteenth century, with an aristocratic/wealthy milieu for the proud dark one, a lesser rank and relative poverty for the modest fair one. There must be authentic detail (Joanna has set her story in England and keeps reminding herself to look things up: did "Chippendale" make plates?).[72] There must be mystery, probably about an inheritance. There must be villainy, incidents, and *doubts* to prevent the lovers from consummating their affections for a decent number of pages. The adventure of "Lady Mary de Soycourt" and "Fanny Goodwood" is drawn out over several exchanges. Susan Koppelman's supposed responses are not shown, but it seems she's a useful confidant, always coming up with the plot device or revelation that will help Joanna keep the end away from the beginning. Mary, disguised as a dashing young highwayman, holds up the public coach in which Fanny is humbly approaching the castle—and steals a kiss? The proud heiress refuses all partners at the ball, until she can steal away—to dance with Fanny? Mary's dead mother (Alice Tiptree, of the Deepdene Sheldons[73]) gave birth to Mary and her twin brother in an Italian forest during a snowstorm: there's some mystery about that event. A secret in Mary's past makes her love for Fanny inconceivable, but not for the conventional reason. But it would be superfluous to summarize this summarized novel further. Joanna wrote her study of the *modern* gothic, *Somebody's Trying to Kill Me and I Think It's My Husband*, in 1973. The "gay gothic" is similar enough to explain why she genuinely *did* consider writing *Lady Sappho* and, equally, why she didn't go through with it. She didn't need to. This sketch, expertly dashed off, is complete and entertaining in itself.

Just as the marvelous visitor (a consoling fiction, invented by the protagonist) in "The Second Inquisition" brings the "Alyx" stories to a conclusion Joanna calls "tragic," *Extra(Ordinary)People* insists on authorship.[74] This isn't a natural object. Someone made this, someone did this; look behind the curtain. Perhaps that was always Joanna's core message, as a writer, a critic, a teacher, and as a feminist. But her demand for utopia is here too, and she's still using science fiction tropes as the ideal form for radical thought. The first step in creating a better world (always *creating*: utopia never becomes stable) is an act of the imagination.

# "POSTSCRIBBLE"
## An Afterword

Joanna retired and moved to Tucson, Arizona in 1994. A long-term relationship had ended, there was nothing to keep her in Seattle, and the warm, dry Arizona climate was better for her health.

In her commentary for the 1993 reissue of the *Khatru* Symposium she gave first place to Kate Wilhelm's socialist politics: "How very radical Kate Wilhelm was then and how little I (or many of the other participants) perceived this."[1] Her introduction for Clare Fraser's *Revolution, She Wrote* (1995) confirms this new direction.

> *The logic of feminism is to expand inexorably into generalized radicalism.*
>
> I came to this conclusion only a few years ago, after 23 years of feminist activism, work and study. I came to a whole host of related conclusions, too: that single-issue activism is a dead end, that class, sexism and racism depend upon each other and that the feminism which doesn't understand this will inevitably decay into careers-for-well-to-do white ladies.[2]

Her feminist work *What Are We Fighting For?* was published in 1997[3] and made little impact, though twenty-first-century sf feminists may find it interesting.[4] "Invasion" (*Isaac Asimov's Science Fiction Magazine* [January 1996]; anthologized in *Best SF 5*, edited by David Hartwell [1997]), a gentle comedy of misunderstandings set on a human-run spaceship that has been invaded by the naughty children of aliens from planet Ulp, was her last published story. A live telephone interview with Samuel Delany, at the 2006 Wiscon 30, the "feminist" science fiction convention, was her last, vicarious, public performance.

Her pioneering science fiction scholarship, her teaching, and her criticism would be a remarkable legacy in themselves. She also produced one of the finest bodies of short fiction of any sf author, past or present. Her novels are dazzling experiments: each of them a new beginning, each examining a new facet of her personal and political experience, her passionate sense of wonder, and, of course, the costs and pleasures of being female. *The Female Man* is only the most famous episode. The whole story is worth the same attention.

In April 2011 Joanna was admitted to hospital after suffering a series of strokes. Her file had been marked "Do Not Resuscitate" for a long time. She slipped away quietly and died on April 29. She was seventy-four. She'd collected (despite her careless attitude to such details) most of the honors the genre has to offer, including the Pilgrim Award, the Hugo Award, the Nebula Award, the Locus Award, and many nominations. Her name was entered in the Science Fiction Hall of Fame in 2013.

## KATHRYN CRAMER: ON JOANNA RUSS
## AS FEMINIST, MENTOR, AND TEACHER

Interview conducted by email in 2017–18

GWYNETH JONES: *You met Joanna Russ when you were at the University of Washington, and she became your self-chosen mentor—for a while. Could you tell me how that came about?*

KATHRYN CRAMER: When I was in high school, my father got back in contact with Gene Wolfe, whom he had known as a child. Gene came to Seattle to attend Norwescon and suggested that we come out. That was my first sf convention. I'm not sure if it was at that Norwescon or one a few years later, but I saw Joanna Russ speak on panels and found out she was on the University of Washington faculty. She was an amazing, charismatic speaker, and I decided that I wanted to take courses with her and looked her up in the university catalog after the convention. I took several quarters of her science fiction writing class. I don't remember if I had read any of her work before I started taking her class. I think I may have read a couple of her novels as preparation. But I had already decided to take her class based on listening to her talk at Norwescon. Many of her students were a bit scared of her and so her office hours were very open timewise. I would just go and talk to her for as much of the time as was available. If anyone else showed up, I would defer. A guy named Michael Gilbert, who later went to Clarion West with me, usually was there, too. My big regret is that she taught a science fiction criticism course and I didn't take it. Michael took it; I was involved in student government and didn't have the time. But I heard all about what they studied from Michael.

GJ: *How much did you know about Joanna's "feminist sf" involvement when you met her, which I think was in 1982?*

KC: I don't think I had any idea how important she was initially. The more literary end of Seattle fandom worshiped her, and I was gradually inducted into those circles. I remember being introduced to Patrick and Teresa Nielsen Hayden on a city bus in Seattle. Michael knew them and had gotten into these circles before me, so he acted as sort of a gatekeeper. He was impressing me by introducing me to the Nielsen Haydens. They were, at the time, doing a lot to help Joanna with her work. I met them again later when they moved to New York. What I remember most vividly about what she wanted to talk about then was the Kirk/Spock stuff. I think she was working on *How to Supress Women's Writing*, or else it had been recently published. But the whole sphere around her was permeated with those ideas. Also, when she taught sf, she mostly taught us Delany's critical methods, though I didn't understand that 'til later.

GJ: *Can you talk about her class teaching?*

KC: She taught the class essentially Clarion/Milford style, though most of what we as a class wrote was pretty bad. Although she had a reputation as a ferocious critic, she was very gentle and tactful in her criticisms of student work. This was true for both male and female students. Given her reputation as a man-eater, one might have expected major slap-downs, of male students off the rails, but I don't remember her ever humiliating anyone in class. She was very kind. She taught the basic "Aspects of the Novel" framework in tandem, with sf criticism blended in (both her own and Delany's, mostly). She had gone to Yale drama school, and one of the things I remember most is her reading passages of sample text aloud. I can still hear them. And when I read her writing now, I can also hear it. I suspect that part of what she was trying to teach us was dramatic structure that she would have learned at Yale. Ted Cornell, my current collaborator and partner, attended Yale drama school a few years later, and I sometimes see echoes of Joanna in his approach.

GJ: *Joanna's change of focus, from feminist sf to literary and political feminism: Did she talk about that?* How to Suppress Women's Writing *was published in 1983, did you read it at the time?*

KC: There was an organization called Radical Women in Seattle that had a monthly dinner. They were socialist/communist. They valued Joanna for her nonfiction political stuff. At a certain point she stopped going, and I asked why. It was because they thought her writing fiction instead of political essays was somehow counterrevolutionary and a capitulation to capitalism. Apparently, this had gone back and forth for years, and eventually she got fed up. Regarding *How to Suppress*, Patrick and Teresa did editorial work on the drafts. And I think I had heard a lot of what was in it before publication. I think I bought it and read it immediately upon publication.

GJ: *Your late husband, David Hartwell was Joanna's champion for a long time. I've realized, researching this study, how important he was to her, as an editor and as a close friend. Can you tell me about their relationship?*

KC: They had a very close friendship, and Delany was also part of that space. Joanna told me, and several other students in her classes, to go to Clarion West. After she died, I was looking through his Russ papers and came across their letters. She wrote him VERY flirtatious letters. And in one of those very flirtatious letters, they discussed that he was coming to Seattle to teach Clarion. And she told him "I have a student for you," like the student was a present. And the student in question was me. That would be why, in retrospect, he paid such close attention to me at Clarion West, even though in my opinion the work I was turning in wasn't good. And that attention changed my life. As far as I know, Joanna and David never had sex. Greg Benford, on the other hand, says she was explosively orgasmic in bed. (She apparently picked Greg up, not the other way around.) There was a kind of force field around David. His wife Pat, an anaesthesiologist, appeared at the time as a feminist ideal, a Heinlein individual. She had a copy of Heinlein's *Friday* signed to her by Heinlein. There were lots of sf feminists with crushes on David who desired but wouldn't touch because of his iconic wife. Again, I was not in on this secret.

GJ: *Vladimir Nabokov taught Joanna at Cornell, and she dedicated* And Chaos Died *to him. He was a great modernist writer, but in ways it's a puzzling association, given she was a radical feminist and he wrote* Lolita *(which she had read: she mentions it in an early academic sf essay). Did she ever talk about Nabokov as a teacher?*

KC: She talked about the opening of *Pale Fire* and how the narrator goes further and further off the rails—this as the framing device of what is to come. I remember in particular her reading aloud the sentence, "There is a very loud amusement park right in front of my present lodgings." If I recall correctly, she signposted that as the first moment we knew we were working with an unreliable narrator.

GJ: *I've seen very late dates for her coming out (as a lesbian). I think in some sf/public areas people didn't know for quite a while. Was it at all difficult for a professor of English to be out at your university in the eighties?*

KC: She was out. I think I recall a lot more grumbling about disrespect for being an sf writer than for her sexuality. As I mentioned above, her life consisted of playing to various audiences that were difficult to reconcile. She wanted to be respected as fully as her colleagues in the English Department, even though she wrote sf. She wanted to be respected by the Radical Women for her feminist sf for which they had no use. And at the same time she wanted the respect of major figures in science fiction even though she was a woman, a lesbian, a feminist, and a socialist. She held her own there through rigor, but rigor plus depression made her a harsher critic than she wanted to be, so she eventually gave up reviewing.

GJ: *Arguably she had a lot to be angry about, in science fiction's attitude to gender, but in her last columns for* Fantasy and Science Fiction *it's as if her patience is close to exhausted. I think you've said that if she was bad-tempered, it was because she was often in pain, but did anger define her?*

KC: For one thing, I think in retrospect Joanna at her peak, were she living in 2016, would be recognized as an Asperger's type. Second, Joanna had a major problem with depression. She had electroshock. (As I recall the story, people like Marilyn Hacker were completely beside themselves that Joanna was going to have electroshock, and David's wife Pat explained to those dead-set against it that Joanna would be helped by this.) She took a wide variety of antidepressants, which screwed up her short term memory. Also, Joanna was cheap and was sometimes offended if she thought things cost too much. She was also in chronic back pain that was not adequately treated by 2016 standards. So, yes, there was anger there, but it was anger in the context of obliviousness to some social signals, depression, medication, and other treatment side effects, financial anxiety, and chronic pain.

There was a dinner David and I had with Joanna and Norman Spinrad in which the topic somehow got off onto something like Phil Dick's story "The Pre-Persons," and just when David and I thought this would devolve into a screaming argument, Joanna and Norman looked at each other across the table and just let it go and changed the subject, and the rest of the dinner was wonderful. She could choose whether to take a stand. Sometimes she chose not to.

## REFLECTIONS ON SCIENCE FICTION—AN INTERVIEW WITH JOANNA RUSS

From *Quest*, a feminist quarterly, Summer 1975

Q:  *How did you begin writing science fiction?*

J:  I started writing science fiction in my last year of graduate school, after three years of doing nothing but playwriting for an MFA from Yale Drama School. I had never written any science fiction before but had read it since I was twelve and I loved it.

Q:  *Why did you choose this particular form? Did you see it as having political, social, or moral implications for contemporary life?*

J:  First, science fiction is a mode rather than a form (a form would be something like the sonnet, the short story, etc.). It is basically anything that is about conditions of life or existence different from what typically is, or what typically was, or whatever was or is. It is allied to fantasy (which I also write) but is not fantasy—which incorporates as part of its pleasure the impossibility of the material. Science fiction is about the possible-but-not-real. Second, I do not believe that any artist (as opposed to a hack) chooses a form; the form chooses the artist, if anything. I did not "choose" sf because I saw it has having political, social or moral implications for everyday life. I did not choose sf at all. I had always loved it. I read it because horror stories and sf seemed to me, from the age of eleven to twelve on, to be about real life in a way that the classics we were assigned at school were not. Both horror stories and sf seem to me in many ways freer and more imaginative that "straight" fiction (although most avant-garde fiction has abolished the distinction between realism and fantasy, something nobody taught us in high school). Does sf have "moral implications"? Good

Lord, is there *anything* that doesn't have moral implications? I don't want to go into the old, idiot song-and-dance routine about sf being prophetic (it isn't) or wonderful for developing the imagination (it rarely succeeds after the first addiction wears off) . . . yet I'm still addicted to it. Possibly it's the appeal of the utterly impossible, for a truly first-rate sf novel would have to be a great novel, period, and in addition have to surmount the most extraordinary technical difficulties. Forty years ago those who cried out that sf was good were voices crying in the wilderness. Now there are ghastly textbooks put out by Prentice-Hall.

Q: *Have your ideas about the role and importance of science fiction changed?*

J: What has changed in my feelings about sf is the result of reading it for twenty-five years. So little of it really reaches the potential of the mode that reading most of it is becoming a chore. Let's say that, like a great many critics and readers, I remain faithful to the ideal but deplore most of the practice. Now that sf is beginning to be academically respectable, my feelings about its "role" (whatever that is) are mixed. Sf should *ideally* be able to say more about more than any other fiction.

Q: *Do you view your science fiction writing as feminist? How do your feminist views affect the science fiction you write?*

J: I am a feminist. Therefore all my writing comes from a gestalt or ground-of-being that includes my feminism. I say "feminism" as if it were a set of explicable beliefs, which in part it is, but there is also a kind of basic experience of which I was aware most of my life but which did not find political expression or a vocabulary until about seven years ago. If you want to call both of these "feminist," then yes, of course my writing (all of it, including non-sf fiction) is feminist. And it affects what I write, just as everything else I am or have been or have experienced affects what I write. I am currently being beaten over the head in an sf magazine by a reviewer of *The Female Man* for this reason. The novel has a great deal of rage in it, which discomforts not only this one reviewer but some women who read and write sf. The novel is even treated as a blueprint for the future, despite the fact that none of the conditions I describe in the novel exist now or probably ever will. But of course the real target is the taboo against rage, specifically rage against men. Long before I became a feminist in any explicit way (my first reaction upon hearing Kate Millet speak in 1968 was that of course every woman *knew* that, but if you ever dared to formulate it to yourself, let alone say it out loud, God would kill you with a lightning bolt), I had turned from writing love stories about women in which women were the losers, and adventure stories about men in which men were winners, to writing adventure stories about a woman in which the woman won. It was one of the hardest things I ever did in my life. These are stories about a sword-and-sorcery heroine called Alyx, and before writing the first [story] I spent about two weeks in front of my typewriter shaking, thinking of how I'd be stoned in the streets, accused of penis envy, and so on (after that, it is obligatory to commit suicide, of course).

It was shifting my center of gravity from Him to Me, and I think it's the most difficult thing an artist can do—a woman artist, that is. It's OK to write about an artist-female with feet in the center of her own stage as long as she suffers a lot and is defeated and is wrong (the last is optional). But to win, and to express the anger that's in all of us, is a taboo almost as powerful as the taboo against being indifferent to The Man. Some criticisms I've heard about my latest novel are, for example, that there are no sympathetic male characters in it. Actually, the people in it (of both sexes) are not a choice lot, objectively considered, but then I do not think it any artist's business to pretend to a false objectivity. Objectivity is for God and She's not telling. The book is somewhat more complex, inasmuch as the women in it (except for Laur) are really parts of one woman, and the two men (leaving out the spear-carriers) are the extremes of sexism *as it impinges on women's lives.* The shift of sympathy is what's being complained about. There are no men portrayed sympathetically because when you are writing about what mounts to a sex war, it is *tempo rubato* to get all misty-eyed about the poor oppressor, as well as uneconomical, aesthetically speaking.

As you can see, I respond to criticism as every writer I know does, by screaming blue murder. But it is hard to convey a distinction that I think is very important: that *The Female Man* and "When It Changed" are explicitly feminist because that's what they are about, but that everything else I write must of necessity bear the imprint of the consciousness and sensibility it came from, and that is, of course, feminist. I spent three years after *The Female Man* trying to get together some theory of propaganda or persuasion or social analysis in art, and I haven't managed it yet. I only hope I built some of the difficulties and ambiguities *into* the novel itself, as I had tried to do.

Mind you, writing what I call propaganda is no different from writing anything else. But the specific problems (for example, the unconscious picture writers have of the reader) are different.

In the end *The Female Man* came over as possibly the only kind of propaganda there can be: either a celebration (to those who agree) or a construct that forces you through a certain cluster of experiences and states of mind. If you do not agree with the assumptions underlying the "portrait" of this experience, reading the book will be torture and it will make you very angry, but perhaps the only propaganda there can be for a forbidden feeling or belief or existence is to present it, as Rita Mae Brown and Jean Genet do. Social analysis or argument (as in Brecht, Ibsen, Shaw) is infinitely more difficult in narrative and may do much better on stage, where the dialectic of argument is live and much easier to make compelling, or comic, or at least interesting.

To be blunt, I wrote my explicitly feminist work in the same way and out of the same motives and ground I write everything. I did not "decide" to do it. It's an attempt to get my head together—literally, in the novel, where there are at least four women with one head apiece, none of whom is a whole woman until they finally do get together . . . for Thanksgiving dinner. I still think that was a witty bit, you know. Thanksgiving. Hem. Anyway.

Q:  *How important is it to emphasize female characters as strong and independent?*

J:  The crucial question about the feminism of a work is not whether the women in it are strong and independent (though I understand your concern perfectly, having been subjected to generations of Supersimps myself in literature) but whether the assumptions underlying the entire narrative are feminist. A sexist story can exist in which all the characters are crystalline life forms living on a planet of Betelgeuse—yes, and a racist one, too—because although the characters aren't human, the writer and the readers are. What's important is who wins and who loses; a remake of Madam Butterfly, with lots of tears, is not a feminist piece of art, no matter who's written it and no matter what sympathy is extended to the poor victim. Many women are guilty of this kind of thing as writers (I like to call it the Joan Didion Syndrome.) Whatever its worth as art (and I think its sentimentality inevitably vitiates it), feminism it ain't. Art is not simple.

Q: *Does the women's movement need science fiction and fantasy? Do you think the women's movement has had difficulties in fantasizing, has suffered from the inability to dream?*

J: May the Heavenly Couple bless me, I don't know enough about "the women's movement" per se to know if we should be dreaming more. The inability to dream is just what sf is supposed to remedy—and not like pure fantasy. No, I shouldn't say that about fantasy; fantasy is inner space. Most of what publishers call "fantasy" had been written either by men or by women simply imitating the tradition of what already existed. There have always been some women writing sf, but now that Marge Piercy is doing it, and there is a novel about Ishtar returning as a Bronx housewife, it does seem to be thriving. Fantasy is extremely difficult in another way, though; there is in it (as Ursula Le Guin points out), at least in the heroic-romance form, *nothing but words.*

Inability to dream—well, everybody needs to dream. It is our spiritual and moral guide. Politics certainly can't be divorced from ultimate goals or ideas about possibilities. The only difficulty I ever encountered with feminists over sf was several years ago in the Labryis Bookstore, into which I barged cheerfully (a perfect stranger) and proposed to give the woman there a list of sf titles. She seemed rather suspicious and probably with reason—I would imagine they'd had considerable hassling in their existence—yet I learned later they simply could not keep Le Guin's *The Left Hand of Darkness* in stock. It always sold out. I say very angry things about Ursula Le Guin quite often, but it's the anger of disappointed adoration; in some daughterly part of me I feel she's capable of writing something like *War and Peace* about *women*, damn it, and I keep nipping her feet to get her to do so. But *The Left Hand of Darkness* is the nearest thing we have to an androgynous vision. I would like to think that *The Female Man* is a gynandrous vision, so if you put the two in a blender (that is, into your head) and mix well, you may end up with something. To return to your question, some of the distrust some feminists *may* have for sf is quite reasonable, since a great deal of sf is a kind of misogynist power-tripping of a very absurd and adolescent kind. And since it is sf and not realism, this shows far more baldly than in realistic fiction. The mode contains perhaps one hundred serious, full-time writers and altogether perhaps three hundred from neophyte aspirants to old professionals, so that every range of quality and content is there. A feminist who goes to the novel rack (under "sf") and picks at random is likely to be not only bored but genuinely insulted. I can only account for my early addiction by adducing the other, mind-expanding quality of the sf works available to me then and the fact that, whatever its faults, sf does present possibilities per se.

Q: *How do you see the relationship between the visions you have described and possibilities for political change, for example, in the different worlds you see in* The Female Man?

J: Impossible question! Books are not blueprints. They are experiences. The worlds in *The Female Man* are not futures, they are here and now writ large. One man just wrote me a lovely fan letter in which he not only described the structure of the book with a precision that astonished me ("an inward descending spiral") but also mentioned casually that Manland/Womanland was *here-and-now*. A flat statement of it would be that Jeannine's world is the past (but still very much present); that Janet's world is a kind of ideal (into which I put all sorts of quirky things I happen to like, like public comic statuary); and that Jael's world is here-and-now carried out to its logical extreme. Joanna keeps running from one to the other. Janet's world is the potential one, not Jael's. I've been asked why there are no men in Whileaway, and my only answer is that I tried but the Whileawayans wouldn't let me.

I can't imagine a two-sexed egalitarian society, and I don't believe anyone else can, either, though Samuel Delany comes closer in *Trouble on Triton* than anything else I've ever read. Well, here you have the whole thing about sf. Where else could one even try out such visions? Yet in the end we will have to have models for the real thing, and I can find none yet, and that is why Whileaway is single-sexed. So is Gethen in *The Left Hand of Darkness*, really.

Q: *What should women science fiction writers be doing?*

J: Why, writing sf, of course. Obviously, work that deals with sexism and feminism will have an effect on feminism, on antifeminism, and (one would think) on all its readers. The effect could easily be reactionary: there seems to have been a mini-upsurge in antifeminist sf, some of it quite naïve—for example, John Boyd's "Pollinators of Eden," in which a frigid female biologist is converted to love and orgasm by making it with a giant sentient orchid. She later gives birth to a pod. (I have never been able to figure out quite how serious Boyd's work is, by the way. Yes, I know it's intended to be funny, but *how* funny?) Or even his *Sex and the High Command*, an extremely sexist book in which women win the sex war and exterminate men. That's what I mean about carefully watching a book's assumptions, not just its obvious statements. You don't have to "mean" sexism, you just have to remain comfortable and unthinking, if you're male.

By the way, James Blish said he invented the words "hard science" to mean *correct* science, as in "hard copy." Popular usage—"hard" means the masculine range of physics, chemistry, astronomy, engineering, and "soft" means the social sciences—is as neat an example of sexist language as I have ever heard. Phallus worship invades the domain of Sacred Reason. Even "hard" to indicate "correct" or "precise" suggests the same thing. (I prefer "winged" myself.)

To be female or feminine or inaccurate or sloppy is to be "soft." Sexual excitement makes women physically mushy and probably does the same to their minds, if they ever had any. All of Western history (and probably Asiatic, too) is in that pair of words. The horrors of the swamp, the split between mind and body, between power and emotion. Oh dear.

This is the effect of reading sex-war books written by men. In one of them God invents a specific form of syphilis (which doesn't show up on a Wasserman test) to give five thousand insurgent American business-women (who have masculinized themselves via androgens because they can't get raises and promotions any other way, and who immediately do take over American business, since they are far more intelligent than their male colleagues) terminal paresis. Well, *that* one dated back to the "teens." The frequency with which these books drag in God or "love" (woman falls on knees, melts—see "soft"—confesses sins, licks toesies, is converted) suggests to me that men are very uneasy about being able to hold their own without divine intervention.

Q: *What has been the role of women and feminism in science fiction writing?*

J: Women have been in the minority in sf from the beginning (if you characterize the beginning as the 1920s or as the Wells/Verne period). This is hardly surprising. The only literary genre in which women have reached anything like substantial number of writers working is the detective story. I don't know why. Perhaps 1920s sf, with its emphasis on pulp, he-man adventure, and (later) on the "hard" sciences, which were assumed to be a closed book to women, simply did not attract women writers. There were always some, though to my sloppy historical memory they wrote either (generally) adventure stories about he-men or sexless stories about phenomena in engineering or strange gimmicks/inventions, just as the men did. There have been a few sentimental ladies' magazine story writers and stories. Pulp fiction was not a place for any artist; the assumption was that the product was (within limits) standard and that one ought not to be able to tell a man's writing from a woman's . . . as if Dickens ought to sound like Thackeray and both of them should be indistinguishable from Tolstoy, on the grounds that little things like a writer's era or nationality ought not to "show"! This commercial attitude still persists. After all, you can't tell from the Kleenex box whether the assembly line was staffed by women or men, so why should a story be different?

Women are still in the minority. In 1973 the membership of the Science Fiction Writers of America was, roughly, two women to eleven men. However, the women have been winning a disproportionate number of the prizes given in the field. This suggests to me that (as in many other fields) women sf writers are more rigorously self-selected than the men.

Q: *Can women science fiction writers play a political role in the field of science fiction and within the women's movement?*

J: Of course they can have a political role within science fiction—if you mean by this the internal politics of the field. It is happening now. One young man has started "The Pig Runner's Digest" to flout and attack sexism (and its more easily spottable symptom, misogyny) in sf. Equal pay is another matter—everybody is poor and publishers generally print any novel that holds together (as long as they can underpay you for it). On the other hand, I have heard stories of "Oh, we can't print that, women writers don't sell," and so on. As in any freelance field where the machines are always hungry for cotton to be woven, nobody cares who picks it. At least I hope so. If things get much more lucrative, they may change. Then, again, I am in no position to be told to my face that X won't print my novel because I'm female. Or because the novel is feminist. Or because it scared the hell out of the senior editor.

Within the women's movement, certainly women sf writers can provide spiritual nutriment and visions and (probably) annoyance and everything else to women's movement readers—that is, as writers. As private citizens they can do all sorts of things, obviously. Some women sf writers will undoubtedly continue to write about Superduperman (but even there he will be more likely to have a stubborn "girl sidekick"), and some won't. The newest generation of sf writers of both sexes is largely a generation trained primarily in literature, not science (or science only secondarily), and since the concerns of science fiction are shifting from "hard" science to social structures and psychology/anthropology, it is easier for women (since most women are not trained in science) to enter sf. What I would like to see, for the health of feminism and the health of feminist sf, is an influx of new women writers.

## FICTION

*Novels*

*Picnic On Paradise*. New York: Ace, 1968.

*And Chaos Died*. New York: Ace, 1970.

*The Female Man*. New York: Bantam, 1975; London: Allen, 1977 (references in the text are to this edition).

*We Who Are About To. . . .* New York: Dell, 1977 (serialized in *Galaxy*, January and February 1976); London: Namara/Women's, 1987 (references in the text are to this edition).

*Kittatinny*. New York: Daughters, 1978.

*The Two of Them*. New York: Berkley, 1978; London: Namara/Women's, 1986 (references in the text are to this edition).

*On Strike against God*. Trumansburg, N.Y.: Out and Out, 1980; London: Namara/Women's, 1980 (references in the text are to this edition).

*Extra(Ordinary)People*. New York: St Martin's, 1984; London: Namara/Women's, 1985 (references in the text are to this edition).

*Story Collections*

*Alyx*. Introduction by Samuel Delany. Boston: Gregg, 1976.

*The Adventures of Alyx*. New York: Simon and Schuster, 1983; London: Namara/Women's, 1985 (references in the text are to this edition).

*The Zanzibar Cat*. Illustrated, with an introduction by Marge Piercy. Sauk City, Wisc.: Arkham House, 1983; New York: Baen, 1984.

*The Hidden Side of the Moon*. New York: St. Martin's, 1987.

*Stories (First Publication)*

"Innocence." *Cornell [University] Writer*, May 1955. Reprinted in *Magazine of Fantasy and Science Fiction*, February 1975.

"Martyr." *Cornell [University] Writer*, 1957.

"The Wise Man." *Cornell [University] Writer*, 1957; *Cimarron Review* 13 (October 1970).

"Nor Custom Stale." *Magazine of Fantasy and Science Fiction*, September 1959.

"My Dear Emily." *Magazine of Fantasy and Science Fiction*, July 1962.

"There Is Another Shore You Know, upon the Other Side." *Magazine of Fantasy and Science Fiction*, September 1963.

"I Had Vacantly Crumpled It into My Pocket . . . but By God, Eliot, It Was a Photograph from Life!" *Magazine of Fantasy and Science Fiction*, August 1964.

"Wilderness Year." *Magazine of Fantasy and Science Fiction*, December 1964.

"Come Closer." *Magazine of Horror*, August 1965.

"Life in a Furniture Store." [Cornell University] *Epoch* 15, no. 1 (Fall 1965).

"The New Men." *Magazine of Fantasy and Science Fiction*, February 1966.

"Mr. Wilde's Second Chance." *Magazine of Fantasy and Science Fiction*, October 1966.

"This Night at My Fire." [Cornell University] *Epoch* 15, no. 2 (Winter 1966).

"Bluestocking." First published as "The Adventuress." In *Orbit 2*, edited by Damon Knight. New York: Berkley, 1967.

"I Thought She Was Afeared, until She Stroked My Beard." First published as "I Gave Her Sack and Sherry." In *Orbit 2*, edited by Damon Knight. New York: Berkley, 1967.

"Visiting." *Manhattan Review*, Fall 1967.

"The Barbarian." In *Orbit 3*, edited by Damon Knight. New York: Berkley, 1968.

"Harry Longshanks." In *Fiction as Progress*, edited by Carl Hartmann and Hazard Adams. New York: Dodd and Mead, 1968.

"Scenes from Domestic Life." *Consumption* 2, no. 1 (Fall 1968).

"This Afternoon." *Cimarron Review* 6 (December 1968).

"Oh! She Has a Lover." *Kinesis* 1 (February 1969).

"The Throaways." *Consumption* 2, no. 3 (Summer 1969).

"A Short and Happy Life." *Magazine of Fantasy and Science Fiction*, June 1969.

"What Really Happened." *Just Friends*, October 1969.

"The Man Who Could Not See Devils." In *Alchemy and Academe*, edited by Anne McCaffrey. New York: Doubleday, 1970.

"The Second Inquisition." In *Orbit 6*, edited by Damon Knight. New York: Berkley, 1970.

"The View from This Window." In *Quark*, edited by Marilyn Hacker. New York: Paperback Library, 1970.

"Visiting Day." *South* 2, no. 1 (1970).

"Window Dressing." In *New Worlds of Fantasy 2*. New York: Ace, 1970.

"Initiation" (from *And Chaos Died*). *Magazine of Fantasy and Science Fiction*, February 1970.

"Cap and Bells." *Discourse*, Summer 1970.

"Not for Love." *Arlington Quarterly*, Fall 1970.

"Suffer a Sea Change." *William and Mary Review*, Fall 1970.

"The Precious Object." *Red Clay Reader* 7 (November 1970).

"Gleepsite." In *Orbit 9*, edited by Damon Knight. New York: Putnam's 1971.

"Poor Man, Beggar Man." *Universe 1*, edited by Terry Carr. New York: Doubleday, 1971.

"The Zanzibar Cat." In *Quark 3*, edited by Samuel Delany and Marilyn Hacker. New York: Paperback Library, 1971.

"Foul Fowl." *Little Magazine* 5, no. 1 (Spring 1971).

"Nobody's Home." In *New Dimensions*, edited by Robert Silverberg. New York: Doubleday, 1972.

"Useful Phrases for the Tourist." In *Universe 2*, edited by Terry Carr. New York: Ace, 1972.

"When It Changed." In *Again, Dangerous Visions*, edited by Harlan Ellison. New York: Doubleday, 1972.

"Dear Diary." *North West Review* 12 (Fall 1972).

"The Soul of a Servant." In *Showcase*, edited by Roger Elwood. New York: Harper and Row, 1973.

"Laura, the Camp, and That Terrible Thing." *Monmouth Review*, Spring 1973.

"Old Pictures." *Little Magazine*, Winter 1973.

"An Old-Fashioned Girl" (from *The Female Man*). In *Final Stage*, edited by Edward L. Ferman and Barry N. Malzberg. New York: Charterhouse, 1974.

"Reasonable People." In *Orbit 14*, edited by Damon Knight. New York: Harper and Row, 1974.

"Passages." *Galaxy*, January 1974.

"A Game of Vlet." *Magazine of Fantasy and Science Fiction*, February 1974.

"A Few Things I Know about Whileaway." In *The New Improved Sun*, edited by Thomas Disch. New York: Harper and Row, 1975.

"Innocence." *Magazine of Fantasy and Science Fiction*, February 1975.

"The Experimenter." *Galaxy*, October 1975.

"Existence." In *Epoch*, edited by Roger Elwood and Robert Silverberg. New York: Berkley/Putnam, November 1975.

"Daddy's Little Girl." [Cornell University] *Epoch* 24, no. 2 (Spring 1975).

"The Clichés from Outer Space." *Witch and the Chameleon*, April 1, 1975; reprinted in a longer form in *Women's Studies International Forum* 7, no. 2, 1984.

"Risk." *Magazine of Fantasy and Science Fiction*, June 1975.

"The Autobiography of My Mother" [Cornell University] *Epoch* 24, no. 2 (Fall 1975).

"Corruption." In *Aurora: Beyond Equality*, ed. Susan Janice Anderson and Vonda McIntyre; New York: Fawcett Gold Medal/Ballantine, 1976.

"My Boat." *Magazine of Fantasy and Science Fiction*, January 1976.

"How Dorothy Kept Away the Spring." *Magazine of Fantasy and Science Fiction*, February 1977.

"Kit Meets the Dragon" (from *Kittatinny*). *Sinister Wisdom* 4 (Fall 1977).

"The Extraordinary Voyages of Amélie Bertrand." *Magazine of Fantasy and Science Fiction*, September 1979.

"Dragons and Dimwits." *Magazine of Fantasy and Science Fiction*, December 1979.

"It's Important to Believe." *Sinister Wisdom* 14, 1980.

"Little Tales from Nature." In *WomanSpace*, edited by Claudia Laperti. Lebanon, N.H.: New Victoria, 1981.

"Russalka; or, The Seacoast of Bohemia" (from *Kittatinny*). In *Don't Bet on the Prince*, edited by Jack Zipes. London: Methuen, 1981.

"The Little Dirty Girl." In *Elsewhere*, vol. 2, edited by Terri Windling and Mark Alan Arnold. New York: Ace, 1982.

"The Mystery of the Young Gentleman." *Speculations*, edited by Isaac Asimov and Alice Laurance. New York: Houghton Mifflin, 1982.

"Souls." *Magazine of Fantasy and Science Fiction*, January 1982.

"Elf Hill." *Magazine of Fantasy and Science Fiction*, November 1982.

"Swordblades and Poppy Seed." *Heroic Visions*, edited by Jessica Amanda Salmonson. New York: Ace, 1983.

"What Did You Do During the Revolution, Grandma?" *Seattle Review* 1, no. 1 (Spring 1983).

"Main Street: 1953." *Sinister Wisdom* 24 (Fall 1983).

"Let George Do It." *Women's Studies International Forum* 7, no. 2, 1984.
"Invasion." *Isaac Asimov's Science Fiction Magazine*, January 1996.

## Slash Fiction

Joanna's Slash Fiction (in manuscript) and K/S (Kirk/Spock) correspondence can be accessed by arrangement (https://library.uoregon.edu/special-collections/registration) at the University of Oregon, Special Collections: "Archive West, Joanna Russ Papers 1968–1989"

## NONFICTION

### Monographs

*How to Suppress Women's Writing.* Austin: University of Texas Press, 1983; reprinted 2018 with a foreword by Jessa Crispin.
*What Are We Fighting For?* New York: St Martin's, 1997.

### Collections

*Magic Mommas, Trembling Sisters, Puritans and Perverts: Essays on Sex and Pornography.* Trumansburg N.Y.: Crossing, 1985.
*To Write Like a Woman.* Bloomington: Indiana University Press, 1995.
*The Country You Have Never Seen.* Liverpool: Liverpool University Press, 2007.

### Reviews (Collected in The Country You Have Never Seen)

*Appearing originally in "Books," Magazine of Fantasy and Science Fiction*

*Strange Signposts: An Anthology of the Fantastic*, edited by Roger Elwood and Sam Moskowitz. December 1966.
*The Warriors of the Day*, by James Blish; *Stealer of Souls* and *Storm Bringer*, by Michael Moorcock. October 1967.
*Lord of Light*, by Roger Zelazny; *The Mind Parasites*, by Colin Wilson. January 1968.
*The Best of the Best*, edited by Judith Merril; *Ashes, Ashes*, by Rene Barjeval, translated by Damon Knight; *A Torrent of Faces*, by James Blish and Norman L. Knight. July 1968.
*Black Easter*, by James Blish; *The Final Programme*, by Michael Moorcock; *The Still Small Voice of Trumpets*, by Lloyd Biggle; *The Doomsday Men*, by Kenneth Bulmer; *Flesh*, by Philip José Farmer. December 1968.
*Pavanne*, by Keith Roberts; *The Age of the Pussyfoot*, by Frederick Pohl; *The Santaroga Barrier*, by Frank Herbert; *Transplant*, by Margaret Jones; *Omar*, by Wilfrid Blunt. April 1969.
*The Sword Swallower*, by Ron Goulart; *The Phoenix and the Mirror*, by Avram Davidson; *Small Changes*, by Hal Clement; *The Best SF Stories from New Worlds 2*, by Poul Anderson; *7 Conquests*, by Poul Anderson. August 1969.
*The Prometheus Project*, by Gerald Feinberg; *Let the Fire Fall*, by Kate Wilhelm; *World's Best Science Fiction: 1968*, edited by Donald A. Wollheim and Terry Carr; *The Last Starship from Earth*, by John Boyd; *The Da Vinci Machine*, by Earl Conrad. September 1969.

*The Day of the Dolphin*, by Robert Merle; *Bug Jack Barron*, by Norman Spinrad; *Emphyrio*,
by Jack Vance; *Best SF: 1968*, edited by Harry Harrison and Brian Aldiss; *The Empty
People*, K .M. O'Donnell. January 1970.

*The Ship Who Sang*, by Anne McCaffery; *Satan's World*, by Poul Anderson; *Report on
Probability A*, by Brian Aldiss; *I Sing the Body Electric*, by Ray Bradbury. July 1970.

*This Perfect Day*, by Ira Levin; *The Simultaneous Man*, by Ralph Blum; *The Dark Symphony*,
by Dean R. Koontz; *Sea Horse in the Sky*, by Edmund Cooper. February 1971.

*The Bed Sitting Room*, by Richard Lester (movie); *First Flights to the Moon*, edited by Hal
Clement; *SF: Authors' Choice 2*, edited by Harry Harrison; *One Step from Earth*, by Harry
Harrison; *The Cube Root of Uncertainty*, by Robert Silverberg; *Time Rogue*, by Leo P.
Kelley; *Operation Ares*, by Gene Wolfe. April 1971.

*The Dialectic of Sex*, by Shulamith Firestone; *Abyss*, by Kate Wilhelm; *The Light Fantastic*,
edited by Harry Harrison; *Partners in Wonder*, edited by Harlan Ellison (collaborations);
*The Day after Judgement*, by James Blish. November 1971.

*Moderan*, by David R. Bunch; *The Falling Astronauts*, by Barry N. Malzberg; *In the Pocket
and Other SF Stories* and *Gather in the Hall of the Planets*, by K. M. O'Donnell; *Humanity
Prime*, by Bruce McAllister; *The Committed Men*, by M. John Harrison; *Pig World*,
by Charles W. Runyon; *Can You Feel Anything When I Do This*, by Robert Shackley.
December 1972.

*Pandora's Planet*, by Christopher Anvil; *The Light That Never Was*, by Lloyd Biggle;
*Midsummer Country*, by James Blish; *Beyond Apollo*, by Barry Malzberg; *What Entropy
Means to Me*, by George Alec Effinger. February 1973.

*Eros in Orbit*, edited by Joseph Elder; *Strange Bedfellows*, edited by Thomas N. Scortia; *The
Iron Dream*, by Norman Spinrad; *The Listeners*, by James Gunn; *Dying Inside*, by Robert
Silverberg. July 1973.

*Bad Moon Rising: An Anthology of Political Forebodings*, edited by Thomas Disch; *Paradox
Lost*, by Frederic Brown; *The Star Road*, by Gordon Dickson; *Complex Man*, by Marie
Farca. February 1974.

*Born with the Dead*, by Robert Silverberg; *Some Dreams Are Nightmares*, by James Gunn;
*Total Eclipse*, by John Brunner; *Flow My Tears the Policeman Said*, by Philip K. Dick; *The
Texas Israeli War*, by Howard Waldrop and Jake Saunders. January 1975.

*Frankenstein Unbound*, by Brian Aldiss; *The Dispossessed*, by Ursula K. Le Guin; *Joy in Our
Cause*, by Carol Emshwiller, *Stellar 1*, edited by Judy-Lynn del Rey. March 1975.

*Cliff Notes: Science Fiction; An Introduction*, by L. David Allen; *Political Science Fiction:
An Introductory Reader*, edited by Martin Harry Greenberg and Patricia S. Warrick;
*As Tomorrow Becomes Today*, edited by Charles Wm. Sullivan III; *Speculations: An
Introduction to Literature Through Fantasy and Science Fiction*, edited by Thomas E.
Sanders; *Modern Science Fiction*, edited by Norman Spinrad; *Science Fiction: The Classroom
in Orbit*, by Beverley Friend; *The English Assassin*, by Michael Moorcock. April 1975.

*The Clewiston Test*, by Kate Wilhelm; *Millennium*, by Ben Bova; *Star Mother*, by Sydney J.
van Scyoc; *Cloned Lives*, by Pamela Sargent; *Star Trek: The New Voyages*, edited by Sondra
Marshak and Myrna Culbreath. November 1976.

*What Happened to Emily Goode after the Great Exhibition*, by Raylyn Moore; *Rime Isle*, by
Fritz Leiber; *The Year's Finest Fantasy*, edited by Terry Carr; *Lord Foul's Bane*, by Stephen
Donaldson; *The Grey Mane of Morning*, by Joy Chant. February 1979.

*Immortal: Short Novels of the Transhuman Future*, edited by Jack Dann; *Anticipations, Eight New Stories*, edited by Christopher Priest; *Ursula K. Le Guin's Science Fiction Writing Workshop: The Altered I*, edited by Lee Harding; *A Place Beyond Man*, by Cary Neeper. June 1979.

"Joanna Replies." November 1979. Reprinted in *The Best From Fantasy and Science Fiction 23*, edited by Edward L. Ferman, 1980.

*On Wings of Song*, by Thomas M. Disch; *Painted Death*, by Robert Aickman; *Kindred*, by Octavia Butler; *Universe 9*, edited by Terry Carr; *New Dimensions 9*, edited by Robert Silverberg; *The Language of the Night: Essays on Fantasy and Science Fiction*, edited by Susan Wood. February 1980.

*Appearing originally in other venues*

"Never Draw Pentagrams in the Bathroom." Reviews of *The Satanists*, edited by Peter Haining; *The Complete Book of Magic and Witchcraft*, by Kathryn Paulson; *Practical Candle Burning*, by Raymond Buckland; *Diary of a Witch*, by Sybil Leek; *Master Guide to Psychism* by Harriet A. Boswell; *Here, Mr. Splitfoot*, by Robert Somerlot. *Village Voice*, September 9, 1971.

*The Shape of Utopia*, by Robert C. Elliott; *Into the Unknown: The Evolution of Science Fiction from Francis Godwin to H. G. Wells*, by Robert N. Philmus. *College English* 33, no. 3 (December 1971).

"Mystification about (gulp) Marriage." Reviews of *The Future of Marriage*, by Jessie Bernard; *Marriage For and Against*, edited by Harold H. Hart. *Village Voice*, June 16, 1973.

*The High Cost of Living*, by Marge Piercy. *Frontiers*, 3, no. 3 (Fall 1978).

*Gyn/Ecology: The Metaethics of Radical Feminism*, by Mary Daly. *Frontiers* 4, no. 1 (Spring 1979).

*In Memory Yet Green: The Autobiography of Isaac Asimov, 1920–1954*; *Opus 200*, by Isaac Asimov. "Book World," *Washington Post*, April 1, 1979.

*On Lies, Secrets, and Silence: Selected Prose, 1966–1978*, by Adrienne Rich. "Book World," *Washington Post*, May 9, 1979.

*The Mermaid and the Minotaur: Sexual Arrangements and Human Malaise*, by Dorothy Dinnerstein. *Frontiers* 4, no. 2 (Summer 1979).

"When We Were Everybody: A Lost Feminist Utopia." Review of *Herland: A Lost Feminist Utopian Novel*, by Charlotte Perkins Gilman. *Feminist Review* 5 (in *New Women's Times* 5, no. 14 [July 16–19, 1979]).

*The Beginning Place*, by Ursula K. Le Guin; *Fireflood and Other Stories*, by Vonda McIntyre; *Yesterday's Children*, by David Gerrold; *The Demon of Scattery*, by Poul Anderson and Mildred Downey. "Book World," *Washington Post*, January 24, 1980.

"Listen, There's a Story for You . . ." Review of *Retreat as It Was!* by Donna J. Young. *Sinister Wisdom* 12 (Winter 1980).

*Surpassing the Love of Men: Romantic Friendship and Love between Women from the Renaissance to the Present*, by Lilian Faderman. "Book World," *Washington Post*, May 10, 1981.

*Women's Creation: Sexual Evolution and the Shaping of Socicty*, by Elizabeth Fisher. *Frontiers*, 5, no. 3 (Fall 1981).

*Essays*

"Daydream Literature and Science Fiction." *Extrapolation* 11, no. 1 (December 1969).

"The Image of Women in Science Fiction." *Red Clay Reader* 7 (November 1970).
"Communique from the Front: Teaching and the State of Art." *Colloquy* 4, no. 5 (May 1977).
"Genre." *Clarion*, edited by Robin Wilson. New York: Signet, 1971.
"The Wearing Out of Genre Materials." *College English* 33, no. 1 (October 1971).
"What Can a Heroine Do? or, Why Women Can't Write." *Images of Women in Fiction*, edited by Susan Koppelman Cornillon. Bowling Green, Ohio: Bowling Green University Popular Press, June 1972.
"The New Misandry." *Village Voice*, October 12, 1972.
"Setting." *Those Who Can: A Science Fiction Reader*, edited by R. S. Wilson. New York: New American Library, Mentor, 1973.
"Speculations: The Subjunctivity of Science Fiction." *Extrapolation* 15 (December 1973).
"Somebody's Trying to Kill Me and I Think It's My Husband: The Modern Gothic." *Journal of Popular Culture* 6, no. 4 (March 1973).
"'What If' Literature." *The Contemporary Literary Scene*, edited by Frank N. Magill. Englewood N.J.: Salem, 1974.
"Dear Colleague: I Am Not an Honorary Male." *Colloquy: Education in Church and Society* 7, no. 4 (April 1974).
"On the Nature of Concrete Phenomena and Rhetorical Sleight of Hand." In *Khatru 3 and 4. Symposium: Women in Science Fiction*, edited by Jeffrey D. Smith. Baltimore, Md.: Phantasmicon, 1975. Repr. by the Corflu 10 Convention Committee, edited by Jeanne Gomoll. Madison Wisc.: Obsessive, 1993. Quotes in this book are from this edition.
"This Is Your Life." In *Khatru 3 and 4. Symposium: Women in Science Fiction*, edited by Jeffrey D. Smith. Baltimore, Md.: Phantasmicon, 1975. Reprinted by the Corflu 10 Convention Committee, edited by Jeanne Gomoll. Madison Wisc.: Obsessive, 1993. Quotes in this book are from this edition.
"On Mary Wollstonecraft Shelley." Introduction to *Tales and Stories*, by Mary Shelley. Boston: Gregg, 1975.
"The Scholar as Translator (Contra)." *Translators and Translating Selected Essays from the American Translators Association Summer Workshops, 1974*, edited by T. Ellen, Crandell, Binghamton: State University of New York Press, 1975.
"Towards an Aesthetic of Science Fiction." *Science Fiction Studies* 6, no. 2.2 (July 1975).
"*A Boy and His Dog: The Final Solution.*" *Frontiers* 1, no. 1 (Fall 1975).
"Outta Space: Women Write Science Fiction." *Ms.*, January 1976.
"Alien Monsters." Speech at the Philadelphia Science Fiction Conference, November 9, 1968, in *Turning Point*, edited by Damon Knight. New York: Harper and Row, 1977. See also "The He-Man Ethos in Science Fiction," *Clarion* 2 (1972).
"'Technology': The Immense Red Herring." *Forum on Technology and the Literary Mind*, Proceedings of the MLA Association (December 1977).
"SF and Technology as Mystification." *Science Fiction Studies* 16, no. 5.3 (November 1978).
"Is 'Smashing' Erotic?" *Chrysalis* 9 (Fall 1979).
"Not for Years but for Decades." *The Coming Out Stories*, edited by Julia Penelope Stanley and Susan J. Wolfe. Watertown, Mass. Persephone 1980.
"Amor Vincit Foeminam: The Battle of the Sexes in Science Fiction." *Science Fiction Studies* 20, no. 7.1 (March 1980).
"On the Fascination of Horror Stories, Including Lovecraft's." *Science Fiction Studies* (Notes and Correspondence) 22, no. 7.3 (November 1980).

"H. P. Lovecraft." *Twentieth-Century Science Fiction Authors*, edited by Curtis Smith. New York: St Martin's, 1981.

"Power and Helplessness in the Women's Movement." *Sinister Wisdom* 18 (1981).

"Recent Feminist Utopias." *Future Females: A Critical Anthology*. Edited by Marleen Barr. Bowling Green, Ohio: Bowling Green University Popular Press, 1981.

"Being against Pornography." *13th Moon* 6, no. 1–2 (1982).

"How to Write Book Reviews." *Feminist Review/New Women's Times* (July/August 1982).

"Introduction." *Uranian Worlds*, edited by Camilla Decarnin, Eric Garber, and Lyn Paleo. Boston: Hall, 1983.

"News from the Front." In *Magic Mommas*, 1985.

"Pornography by Women, for Women, with Love." Extended version of an essay published in *Nome* 8 (May 1985). In *Magic Mommas*, 1985.

"Pornography and the Doubleness of Sex for Women." In *Magic Mommas*, 1985.

"To Write 'Like a Woman': Transformations of Identity in the Work of Willa Cather." *Journal of Homosexuality* 12, no. 3–4 (1986).

"On 'The Yellow Wallpaper.'" Letter addressed to the NWSA journal, Autumn 1988; published in *To Write Like a Woman*.

"Letter to Susan Koppelman." November 1984. Published in *To Write Like a Woman*.

"Writers Comment on Their Own Work." *Women's Review of Books*, 6, no. 10–11 (July 1989).

"Introduction." *The Penguin Book of Fantasy by Women*, edited by A. Susan Willams and Richard Glyn Jones. London: Penguin, 1995.

"Introduction." In *Revolution, She Wrote*, by Clara Fraser. Seattle, Wash.: Red Letter, 1998.

*Letters*

On the inhibitions lesbian-feminist politics seeks to place on artistic talent. *Sinister Wisdom* 11 (Fall 1970).

On a shockingly sexist review of Phyllis Chesler's *Women and Madness*. *Village Voice*, October 1972.

"Comment on '"The Exquisite Slave': The Role of Clothes in the Making of the Victorian Woman," and "Dress Reform as Anti-Feminist.'" *Signs* 2, no. 3 (Spring 1977).

"Comment on 'Prostitution and Medieval Canon Law,' by James Brundage." *Signs* 2, no. 4 (Summer 1977).

On the fear of erotic intensity between women. *Frontiers* 4, no. 2 (1979).

"Writing Pays Very Badly." With facts and figures. *Feminist Review/New Women's Times*, February 29–March13, 1980.

On gay male non-verbal signaling. *Gay Community Center Newsletter*, July 1980.

Women and SF, three letters. *Science Fiction Studies* 2, no. 7.2 (July 1980).

To *Venom: The Magazine of Killer Reviews*, November 1981.

Comment on *There Is No Natural Human Sexuality*, by Ruth Hubbard. *Sojourner* 10, no. 8 (June 1985).

Comment on *Solstice*, by Joyce Carol Oates. *Women's Review of Books* 2, no. 9 (June 1985).

Comment on *Gender Justice*, by David L. Kirp et al. *Women's Review of Books* 3, no. 6 (March 1986).

On the difference between separatism and segregation. *Seattle Source*, April 11, 1986.

Comment on *A Passion for Friends*, by Janice Raymond. *Women's Review of Books* 3, no. 12 (September 1986).

"Writers Choose Their Reading: Susan Koppelman's Short Story Anthologies (*Old Maids*, *The Other Woman; Mothers and Daughters*) and *Close To Home: A Materialist Analysis of Women's Oppression*, by Christine Delphy." *Women's Review of Books* 4, no. 10–11 (July/ August 1987).

"On Lesbian Gentile Semantics: Untangling Butch/Femme, Masculine/Feminine Talk." *Lesbian Ethics* 2, no. 3 (Summer 1987).

"Atheist Mysticism." *Gay Community News*, January 22–28, 1989.

Comment on *Gender and the Politics of History*, by Joan Wallach Scott. *Women's Review of Books* 4, no. 7 (April 1989).

Comment on Veronica Hollinger's essay "On James Tiptree Jr." *Extrapolation* 31, no. 1 (Spring 1990).

Comment on "The Counterdiscourse of the Feminine" in three texts by Wilde, Huysmans, and Sacher-Masoch, discussed in a publication of the Modern Language Association, March 1992.

"Rewind after Viewing." Review of *Ishtar*, a movie by Elaine May. *Sojourner: The Women's Forum* (September 1993).

Comment on *The Persistent Desire: A Femme-Butch Reader*, edited by Joan Nestle. *Lesbian Review of Books* 1, no. 3 (1995).


## PLAYS

"Window Dressing." *Confrontation*, Spring 1973; reprinted in *The New Women's Theatre*, edited by Honor Moor. New York: Vintage, 1977.


## POEMS

"To R. L." *Epoch* 6 (1953–1955): 242.

"Family Snapshots—Botanical Gardens" and "A La Mode." *Epoch* 7 (1955–1957): 35.

Other poems published in the *Cornell [University] Writer* and in *[Cornell University] Epoch* include "Death and the Gentleman," "Never Forgive Me," "The Queen at Ur," "A Schoolteacher's Daughter Speaks," and "Down White Park Street." The poems from 1957 are "the last of Russ's career" (Brit Mandelo).

Poetry manuscripts, with some print copies. Brown Popular Culture Library Joanna Russ Collection (PCL MS 007), Bowling Green State University, Bowling Green, Ohio.


## JUVENILIA

Early stories and notebooks (from 1942). Brown Popular Culture Library, Joanna Russ Collection (PCL MS 007), Bowling Green State University, Bowling Green, Ohio.


## INTERVIEWS

"Reflections on Science Fiction: An Interview With Joanna Russ." In *Building Feminist Theory: Essays from Quest*, edited by Charlotte Bunch, 243–50. New York: Longman, 1981.

Walker, Paul. *Speaking of Science Fiction: The Paul Walker Interviews.* Oradel, N.J.: Luna, 1978, 242–52.

Johnson, Charles. "A Dialogue: Samuel Delany and Joanna Russ on Science Fiction." *Callaloo* 7, no. 3 (22) (1984): 27–35.

McCaffery, Larry. *Across the Wounded Galaxies: Interviews with Contemporary American Science Fiction Writers.* New Brunswick N.J.: Rutgers University Press, 1990, 176–210.

Bengels, Barbara. "As the Twig Is Bent: SF Writers Talk about Their Childhood." *New York Review of Science Fiction* 22, no. 9 (May 2010).

## CHAPTER 1. JOANNA RUSS, TRANS-TEMP AGENT

1. *Country You Have Never Seen*, 284.

2. Bengels, "As the Twig Is Bent," 10–19.

3. Joanna Russ Collection, PCL MS 007, Browne Popular Culture Library, Bowling Green State University, Bowling Green, Ohio.

4. Bengels, "As the Twig Is Bent," 10–19.

5. Russ interview in Walker, *Speaking of Science Fiction*.

6. Arthur March and Ira Maximilian Freeman, *The New World of Physics*, Random House, 1962. Expanded from a 1957 paper.

7. *Magic Mommas*, 115.

8. Smith, *Khatru*, 88.

9. "The special tie women have with children is recognized by everyone. I submit, however, that the nature of this bond is no more than shared oppression." Firestone, *Dialectic of Sex*, 74.

10. I suppose only outright porn has a lower score; Joanna made forays into that genre too.

11. Wolfe, "Alyx among the Genres," 5.

12. Russ interview in Walker, *Speaking of Science Fiction*.

13. Harlan Ellison's introduction to "When It Changed" in *Again, Dangerous Visions*.

14. A slide from the experiment can be seen at https://femscifi.wordpress.com/2013/11/27/joanna-russ-and-the-westinghouse-science-talent-search.

15. See Brit Mandelo, "Poetry of Joanna Russ," at *Stone Telling*: http://stonetelling.com/issue6-dec2011/mandelo-russpt1.html.

16. See *Female Man*, 131 ("there but for the grace of God go I"), and *Magic Mommas*, 27. Like Jeannine, who finally elects to marry her gentle boyfriend, though she hates having sex with him, Joanna took flight into marriage, briefly, and out of sheer desperation.

17. *Country You Have Never Seen*, 284

18. Walker, *Speaking of Science Fiction*, 247.

19. Honor Moore, *The New Women's Theatre: Ten Plays by Contemporary American Women* (New York: Random House, 1977).

20. Biographical note for *And Chaos Died*.

21. Smith, *Khatru*, 72–73, original emphasis.

22. *Magic Mommas*, 25.

23. All fictional futures are recognizable, in hindsight, as having been conceived a specific point in real history.

24. May, *Homeward Bound*, 16–18.

25. Yaszek, "History of One's Own," 43–45.

26. May, *Homeward Bound*, 3.

27. *Zanzibar Cat*, 116.

28. Cortiel, *Demand My Writing*, 24–35.

29. A shared fictional universe, based on the works of H. P. Lovecraft; the term was coined by August Derleth.

30. See also *Female Man*, 192–94.

31. *Magic Mommas*, 27–29.

32. https://www.flickr.com/photos/42080330@No3/8218051315.

33. *Building Feminist Theory*, 243–50.

34. Wolfe, "Alyx among the Genres," 3.

35. *Weird Tales*, October 1934.

36. Wolfe, "Alyx among the Genres," 4.

37. *Magic Mommas*, 52.

38. *Adventures of Alyx*, 26. Alyx's gorgeous pirate is homage to the hero of Fritz Leiber's "Fafhrd and the Grey Mouser" stories. Leiber returned the compliment, placing Alyx in "The Two Best Thieves in Lankhmar" (1968) and "Under the Thumbs of the Gods" (1975).

39. "The Old Man of the Mountain" is the title of the manuscript at the Bowling Green State University archive.

40. Wolfe, "Alyx among the Genres," 10–11.

41. *Adventures of Alyx*, 62. The dangerous pressure points are in the *front* of the neck (the throat), where the carotid arteries pass either side of the windpipe. The error would be corrected in *Picnic on Paradise*.

42. *Adventures of Alyx*, 44. In "Bluestocking" there's an unfamiliar creation myth, and humans have six fingers, generally only on the right hand for women.

43. *Picnic on Paradise*, 20. The first appearance of this enduring institution in Joanna's sf.

44. Wolfe, "Alyx among the Genres," 11–12.

45. Piercy, *Parti-Colored Blocks*, 252. Group therapy may have been an inspiration for this dreadful crew. One might also recall Joanna spent several years working in theater.

46. Gregory Feeley, *Foundation 30*, 1984.

47. Niall Harrison, https://sfmistressworks.wordpress.com/2011/08/05/the-adventures-of-alyx-joanna-russ, emphasis added. "Fafhrd" was Fritz Leiber's not-too-bright fantasy adventure hero; Elric of Melniboné was British "New Worlds" author Michael Moorcock's moody, introspective fantasy protagonist.

48. First collected in *The Adventures of Alyx* (Boston: Gregg, 1976).

49. 1926 was the year Hugo Gernsback founded *Amazing Stories*.

50. Iris Storm ("March" was her maiden name), heroine of *The Green Hat*, tragically doomed by her first husband's suicide, drives a yellow Hispano-Suiza and pays the price for glamorous depravity in septic abortions. I'd rather take the bus, myself.

51. Morlocks and Eloi are the degenerate, far-future human types in Wells's *The Time Machine*. The feckless, luxurious Eloi are kept for meat by the Morlocks, who do the world's work but live in hiding underground. (Wells's reference is to the upper classes and their servants in nineteenth century England.)

52. Wolfe, "Alyx among the Genres," 14.

53. *Adventures of Alyx* (Women's Press), 161. "I found myself at the archway, by the foot of the stairs, with *The Green Hat: A Romance* in my hand."

54. "'The Second Inquisition' *is* an Alyx story—the character in it is Alyx's great-granddaughter. I wanted the stories to form a closed piece, a kind of Klein bottle thing, with its tail in its mouth, to imply that the protagonist of the Inquisition went on to write the other stories." Cortiel, *Demand My Writing*; letter from Joanna Russ, September 21, 1995.

55. "If a man can resist the influence of his townsfolk, if he can cut free from the tyranny of neighbourhood gossip, the world has no terrors for him; there is no second inquisition."

## CHAPTER 2. JOANNA RUSS AND THE NEW WAVE

1. Cover copy of the 1951 Compact Books edition of Merril's bleak domestic revival/anti-nuclear-war novel *Shadow on the Hearth*.

2. Merril, *Merril Theory*. Not entirely a compliment, according to William Gibson: "You could write whatever you wanted in science fiction, because it was beneath contempt." *Guardian*, May 3, 2003.

3. *Galaxy*, December 1966

4. In the aftermath of a chemical weapons holocaust, "reality has become," according to Aldiss's publicity, "a fluid mixture of the real, the imaginary and the nightmarish."

5. "Perhaps the high-water mark . . . came on August 18, 1969, when guitarist Jimi Hendrix stood on stage at Woodstock and played his version of 'The Star-Spangled Banner.'" https://www.gilderlehrman.org/history-by-era/sixties/essays/protest-music-1960s.

6. *Country You Have Never Seen*, 7.

7. "I mean, I didn't believe *anything*: not the character of the protagonist, nor (except in brief flashes) any of the other characters. . . . When it all got too much for me I didn't stop, I just switched over to a (highly necessary) 'suspension of disbelief' and went on reading into the small hours of the night, for the sheer pleasure of the prose." Merril, "Books" *Magazine of Fantasy and Science Fiction*, September 1968.

8. James, "Russ on Writing," 19–20. According to Gordon Van Gelder, "Ed Ferman was the editor of all the book columns—those of Blish, Merril, Budrys, and Russ. And Ed always sang the praises of Joanna's columns to me. To quote from a recent email of his, 'I don't recall that Judy Merril or Jim Blish edited any of her columns. Just me, and she hardly needed any editing.'"

9. "The evaluative critic—who pronounces on the absolute merits of the work he is considering, is not very useful to either the writer or the reader." Blish, *More Issues at Hand*.

10. "*Conquests* [by Poul Anderson] . . . (not first-rate Anderson) . . . stuck with me and made me think. . . . Zelazny's "For a Breath I Tarry" is an emotional orgy that made me cry, but I didn't respect the story for making me cry, or like myself any better for it." *Country You Have Never Seen*, 24.

11. Blish, *More Issues at Hand*, introduction.

12. *Country You Have Never Seen*, 14–15

13. Ibid., 29–31.

14. A fix-up is a novel constructed from several stories on the same theme, previously published separately, more or less revised for the novel form. (See also chapter 7 herewith.)

15. *Country You Have Never Seen*, 18.

16. Ibid., 33; 46

17. Ibid., 62–65

18. Julius Caesar announced his bid for supreme power by crossing the river Rubicon with his army, something no Roman general of the Republic had the right to do. Crossing the Rubicon means making your drastic intentions clear. There's no going back.

19. *A Voyage to Arcturus* was a major influence on C. S. Lewis's "Space Trilogy."

20. David Redd: http://davidredd.co.uk.

21. Dorothy Allison, in her essay collection *Skin*, is frank about science fiction as a masturbation aid: "The honest to god truth is that I spent most of my adolescence, and I'll admit it, even my twenties, jacking off to science fiction books." Cortiel, *Demand My Writing*, 158.

22. *Country You Have Never Seen*, 219.

23. Ibid., 221.

24. Ibid., 226

25. Ibid., 196n.

26. *Hidden Side*, 175. Compare with the first appearance of "Jael" (*Female Man*, 19) and with Janet Evason's arrival in the Pentagon (*Female Man*, 22–3)

27. http://www.pseudopodium.org/repress/TheStarPit/SamuelRDelany-NotesOn TheStarPit.html. Pacifica lists Joanna as "dialogue director," not continuity girl: https://pacificaradioarchives.org/recording/bb383013c.

28. Timothy Leary, 1966: possibly quoting Marshal McLuhan. In his memoir *Flashbacks* (Los Angeles: Tarcher, 1983) Leary elaborated: "'Turn on' meant go within, to activate your neural and genetic equipment. . . . Unhappily my explanations of this sequence of personal development were often misinterpreted to mean 'Get stoned and abandon all constructive activity.'"

29. "[A]n impressionist mode in which through violent and startling leaps of imagery and logic, she attempts, and succeeds, in providing for the reader a direct knowledge of the unknowable" Robert Silverberg, introduction to the Gregg Press edition of *And Chaos Died*.

30. See Brit Mandelo, "Reading Joanna Russ—*And Chaos Died*," http://www.tor.com/2011/07/19/reading-joanna-russ-and-chaos-died-1970.

31. *And Chaos Died*, 35.

32. Delany, "Orders of Chaos," 117.

33. The date of the archived manuscript at Bowling Green State.

34. Cortiel, *Demand My Writing*, 219. "Jai Vedh . . . rejects most components of masculinity in science fiction. . . . His partially displaced homosexuality and his unstable physical existence in the text let him occupy a number of different subject conditions. . . . [O]ne may read him as a gay man, a bisexual man or even a lesbian woman—ultimately he resists each of these identifications."

35. *And Chaos Died*, 72. "He had been loved, and he still lived. It was a miracle."

36. Jai Vedh's "Initiation," an extract from *And Chaos Died*, appeared in the *Magazine of Fantasy and Science Fiction*, February 1970.

37. *And Chaos Died*, 84.

38. Cortiel, *Demand My Writing*, 60.

39. *And Chaos Died*, 107.

40. *And Chaos Died*, epigraph: "Chaos, the God of the Center, has no sensory apertures, while other beings have seven. Two Gods decided to do him a favor by boring holes in him, one hole a day. On the seventh day, Chaos died."

41. Fritjof Capra, *The Tao of Physics* (Boulder, Colo.; Shambhala, 1975).

42. Delany (in *Orders of Chaos*) named the lost colony planet "Lys" after a garden city oasis on the dying earth of "The City and The Stars," by Arthur C. Clarke. It is nameless in Russ's text, which I suppose was intentional.

43. *And Chaos Died*, 9: "on which every place was like every other place"—globalization's maximum entropy has been reached.

44. Delany: "not a flashback in it." *Orders of Chaos*, 112.

45. *And Chaos Died*, 133.

46. *And Chaos Died*, 143. Landru: either a historical French serial killer or a mad supercomputer—convinced by Captain Kirk to destroy itself, in *Star Trek* S1:E21, "Return of the Archons."

47. Delany, "Orders of Chaos," 116.

48. Introduction to the Gollancz SF Masterworks edition of Delany, *Dhalgren*.

49. Unsurprisingly, since she seems to have read it as utopian fiction, Joanna didn't have a high opinion of *Dhalgren*; see *Khatru*, 105

50. Letter from Merril to Brian Aldiss. Mendlesohn, *On Joanna Russ*, 72.

51. Mendlesohn, *On Joanna Russ*, 78

52. Stephen Jones, BBC Music magazine, September 2002 http://www.stephen-johnson .co.uk/publications/bbc-music-magazine.php.


## CHAPTER 3. YEAR ZERO ART

1. Yaszek and Sharp, introduction, xx.

2. May, *Homeward Bound*, "Fanning The Home Fires," 58–92.

3. May, *Homeward Bound*, 94.

4. "With regard to female students, chances for marriage are greatly reduced if they do not make a permanent attachment during college years." May, *Homeward Bound*, 79–80.

5. Joanna would repent, but in *The Female Man* her own focus was equally narrow, white, and middle class.

6. "[T]hat disgusting decade." Joanna, as an adult, became well aware of what the fifties had done to her generation. *Magic Mommas*, 69.

7. *Female Man*, 104

8. *Country You Have Never Seen*, 68. Sam Moskowitz is usually credited as teaching the first science fiction course, at City College New York in 1953.

9. *Cornillon*, "Images of Women In Fiction," 12.

10. *Country You Have Never Seen*, 74.

11. See *The Right Stuff*, by Tom Wolfe (New York: Farrar, Straus and Giroux, 1979).

12. *Country You Have Never Seen*, 83. (Joanna's emphasis).

13. Ibid., 79.

14. Ibid., 88.

15. Ibid., 103.

16. Ibid., 106–7.

17. Ibid., 109.

18. Aldiss, *Frankenstein Unbound* (London: House of Stratus, 2000), 103.

19. *Country You Have Never Seen*, 110. Ironically, Anarres ends up paying the same lip service to gender equality as Mao's China, the real world "ambiguous utopia" (allegedly fostering women's liberation) Le Guin's Anarres very loosely resembles.

20. Like men habitually infantilizing women (baby), Joanna, and Judith Merril habitually used the slur of junior status to belittle other female (and only female) writers. I wonder how Whileaway's fighting-talk (calling anyone "baby" or "little girl" is dangerous) relates to this naughty habit?

21. Robert Silverberg provided a perceptive, enthusiastic preface for the Gregg Press hardcover edition of *And Chaos Died*, 1978.

22. See *Zanzibar Cat*, "When It Changed," 19.

23. An uncollected "short," "Wilderness Year" (*Magazine of Fantasy and Science Fiction*, December 1964) suggests the survival experience was another long-standing fantasy.

24. *Courage and Tools: The Florence Howe Award for Feminist Scholarship, 1974–1989*, edited by Joanne Glasgow and Angela J. C. Ingram (New York: MLA, 1990)

25. Merrick, *Secret Feminist Cabal*, 98, cites Dr. Robert S. Richardson, not Campbell, for this bright idea, in a 1955 issue of the *Magazine of Fantasy and Science Fiction*. In the correspondence that followed, the term "feminist" appears, already current in fandom.

26. Heinlein's reputation as a "female friendly" sf writer (inexplicable to me when I met his "adult" works) was pretty tarnished by 1970.

27. A scenario that recalls James Blish's *All The Stars a Stage* (New York: Doubleday, 1971). Men on a forerunner planet die of despair, under a peaceful matriarchy that crushes their manly spirit. A survivor escapes to found Man's hegemony on Earth.

28. "SubCommittee," 1962, collected in Henderson's *The Anything Box*, New York: Doubleday, 1965.

29. Le Guin revised the original "Gethen" story, "Winter's King" for *The Wind's Twelve Quarters* (1975), replacing most masculine pronouns and references with feminine ones. She had concluded that "one does not see [an androgyne] in any role that we automatically perceive as 'female': and therefore, we tend to see 'him' as a man."

30. The Marvel Comics (Stan Lee and Jack Kirby) superhero and his scientist alter-ego Bruce Bannon first appeared in 1962.

31. *Country You Have Never Seen*, 234.

32. Quoted in *To Write Like a Woman*, 127.

33. See *Apex* magazine issue 37: https://www.apex-magazine.com/girl-meets-house
-kitchen-sinks-joanna-russ-and-the-female-gothic/

34. Cortiel, *Demand My Writing*, 84. Bat-winged Jael features in a letter from Joanna.

35. *Zanzibar Cat*, 84.

36. "I wrote that story after an intersession colloquium at Cornell the year I started teaching there, which must have been 1969." Interview in McCaffery, *Across the Wounded Galaxies*, 201. A Cornell-based story, "The View from This Window," suggests that that the associated novel, *The Female Man* also existed, in some form, in 1970.

37. "The first utopian fiction in English by a woman" Donawerth and Kolmerten, *Worlds of Difference*, 207n.

38. Ibid., 107–25.

39. Bamberger, " Myth of Matriarchy."

40. Yaszek and Sharp, *Sisters of Tomorrow*, xxii.

41. Moscowitz, *When Women Rule.*

42. Cornillon, *Images of Women*, 88–89.

43. Accounts differ: in a second report: "I ought to add there was a fourth duel, in which nobody got killed," and Janet nursed her defeated foe through a long recovery. *Female Man*, 48.

44. "The mission statement of the quintessential feminist sf text." Nathalie Rosinsky, *Feminist Futures*, Ann Arbor, Mich.: UMI Research,1984.

45. *Female Man*, 6. Like the serialist composer Karlheinz Stockhausen, Joanna put her faith in "science" as a pure tradition that could still be trusted when all else had failed. Her philosophy of science lecture notes are preserved in the American Institute of Physics archives. https://www.aip.org/history-programs/news/found-archives-joanna-russ-lecture-notes.

46. *Female Man*, 7. Also see the "probability mechanics" stories "Reasonable People" and "What Did You Do during the Revolution Grandma?"

47. *Female Man*, 18: "[In "When It Changed" . . . ] the strangers ask where the 'men' are: the Whileawayans hear 'where are all the *"people?"'(Zanzibar Cat*, 15). "It's a difference in pov, a change in the language." Joanna Russ, from a letter to Sarah Lefanu, August 17, 1987.

48. This is "Jael," the Womanland assassin. She does the dirty work, but she's so ugly. *Nice* feminists don't like radicals.

49. *On Strike against God*, 17.

50. Smith, *Khatru*, 73–74.

51. In Jeannine's probability the Japanese still hold mainland China, annexed in our world in World War II. Chiang Kai-Shek's widow rules in Taiwan, like the real Chiang Kai-Shek after the People's Revolution.

52. Joanna's list closely resembles "lists" of desirable behavior for fifties wives, preserved in the KSL survey: May, *Homeward Bound*, 34.

53. *Female Man*, 5.

54. *Female Man*, 45.

55. Cortiel, *Demand My Writing*, 197–203.

56. *To Write Like a Woman*, 139.

57. Firestone, *Dialectic of Sex*, 72–104. Firestone's relationship with her father was very difficult. She died in tragic circumstances in 2012.

58. One of several "Lauras" in Joanna's works: objects of desire, versions of a young Joanna, or (as here), perhaps both. Julie Phillips suggests that Joanna's "Laura" references, tacitly, the Little House series, and Laura Ingalls Wilder's eponymous heroine. Given the Little House themes of pioneer life, American expansionism, manly virtue, and a glorious, enabling father-figure, this would be a very conflicted nostalgia, yet Phillips may be right.

59. *Female Man*, 82.

60. *Female Man*, 93

61. Martins, "Revising the Future," 408.

62. *Female Man*, 99.

63. The Great Happiness Contest, a favorite with Russ readers, 116–19.

64. *Female Man*, 138–39.

65. See Calvin, "This Shapeless Book."

66. *Female Man*, 2. "187" was Bobby Fischer's score in 1958 (approximately "148" today). Raw "IQ" scores have fallen into disrepute since Joanna's time.

67. The murder of the brothel boss by Jael (or Yael) concludes with a direct quote, "At her feet . . .," from the Song of Deborah, Judges 5.

68. Impossible to contemplate for the "Joanna" of *The Female Man*, this plan is embraced in her late sf stories "Bodies" and "What Did You Do during the Revolution Grandma?"

69. See Cortiel, *Demand My Writing*, 60: Womanland appears equivalent with the Americas, Manland with an extended Soviet Bloc.

70. *Female Man*, 192–94 The "little dirty girl" in this nightmare perhaps returns for healing in the 1984 short story.

71. *Female Man*, 203. The list is long and currently hearteningly unrecognizable. A gender-reversed version features in the *Khatru* symposium.

72. Cortiel, *Demand My Writing*, 123–24.

73. Schrafft's: a modest, respectable New York restaurant chain, now defunct, where women could comfortably eat with other women.

74. McCaffery, *Across the Wounded Galaxies*, 178. See also p. 195: "two of the most 'difficult' and controversial SF novels ever published—*The Female Man* and Delany's *Dhalgren*—have been two of the biggest sellers."

## CHAPTER 4. THE SECRET FEMINIST CABAL

1. From "Siberian Khatru," the best track on the Yes prog rock album *Close to the Edge* (1972). Jeff is a Yes fan.

2. "To hell with talking about 'women in sf.'" Tiptree, *Khatru*, 18.

3. Merrick, *Secret Feminist Cabal*, 115–16.

4. Lisa Tuttle's wonderfully neat summing up (in the chapter's epigraph) of the situation for women in sf is, as best she and I can recollect, from a 1988 panel discussion in Beverley, U.K.

5. Lisa Tuttle, email correspondence, March 2017.

6. Sarah LeFanu, email correspondence, March 2017.

7. Luise White, email correspondence, February 2017.

8. Susan Wood: http://amazingstoriesmag.com/2014/08.

9. Not restricted to feminist writers, or material. The series continued until 1996.

10. New York: Pantheon/Doubleday, 1979. Joanna's review is collected in *The Country You Have Never Seen*, 152–55.

11. Donawerth and Kolmerton, *Worlds of Difference*, 137–52. "Gola" is reprinted in full in Justine Larbalestier's collection *Daughters of Earth*, 2006, with a valuable essay (by Brian Atterbury) on Hugo Gernsback and the early sf feminists (50–66).

12. Chicago: University of Chicago Press.

13. Introduction, xvii–xxi.

14. *Foundation* 46, 2.127 (2017), 119–22.

15. Merrick, *Secret Feminist Cabal*, 118.

16. Matzke, "Weaker(?) Sex?," 6–20.

17. Willis, "Women SF Doesn't See"; October 1992. Willis later conceded that her list of "lost" writers (obliterated by feminism) was a near-match for the early authors in Pamela Sargent's 1975 *Women of Wonder* anthology.

18. Matzke, "Weaker(?) Sex?," 10.

19. Merrick, "Female 'Atlas,'" 55. Susan Wood, convener of the first "women in sf" panel at Worldcon 1974, traced the impact of the women's movement on SF in the early seventies to "the fiction and criticism of Joanna Russ, seconded by Vonda McIntyre."

20. *To Write Like a Woman*, 8. The duodecimal system opens the way to algorithmic calculation, essential to modern technology.

21. Introducing discoveries in pure science to the public through stripped-down narrative, or "dialogues," between characters, is a venerable technique. See Galileo's *Dialogue Concerning the Two Chief World Systems*, 1632 (which might have been more safely published as fiction).

22. The "two cultures" are science and the humanities, a fundamental social division, according to C. P. Snow, British scientist and novelist (1959).

23. I prefer "conventional." The conventions of both classic "nineteenth-century novels" and modern popular fiction are invisible but highly unnatural.

24. *To Write Like a Woman*, 11.

25. Samuel Delany "About 5,760 Words" a paper read at the Modern Language Association, December 1968; published in *The Jewel-Hinged Jaw*, 1977.

26. *To Write Like a Woman*, 19.

27. Ibid., 23. More like a very gentle tap! But Joanna was loyal to all her avant-garde male "allies," and could not admit that Nabokov condones and "mystifies" the rape of a very young girl, without dismissing him from her pantheon.

28. Ibid., 23.

29. Ibid., 24.

30. Ibid., 66.

31. Ibid., 71.

32. Ibid., 67. *A Boy and His Dog*, the movie, could have invented, singlehandedly, the whole concept of the aftermath of global thermonuclear war as an adventure playground. It will be spookily familiar, visually, to anyone acquainted with the video game series *Fallout*, or the later Mad Max movies.

33. Ellison saw the story as a direct commentary on U.S. Cold War politics and enclaves of divided opinion. See Harlan Ellison, interviewed: https://thedissolve.com/features/ interview/73-harlan-ellison-on-taking-flak-for-but-admiring-a-b.

34. The mayor sends malcontents to "the farm," implied to be a death sentence. In *Soylent Green* (1973) the "miracle protein," in a future of nightmarish scarcity, is processed people. The original sf story was Harry Harrison's "*Make Room, Make Room.*"

35. Leni Riefenstahl, 1934. Ethnic cleansing of non-Aryans is a major feature of the plan to make Germany great again.

36. See the *Magazine of Fantasy and Science Fiction* online archive: https://www.sfsite.com/ fsf/blog/2016/02/18/fandsf-february-1975.

37. Undoubtedly, Mirrlees references the same the forbidden fruit as in Christina Rossetti's wonderful poem "Goblin Market."

38. *Khatru*, 9.

39. Ibid., 6.

40. This response initiated a long-running "Tolstoy" thread. Everybody *hated* what he'd done with Natasha.

41. *Khatru*, 12.

42. Ibid., 22–34, later published in *The Jewel Hinged Jaw*, (2nd ed., 2009). Suzy Charnas, in the 1993 Khatru, remembers "how much I enjoyed Chip's first blast" (33).

43. *Khatru*, 35. The "Aurora" anthology included fine stories from Alice Sheldon, under both pseudonyms, and a dour contribution from Joanna.

44. Ibid., 37–39.

45. Ibid., 44.

46. Ibid., 48.

47. Ibid., 56.

48. Ibid., 61. Jean-Paul Sartre, *Anti-Semite and Jew*, 1945, 1946 (originally, *Réflexions sur la question juive*) (New York, Schocken Books, 1948).

49. *Khatru*, 62–66.

50. Ibid., 69.

51. Ibid., 72–73. "Writing about death" must refer to Joanna's fourth novel, *We Who Are about To* (see chapter 5 herewith).

52. *Khatru*, 74; See p. 49 (Yarbro): "Luise . . . [i]f you want to kill somebody, or you think it's a grand thing, count me out. Killing is no way to freedom."

53. Ibid., 80–81.

54. Ibid., 91.

55. Ibid., 392.

56. Ibid., 85: Charnas's 1993 comment that Tiptree's concern "shut me up for the rest of the symposium" reveals Smith's editing process: comments from Charnas carry on appearing, after she'd stopped responding.

57. Ibid., 101–5: the radical feminist sf manifesto.

58. Ibid., 102.

59. "The Female 'Atlas,'" 53.


CHAPTER 5. THE SPOOK BY SCIENCE FICTION'S DOOR

1. *To Write Like a Woman*, 171–76.

2. *To Write Like a Woman*. See "Recent Feminist Utopias," 144.

3. *We Who Are About To*, 152.

4. Sam Greenlee, *The Spook Who Sat by the Door* (London: Allison and Busby, 1969; New York: Baron, 1969); also a movie, 1973.

5. Merril, *Merril Theory*, introduction.

6. "The Female 'Atlas,'" 49–53. It should be noted that Richard Geis, fanzine editor and soft porn sf author, won the fanzine Hugo Award for *Alien Critic* in 1974 and again in 1975.

7. Perhaps Anderson resented this female privilege. In his *Virgin Planet* (1957) a lone male provides the "love interest," and two women in an all-female society spend the whole book fighting over him. See Larbalestier, *Battle of the Sexes*, 87

8. *Alyx*, introduction.

9. Wilhelm, always ahead of the game on socioscientific problems, realized the dangers of this "miraculous" new product. The unease of her scientists, along with their submission to the big business agenda, is chillingly familiar.

10. Larbalestier, *Battle of the Sexes*. See also http://justinelarbalestier.com/blog/2002/08/19/researching-the-battle-of-the-sexes-in-science-fiction.

11. "Tiptree" was unmasked in 1976.

12. *To Write Like a Woman*, 43.

13. Ibid., 45. "Instinctively he had covered his naked loins with his hands but now . . . he removed his hands and boldly thrust his loins forward."

14. Bamberger, "Myth of Matriarchy," 274–75.

15. *To Write Like a Woman*, 41.

16. First published in *Amazing Stories*, March 1927.

17. *To Write Like a Woman*, 62.

18. H. P. Lovecraft died in 1937, before his stories became popular. Decades later the posthumous propagation of his works (*The Cthulhu Mythos*) had become an unstoppable tide.

19. Edited by Curtis C. Smith (New York: Palgrave MacMillan, 1981).

20. From its inception in 1975 to 2015, the World Fantasy Award was a bust of H. P. Lovecraft. The new award, introduced in 2016, is a fine object, the disc of a yellow full moon, in the branches of a leafless tree. It was about time for a change.

21. In the 1989 edition of *Tales of the Cthulhu Mythos* (Sauk City, Wisc.: Arkham House).

22. Lovecraft's technique of nested narrators (as in "The Colour out of Space") presents incredible content at remove, and thereby hopefully more convincing.

23. See *Magic Mommas*, 49–50. By 1976 Joanna could have seen Tyson's theater work, her breakthrough performance in Jean Genet's "The Blacks," and the movie that won her an Oscar nomination (*Sounder*, 1972).

24. "A grim and schizoid tale from a Godawful place I am glad never to have visited again." Foreword to "Corruption," in *Zanzibar Cat*. In her biography of Alice Sheldon (*James Tiptree Junior: The Double Life of Alice Sheldon*), Julie Phillips records a discussion of the *Beyond Equality* project between "James Tiptree" and Joanna (352).

25. The Bowling Green State University archive manuscript is dated 1954–55.

26. The USCSS *Nostromo*, featured in the 1978 Ridley Scott movie *Alien*. Nostromo carried no passengers but might have been on the same scale as the ship lost on the first page of *We Who Are about To*.

27. "Lori" is also the name of a juvenile character in Marion Zimmer Bradley's *Darkover Landfall*. Her father was an indigene, and she is psychically disabled.

28. Joanna describes this gaudy costume as "Grautsark," referring to a 1926 movie set in an imaginary, militarist European state. The novel is peppered with obscure cultural referents (not all of them accurate), perhaps to highlight our narrator's abrasive intellectual isolation.

29. See Joanna's essay "SF and Technology as Mystification" (chapter 6 herewith).

30. A medieval satirical trope, the "ship of fools," with its deluded, insane, gluttonous, criminal, or just plain drunk passengers and crew, was a means of criticizing a corrupt establishment.

31. "X" is the designation Joanna chose for her narrator, in the résumé of the first part of the story, provided with the second part in *Galaxy*, February 1976. She is otherwise nameless until the solo finale.

32. See Larbalestier, *Battle of the Sexes*, 150–52. Randall Garrett's "Queen Bee" (1958), a stunningly nasty story about explorers putting forced pregnancy before "basic issues of survival," may have inspired both *We Who Are about To* and *Darkover Landfall*. *Queen Bee* also assumes that women in this situation will not support each other. A version of the story, probably pirated, is available online at http://galacticjourney.dreamwidth.org/4492.html.

33. *We Who Are About To*, 27 (Women's Press).

34. https://www.tor.com/2011/08/08/reading-joanna-russ-we-who-are-about-to-1977.

35. Algis Budrys, *Benchmarks Continued: F&SF "Books" Columns 1975–82*, edited by David Langford (Ansible Editions, 2012), Lulu.com spotlight, 99–98.

36. A justification countered in X's rebuttal: "Civilization's doing fine. We just don't happen to be where it is." *We Who Are About To*, 31.

37. *The Witch and the Chameleon*, issue 2, edited by Amanda Bankier Hamilton (Ontario: Permanent Press, 1974); for transcripts see https://fanlore.org/wiki/Darkover_Landfall _reviewed_by_Vonda_N. McIntyre

38. *Morituri te salutant* ("Those who are about to die salute thee"). The "gladiators' salute," probably never used in the Roman Empire's arenas.

39. For transcripts see https://fanlore.org/wiki/DARKOVER_SPINOFF. Or_maybe _that_should_read_CONTRARY_MOTION-VERY.

40. Problematic indeed, as later emerged. Bradley was married to Walter Breen, a convicted pedophile, and by her own testimony enabled his activities. She died in 1999. In 2013 her daughter revealed, convincingly, that Bradley had abused her as a child, sexually and physically, for years.

41. As Joanna said of James Gunn's *The Listeners* in *Country You Have Never Seen*, 95.

42. The entire quote from Kurt Vonnegut's *God Bless You, Mr. Rosewater* (St. Albans: Granada/Panther, 1967), 24; cited in Delany's introduction to the Wesleyan University Press edition of *We Who Are about To* [2005]) equates sf's corrupt promise of endless plenty with pornography.

43. See *Khatru*, 89: "the fantasy of immortality . . . isn't the whole revolt against Nature itself something we are trying to get away from."

44. Ibid., 73.

45. The "flying stick's" chief advantage seems to be that it can be called a broomstick, a witch's attribute, by X and her "Mirror Sister."

46. There's been no sign, in this group, that "patriarchy" ever went away.

47. *We Who Are About To*, 47 (Women's Press).

48. Ibid., 75. It was Joanna who "won a lot of scholarships" and planned a dazzling, "coded male" career.

49. Ibid., 77.

50. "She ruined her life before the book begins; ran away from political responsibility from sheer fear." Joanna Russ, letter to Sarah LeFanu, 1987.

51. An allegorical drama in which the characters personify abstractions.

52. This "brilliancy" seems to imply an afterlife, but Neo-Christianity is godless, eternity has no duration, and the art of dying is its own reward.

53. Perhaps Lori died so she could share the "rescue" Elaine/X sought for herself. See Spencer, "Rescuing the Female Child," 167.


CHAPTER 6. JOINING THE CULTURAL MINORITY

1. Nabokov rejected the label, asserting that "literature is the product of individuals, not groups" (Aleksandr Pushkin, *Eugene Onegin: A Novel in Verse*, translated by Vladimir Nabokov [Princeton, N.J.: Princeton University Press, 1975]). But categories are useful tools for critics, not limiting factors for the artist.

2. Interview in McCaffery, *Across the Wounded Galaxies*, 184.

3. Suzy Charnas, quoted in Phillips, *James Tiptree Junior*, 383.

4. *To Write Like a Woman*, author's introduction

5. *The Two of Them*, dedication (Women's Press).

6. Rather late in the narrative, Irene finally names the "Trans-Temporal Authority" (the term "Military" omitted). *Two of Them*, 127.

7. *Country You Have Never Seen*, 140.

8. Ibid., 144.

9. Ibid., 145–47.

10. Ibid., 149–50.

11. Ibid., 154.

12. Ibid., 155–60. *Gyn/Ecology* became an issue seriously damaging to Daly, and to American Second Wave feminism, when Audre Lorde (the African American feminist poet, greatly admired by Joanna) publicly denounced Daly for celebrating only "white" goddesses and for condemning the African "tradition" of female genital mutilation.

13. In the *Khatru* symposium Samuel Delany cited a statistic from *Scientific American*: "The average middle-class American father spends 23.7 seconds a day playing(!) with his less-than-year-old infant." *Khatru*, 23.

14. *The Best from Fantasy and Science Fiction*, 23rd edition, edited by Edward L. Ferman (New York: Doubleday, 1979).

15. *Country You Have Never Seen*, 178.

16. Rebecca West, [Cicely Isobel Fairfield], *Black Lamb and Grey Falcon* (London: Macmillan, 1941), prologue. Joanna's source for this reference may have been from "James Tiptree's" first essay in *Khatru*, 21.

17. See Gérard Klein, "Discontent in American Science Fiction," *Science Fiction Studies* 4 (1977): 1–13.

18. *The Witch and the Chameleon*, 5–6 (1976). Possibly Catherine Masden's only work of fiction.

19. Joanna seems bothered by Wittig's primacy, emphasizing that *Les Guérillères* could not have influenced *The Female Man*, which was seeking a publisher before a translation was available.

20. Carol Pearson, "Women's Fantasies and Feminist Utopias," *Frontiers* 2, no. 3 (Autumn 1977).

21. Theodore Sturgeon, *Venus Plus X* (New York, Pyramid, 1960)—"the first hermaphroditic sf novel."

22. In *Triton* a male character, unhappy with utopian freedoms, seeks a sex change with the intention of providing at least one man with a proper, feminine, and compliant helpmate.

23. A comment on Delany's present day that still applies. Modern warfare makes unarmed civilians more vulnerable, in far greater numbers, than military personnel, even when the battleground has air and gravity.

24. In Gearhart's *The Wanderground*, some Hill Women are in talks with the "Gentles" (gentle men); not all the women approve.

25. See Spencer, "Rescuing the Female Child."

26. In Vonda McIntyre's postcatastrophe society, both the abuser and his victim are seen as in need of rescue. He is "sent to the menders" for therapy.

27. See Joanna's essay "Amor Vincit Foeminam" in *To Write Like a Woman*, 41–59.

28. *To Write Like a Woman*, 144–45.

29. *Chrysalis: A Magazine of Women's Culture*, Los Angeles, ran from 1977 to 1980.

30. Nancy Ann Sahli, a Vassar alum with a very distinguished career, is the biographer of Elizabeth Blackwell, "the first woman doctor."

31. *Chrysalis 8*, 21, letter from the "Yale Courant."

32. Ibid., 18. Cooke is currently distinguished professor of history and women's studies at John Jay College of Criminal Justice, New York.

33. *Magic Mommas*, 17–41.

34. Ibid., 20.

35. Ibid., 28–29.

36. Ibid., 33.

37. *To Write Like a Woman*, 161. Herndl uses the doubled categorizing of a woman's "hereditary estate" in her essay.

38. "The woman novelist must be an hysteric. Hysteria is the woman's simultaneous acceptance and refusal of the organization of sexuality under patriarchal capitalism. . . . I do not believe there is such a thing as female writing, a 'woman's voice.' There is the hysteric's voice which is *the woman's masculine language* talking about feminine experience." Juliet Mitchell "Femininity, Narrative and Psychoanalysis"; in *Women, The Longest Revolution* (New York: Pantheon, 1984), 289–90; quoted in Herndl.

39. *To Write Like a Woman*, 166.

40. *Voyages Extraordinaires* is the general title Jules Verne gave to his project of exploring all the limits of geographical and scientific knowledge. The translation should be "journeys," but then the association would be lost.

41. "Beam Us Home," *Galaxy*, April 1969; collected in Tiptree, *Ten Thousand Light Years from Home*, 1973. "James Tiptree" (Alice Sheldon's) "Star Trek" fan-story. Important to Joanna.

42. In many premodern cultures, including "Native American" societies, the wolf is regarded as a powerful spiritual guide and helper.

43. *Kittatinny*. New York: Daughters, 1978, 15.

44. The story of the water spirit, Rusalka, who unwisely insists on getting herself transformed into human form to win a human male lover. Variants include H. C. Andersen's "The Little Mermaid."

45. See chapter 1, herewith, "The Second Inquisition": the teen narrator and mirrors.

46. The Prime Directive (*Star Trek*; inconsistently applied) prohibits interference with the internal development of alien civilizations; and is perhaps originally a reference to the proxy war fought in Southeast Asia.

47. Irene Adler appeared in one Holmes story, "A Scandal in Bohemia," *Strand*, June 1891. As the only female lead available, she has become a pivotal character in modern Holmes treatments.

48. The first time she learned his name, Irene had the perfect riposte: "It has always been my ambition to love someone of the name of Ernst; that name inspires complete confidence" (*The Two of Them*, 5, quoting Oscar Wilde, *The Importance of Being Earnest*). A high standard of banter is an essential feature of Irene and Ernst's private world.

49. Ibid., 78. The menarche is celebrated with presents and parties on Whileaway (to the disgust, no doubt, of many skeptical twelve-year-olds) The practical details of

menstruation, rarely mentioned in Joanna's fiction, here seem a reminder that Irene may be closer to the women of Ka'abah than to Ernst, or to "the Gang."

50. Ibid., 84. In "For the Sake of Grace" Aunt Grace is kept in solitary confinement in the Women's Discipline Unit, and she's quite mad. In "The Two of Us" Aunt Dunya's *private* prison strongly references "The Yellow Wallpaper," down to the low-level "smooch" made by the woman from behind the wallpaper, bestially crawling round and round, her shoulder to the wall. Joanna's insistence ("On the Yellow Wallpaper") that the prisoner in Gilman's story is not *mad* but haunted or possessed is omitted here.

51. Ibid., 8–9.

52. Ibid., 134.

53. Ibid., 140.

54. "Joanna Russ could have got away with murder, even in 1978; except for her own determination to call Irene's act a transgression. It's the narrative that directs us to see Irene's shame and distress, and not Ernst's abuse of power." Gwyneth Jones, "Postscript to the Fairytale," *New York Review of Science Fiction*, 17, no. 203 (July 2005): 51.

55. Cortiel, *Demand My Writing*, 45.

56. *The Two of Them*, 114. In their tricky exit from Ka'abah, Irene lost her head and started yelling terrible insults. She later couldn't be sure this had really happened; maybe "her anger fooled her . . . at the last minute she held it all back." Maybe she didn't actually shoot Ernst, either.

57. "Shall these bones live?" Ezekiel 37:1–14


## CHAPTER 7. BEYOND GENDER?

1. *Magic Mommas*, 105.

2. McCaffery, *Across the Wounded Galaxies*, 180.

3. Kathryn Cramer, interview, September 2017.

4. *Country You Have Never Seen*, 243.

5. *How To Suppress Women's Writing*, 110.

6. Jeanne Gomoll, email, March 6, 2017.

7. Kathryn Cramer interview, herewith.

8. Timmi Duchamp, email September 11, 2017.

9. See *Science Fiction Studies* 17, no. 2 (July 1990), Joan Gordon: "Concerning the Pilgrim Award."

10. *Country You Have Never Seen*, 250–66.

11. *Science Fiction Studies* 7, no. 2 (July 1980): 232–36.

12. *Country You Have Never Seen*, 270–71. But where is the killer review of *And Chaos Died* Joanna had provided? I know it existed. (A contributor to this "sportive little publication" had to submit a venomous review of their own work before they were allowed to torture someone else).

13. Ibid., 277–78.

14. Ibid., 281.

15. Ibid., "The Other Side," 289; and *SFRA Newsletter* 172 (November 1979).

16. Ibid., 292–94.

17. Ibid., 284–85.

18. Ibid., 286–87. The psi-powered mysticism in *And Chaos Died* bears the mark of these experiences; see also the haunting fragment "Main St. 1953," noted in this chapter.

19. The year was 1986. "The sad truth of the matter is that SF has not been much fun of late . . ." (Sterling's dismissal of the Feminist Seventies is absent in later editions.) For Jeanne Gomoll's "An Open Letter to Joanna Russ," see http://sf3.org/wp-content/uploads/2012/08/25-Vol-10-No-1.pdf.

20. *Country You Have Never Seen*, 287–88.

21. Ibid., 295–97.

22. *To Write Like a Woman*, 150.

23. See https://cather.unl.edu/cs006_gorman.html.

24. *Country You Have Never Seen*, 243.

25. In *The Country You Have Never Seen*, Marion Zimmer Bradley is named in a footnote.

26. A project dear to Suzette Haden Elgin in her "Native Tongue" series.

27. Female but not "feminine," presumably.

28. In fact, "News from the Front" and "Pornography and the Doubleness of Sex for Women" seem to be original to the collection.

29. See Russ, "Scenes from Domestic Life," an early lesbian story (published in *Consumption*) dating from 1968. Cortiel, *Demand My Writing*, 184–90.

30. *Country You Have Never Seen*, 182–85.

31. *Magic Mommas*, 104.

32. *Off Our Backs* 15, no. 11 (December 1985): 18–19.

33. *Magic Mommas*, 76.

34. Ibid., 33.

35. Interview with Joanna Russ by Consuela Francis and Alison Piepmeier, *Journal of Popular Romance Studies* 1, no. 2 (March 31, 2011).

36. *Magic Mommas*, 83.

37. Ibid., 83.

38. See entry "1985" at https://fanlore.org/wiki/Timeline_of_K/S_Fandom.

39. *Magic Mommas*, 118.

40. "To resolve contrarieties, unite them in your own person." *Female Man*, 138.

41. Currently, the "Brocéliande" in Brittany, with Arthurian connections, and a very tired fountain of youth, is Paimpont forest, but the tradition is genuinely ancient: a "haunted forest" in Gaul was known to Lucan in the first century AD.

42. The premiere of *Hernani* by Victor Hugo (February 1830) was a staged ruckus: Victor Hugo's Romantics, versus the Neo-Classicists, had packed the theater and began fighting in the aisles. The play was less interesting than this sounds and is now rarely staged.

43. "All books are either dreams or swords. You can cut or you can drug with words." Amy Lowell's "Sword Blades and Poppy Seed" is the title poem of her 1914 collection.

44. "What should I do with your strong, manly, spirited sketches . . . ? How could I possibly join them on to the little bit (two inches wide) of ivory on which I work with so fine a brush, as produces little effect after much labor?" Jane Austen, from a letter to her beloved nephew, James Edward Austen-Leigh.

45. She wrote at first in collaboration with Jules Sand and adopted their pen name "George Sand" for her first solo novel, *Indiana* (1832).

46. See Cortiel, *Demand My Writing*, 108–13, for a detailed study of this story.

47. *On Strike against God*, 5; all references are to the 1987 Women's Press edition. "My analyst and I often discussed—years ago—my compulsion to always have the last word with men. We worked on it for months but we never got anywhere."

48. *On Strike against God*, 48–49. This life-changing moment is described almost identically in the *The Female Man*, 208. "I knelt down by her chair and kissed her on the back of her smooth, honeyed, hot neck."

49. Postrealist in the blurring, throughout, of fictional and confessional writing, and in touches like the "apparitions" of Esther's vampire analyst, a Tooth Fairy in blue gauze skirts and a talking, Jewish uterus.

50. Mendlesohn, *On Joanna Russ*, 114–30.

51. Esther rates the summer camp, at age twelve "when I necked with my best friend," "a point of peculiar integration from which everything has definitely gone downhill." See "Not for Years but for Decades," 18.

52. The real Merril would probably have been a sharper opponent.

53. See "My Dear Emily," 14.

54. *On Strike against God*, 96.

55. McCaffery, *Across the Wounded Galaxies*, 181.

56. *Speculations* is an eccentric anthology: contributors' names were given in code; readers were invited to work out the authors.

57. McCaffery, *Across the Wounded Galaxies*, 182.

58. *Extra(Ordinary) People*, 24. Radegunde quotes a famous Sappho fragment, and a sensual verse from Virgil, explaining she doesn't want him to die a virgin: "rape isn't sex."

59. McCaffery, *Across the Wounded Galaxies*, 183. She called it "banal."

60. See also chapters 5 and 6.

61. *Extra(Ordinary)People*, 66.

62. Ibid., 92.

63. Another of Joanna's unnamed narrators. Jeanne Cortiel calls her "Rose Marie," but "Rose Marie" (referenced by James, 109), was a thirties movie musical.

64. Probably James died by suicide, a death that can be anticipated fairly precisely, as required for the "capturing the patterns" process.

65. McCaffery, *Across the Wounded Galaxies*, 186. "In fact, all the pieces in *Extra(Ordinary) People* are told to some other character directly or in a letter."

66. *Extra(Ordinary)People*, 95. Joanna's epigraph for this story, quoting the Russian poet "Anna Tsetsaeyva" (Marina Tsvetaeva) defines Utopia as the place where *feelings* matter as they should at last, and our emotional lives are our real lives.

67. Theresa Nielsen Hayden, January 12, 2012, in a comment on Tor.com: https://www .tor.com/2012/01/11/reading-joanna-russ-extraordinary-people-1984-part-2.

68. With drastic consequences, in Joanna's 1974 "probability mechanics" story "Reasonable People."

69. *Female Man*, 188.

70. McCaffery, *Across the Wounded Galaxies*, 183. "You'd have to be pretty dumb not to notice that it's not really a mediaeval world; among other things it's today's America." The characters' names, Art and Bob, Sid and Charlene, ought to be a hint.

71. Vincent Virga, *Gaywyck* (New York: Avon, 1980).

72. In case you were wondering: no. Chippendale made furniture.

73. Alice Sheldon and Joanna were still corresponding in the 1980s. They never met in person (Phillips, *James Tiptree Junior*, 432).

74. McCaffery, *Across the Wounded Galaxies*, 184–85.

## AFTERWORD

1. *Khatru*, 115.

2. Clare Fraser, *Revolution, She Wrote* (Seattle: Red Letter, 1998), introduction, 13.

3. See *Science Fiction Studies*, 81, no. 27.2 (July 2000): Donawerth, Books in Review, "An Indispensible Writer."

4. https://www.tor.com/2012/06/27/reading-joanna-russ-what-are-we-fighting-for-sex-race-class-and-the-future-of-feminism-1998

# SELECT BIBLIOGRAPHY OF SECONDARY SOURCES

Anderson, Poul. "Reply to a Lady." *Vertex: The Magazine of Science Fiction*, June 1974, 6.

Arlen, Michael. *The Green Hat: A Romance*. New York: Doran, 1924

Armitt, Lucie, ed. *Where No Man Has Gone Before: Women and Science Fiction*. London: Routledge, 1991.

Blish, James. *Cities in Flight*. New York: Baen, 1991.

———. [William Atheling Jr.]. *More Issues at Hand: Critical Studies in Contemporary Science Fiction*. Chicago: Advent Publishers, 2014.

Bamberger, Joan. "The Myth of Matriarchy: Why Men Rule in Primitive Society." In *Women, Culture, and Society*, edited by Michelle Rosaldo and Louise Lamphere, 263–80. Stanford, Calif.: Stanford University Press, 1974.

Born, Georgina. *Rationalizing Culture*. Berkeley: University of California Press, 1991.

Bradley, Marion Zimmer. *Darkover Landfall*. New York: Daw, 1972.

Burroughs, William. *Naked Lunch*. New York: Grove, 1959; London: Harper Collins, Flamingo Sixties Classics, 2001.

Calvin, Ritch. "'This Shapeless Book': Reception and Joanna Russ's *The Female Man*." *Femspec* 10, no. 2 (2010).

Charnas, Suzy. *Motherlines*. New York: Berkley, 1978.

———. *Walk to the End of the World*. New York: Ballantine, 1974.

Cornillon, Susan Koppelman, ed. *Images of Women in Fiction Feminist Perspectives*. Bowling Green, Ohio: Bowling Green University Popular Press, 1972.

Cortiel, Jeanne. *Demand My Writing*. Liverpool: Liverpool University Press, 1999.

Delany, Samuel R. *Dhalgren*. New York: Bantam, 1973.

———. "Introduction." *Alyx*, by Joanna Russ. Boston: Gregg, 1976.

———. *The Jewel-Hinged Jaw*. New York: Berkley, 1978.

———. "Orders of Chaos: The Science Fiction of Joanna Russ." In *Women Worldwalkers: New Dimensions of Science Fiction and Fantasy*, edited by Jane B. Weedman, 95–123. Lubbock: Texas Tech University Press, 1985.

———. *Triton*. New York: Bantam, 1976.

Dick, Philip K. "An Open Letter from Philip K. Dick." *Vertex: The Magazine of Science Fiction*, October 1974.

Disch, Thomas M. *The Dreams Our Stuff Is Made Of*. New York: Free Press / Simon and Schuster, 1998.

Donawerth, Jane L. "Science Fiction by Women in the Early Pulps 1926–1930." In Donawerth and Kolmerten, *Worlds of Difference*, 137–52.

Donawerth, Jane L., and Carol A. Kolmerten. *Worlds of Difference: Utopian and Science Fiction by Women*. Liverpool: Liverpool University Press, 1994.

DuPlessis, Rachel Blau. "The Feminist Apologues of Lessing, Piercy, and Russ." *Frontiers* 4, no. 1 (Spring 1979): 1–8.

Elgin, Suzette Haden. "For the Sake of Grace." In Elgin, *At the Seventh Level*, 7–31.

———. *At the Seventh Level*. New York: Daw, 1972.

Firestone, Shulamith. *The Dialectic of Sex*. New York: Bantam, 1970.

Gearhart, Sally Miller. *The Wanderground: Stories of the Hill Women*. Watertown, Mass.: Persephone, 1978.

Gilman, Charlotte Perkins. "The Yellow Wallpaper." 1899. Reprint, Old Westbury N.Y.: Feminist, 1973.

Herland, *The Forerunner*. 1915. Reprint, New York: Pantheon/Doubleday, 1979.

Gomoll, Jeanne. "An Open Letter to Joanna Russ." *Aurora* 10, no. 1 (1986–87): 7–10.

Green, Jen, and Sarah LeFanu, eds. "Introduction." In *Despatches from the Frontier of the Female Mind*. London: Namara/Women's Press, 1985.

James, Edward. "Russ on Writing Science Fiction and Reviewing It." In Mendlesohn, *On Joanna Russ*, 19–30.

Jones, Gwyneth. "*The Two Of Them*: Postscript to the Fairytale." In *Imagination/Space*, 43–57. Seattle, Wash.: Aqueduct, 2011.

———. "Writing Science Fiction for the Teenage Reader." In *Where No Man Has Gone Before: Women and Science Fiction*, edited by Leslie Armitt, 165–77. London: Routledge, 1991.

Khanna, Lee C. "The Subject of Utopia: Margaret Cavendish and Her Blazing World." In Donawerth and Kolmerten, *Worlds of Difference*, 15–34.

Kolmerton, Carol A. "Texts and Contexts: American Women Envision Utopia." In Donawerth and Kolmerten, *Worlds of Difference*, 107–25.

Larbalestier, Justine. *The Battle of the Sexes in Science Fiction*. Middletown, Conn.: Wesleyan University Press, 2002.

———, ed. *Daughters of Earth: Feminist Science Fiction in the Twentieth Century*. Middletown, Conn.: Wesleyan University Press, 2006.

LeFanu, Sarah. *In the Chinks of the World Machine: Feminism and Science Fiction*. London: Namara/Women's Press, 1988

Le Guin, Ursula K. "A Citizen of Mondath." In *The Profession of Science Fiction*, edited by Maxim Jakubowski and Edward James. London: Macmillan, 1992

———. "The Day Before The Revolution." In Le Guin, *Wind's Twelve Quarters*, 263–80.

———. *The Dispossessed*. New York: Harper and Row, 1974.

———. *The Left Hand of Darkness*. New York: Walker, 1969.

———. "The Masters." In Le Guin, *Wind's Twelve Quarters*, 37–54.

———. The Wind's Twelve Quarters and the Compass Rose. London: Gollancz, 2015

———. "Winter's King." In Le Guin, *Wind's Twelve Quarters*, 85–108.

Leiber, Fritz. *Conjure Wife*. New York: Street and Smith, 1943.

Lovecraft, H. P. "The Call of Cthulhu" In Lovecraft, *Complete Fiction*, 355–79.

———. "The Colour Out of Space." In Lovecraft, *Complete Fiction*, 594–616.

———. "The Dream-Quest of Unknown Kadath." In Lovecraft, *Complete Fiction*, 409–89.

———. "The Dunwich Horror." In Lovecraft, *Complete Fiction*, 633–67.

————. *H. P. Lovecraft: The Complete Fiction*. Introduction by S. T. Joshi. New York: Barnes and Noble, 2011.

————. "The Shadow Over Innsmouth." In Lovecraft, *Complete Fiction*, 807–58.

————. "The Strange High House in the Mist." In Lovecraft, *Complete Fiction*, 401–8.

Luis, Keridwen N. "Les Human Beans? Alienation, Humanity and Community in Joanna Russ's *On Strike against God*." In Mendlesohn, *On Joanna Russ*, 114–30.

Malzberg, Barry. *Beyond Apollo*. New York: Random House, 1972.

Martins, Susan. "Revising the Future in the Female Man." *Science Fiction Studies* 32, no. 3 (2005): 405–22.

Matzke, Brian S. "'The Weaker(?) Sex': Women and the Space Opera in Hugo Gernsback's *Amazing Stories*." *Foundation* 126 (2017): 6–24.

May, Elaine Tyler. *Homeward Bound: American Families in the Cold War Era*. New York: Perseus/ Basic, 1998.

McIntyre, Vonda N. and Susan J. Anderson. *Aurora: Beyond Equality*. Greenwich, Conn: Fawcett, 1976.

————. *Dreamsnake*. Boston: Houghton Mifflin, 1978.

Mendlesohn, Farah, ed. *On Joanna Russ*. Middletown, Conn.: Wesleyan University Press, 2009.

Merrick, Helen. "The Female 'Atlas' of Science Fiction? Russ, Feminism, and the SF Community." In Mendlesohn, *On Joanna Russ*, 48–63.

————. *The Secret Feminist Cabal*. Seattle, Wash.: Aqueduct, 2009.

Merrick, Helen, and Tess Williams, eds. *Women of Other Worlds: Excursions through Science Fiction and Feminism*. Nedlands: University of Western Australia Press, 1999.

Merril, Judith. *The Merril Theory of Lit'ry Criticism*. Edited by Ritch Calvin. Seattle, Wash.: Aqueduct, 2016.

————. *Shadow on the Hearth*. New York: Doubleday, 1952.

Moore, C. L. *Black God's Kiss*. Redmond Wash.: Paizo, 2007.

Moscowitz, Sam, ed. *When Women Rule*. New York: Walker, 1972.

Nabokov, Vladimir. *Lolita*. Paris: Olympia, 1955.

————. *Pale Fire*. New York: Putnam's, 1962.

Newell, Diane, and Jenea Tallentire. "Learning the "Prophet Business": The Merril-Russ Intersection." In Mendlesohn, *On Joanna Russ*, 64–82.

Phillips, Julie. *James Tiptree Junior: The Double Life of Alice Sheldon*. New York: St. Martin's, 2007.

Piekut, Benjamin. *Experimentalism Otherwise: The New York Avant-Garde and Its Limits*. Berkeley: University of California Press, 2011.

Piercy, Marge. "An Appreciation of Joanna Russ." In, *Parti-Coloured Blocks for a Quilt*. Ann Arbor: University of Michigan Press, 1982.

————. *Woman on the Edge of Time*. New York: Knopf, 1976.

Sahli, Nancy. "Smashing: Women's Relationships before the Fall." *Chrysalis: A Magazine of Women's Culture* 8, 17–27.

Sleight, Graham. "Extraordinary People: Joanna Russ's Short Fiction." In Mendlesohn, *On Joanna Russ*, 197–209.

Smith, Jeffrey D., ed. *Khatru 3 and 4 Symposium: Women in Science Fiction*. November 1975; reprinted Corflu 10, 1993, edited by Jeanne Gomoll. Madison Wisc.: Obsessive.

Spencer, Kathleen L. "Rescuing the Female Child: The Fiction of Joanna Russ." *Science Fiction Studies* 17, no. 2 (1990): 167–87.

Sturgis, Susanna. Review of *Magic Mommas, Trembling Sisters, Puritans and Perverts*, by Joanna Russ. *Off Our Backs* 15, no. 11 (December 1985): 18–19.

Tiptree, James, Jr. [Alice Sheldon]. "Beam Us Home." In *Ten Thousand Light Years from Home*. New York: Ace, 1973.

———. "Houston, Houston, Do You Read?" In *Aurora: Beyond Equality*, by Vonda N. McIntyre and Susan J. Anderson. Greenwich, Conn: Fawcett, 1976.

———. [Racoona Sheldon]. "Your Faces, O My Sisters! Your Faces Filled of Light." In *Aurora: Beyond Equality*, by Vonda N. McIntyre and Susan J. Anderson. Greenwich, Conn: Fawcett, 1976.

Vest, Jason. "Violent Women, Womanly Violence." In Mendlesohn, *On Joanna Russ*, 157–67.

Vinge, Joan D. "Tin Soldier." In *Orbit 14*, edited by Damon Knight. New York: Harper and Row, 1974.

Vint, Sherryl. "Joanna Russ's *The Two of Them* in an Age of Third-Wave Feminism." In Mendlesohn, *On Joanna Russ*, 83–98.

Wilhelm, Kate. *The Clewiston Test*. New York: Farrar, Straus and Giroux, 1976.

Willis, Connie. "The Women SF Doesn't See." Guest editorial, *Isaac Asimov's Science Fiction Magazine*. New York: Bantam/Doubleday Magazines, October 1992.

Wittig, Monique. *Les Guérillères*. Paris: Les Editions de Minuit, 1969.

Wolfe, Gary K. "Alyx among the Genres." In Mendlesohn, *On Joanna Russ*, 3–18.

Wood, Susan. "Women and Science Fiction." *Algol*, Winter 1978–79.

Yaszek, Lisa. *Galactic Suburbia*. Chicago: University of Chicago Press, 2008.

———. "A History of One's Own: Joanna Russ and the Creation of a Feminist SF Tradition." In Mendlesohn, *On Joanna Russ*, 31–47.

Yaszek, Lisa, and Patrick B. Sharp, eds. *Sisters of Tomorrow*. Middletown, Conn.: Wesleyan University Press, 2016.

avatar: Joanna's viewpoint characters as avatars of herself, 12, 131, 132; of Lovecraft, 8; "Trans Temp" as avatar of the science fiction community, 19

Ballard, J. G.: criticized (by Algis Budrys), 21; reviewed, 23, 24; successful career, 37; UK *New Worlds* writer, 21

Bamberger, Joan, 96

Bankier, Amanda, 69; editor of *The Witch and the Chameleon*, 79, 192n37

Barale, Michele, 137

*Bildungsroman*, 126, 140

Bitch Goddess, 46, 100

Blish, James, 25, 79; editor of first "Alyx" collection, 16; on "evaluative" criticism (as William Athling Jr.), 24, 183n9, 183n11; intended the sf term "hard science" to mean "correct science," 167; Joanna's editor at the *Magazine of Fantasy and Science Fiction*, 41; published anti-feminist novel, 92, 186n27; works reviewed, 22–26

Borges, Jorge Luis, 73, 110

Bradley, Marion Zimmer, 110, 119, 141, 191n27, 192n40, 196n25; *Darkover Landfall*, 101–2

Brecht, Bertholt, 73, 74, 164

British, 21, 25, 37, 42, 47, 48, 182n47, 189n22; influence, 22; pronunciation of "Irene," 127; sf as "more respectable," 42. *See also* Aldiss, Brian; Ballard, J. G.; Moorcock, Michael

Brontë, Charlotte, 8, 46, 113, 118

Brontë, Emily, 8

Bronx, 2, 3, 36, 165

broomstick, 105, 192n45

Budrys, Algis, 25, 37, 93, 192n35; reviles "New Wave" sf, 21; reviles *We Who Are About To*, 101, 111

Bunch, David, 116; reviewed, 42

Canada, 35

capitalism, 40, 100, 117–18, 159, 194n38

Cather, Willa (Wilella Sibert), 137–38, 196n23

Cavendish, Margaret, Duchess of Newcastle, 55–56, 63, 186n37

Charnas, Suzy McKee, 119; on commonality of ideas in feminist sf, 110, 193n3; *Khatru* panelist, 69, 80–89, 190n42, 190n56; *Motherlines*, 117, 119, 120

child, 2, 9, 30, 32, 94, 103, 107, 108, 111, 132, 148, 157, 192n40; child bearers, 66, 101; childbearing, compulsory, 101–3; childcare, gender differentiated, 48, 58, 84, 119; childrearing, gender differentiated, 40, 47, 48; female, rescue of, 100, 109, 120, 148, 192n53; fictional self, 66, 144–45; girl-child, 3, 99; hareem, 129; penis envy, diagnosed in, 5; psychotic, 37. *See also* childhood; children; Russ, Joanna

childhood, 2, 4, 81, 109, 113; dependency, must be abolished, 61; religion, 147; sexual inner life in, 122; sexual shame in, 143; sexually active (fictional), 34, 36

children, 23, 52, 56, 57, 94, 114, 115, 122, 123, 128, 155; conceived by marital rape, 128; idealistic (ironical), 58; "reared in common," 54; in "Recent Feminist Utopias," 120; signifier of domestic revival desperation, 30; special, 129; in Whileaway society, 61; women's public lives, sacrificed to, 67

CIA (Central Intelligence Agency), 91, 93

CIA (Civil Improvement Agency, fictional), 92

Cold War, 3, 6, 39–40, 71, 189n33; Elaine Tyler May study, 40

comics, 81, 122, 186n30

coming out (as a lesbian), 11, 64, 121, 146, 160

Communism, 40

community, 2, 85, 102, 136; community doctor, 33; gay newsletter, 135; Queensborough Community College, 11; science fiction community, 5, 19, 22, 93, 100, 118, 131, 135; of women in science fiction, 71

*Conjure Wife* (Leiber), 40

consciousness-raising group, 70, 140

contraceptive pill, 22

Cornell University, 4, 5, 9, 11, 53, 159; brewing Second Wave feminism, 22; conference on women, 86, 186n36; *Cornell Writer*, 76; as a fictional setting, 146–47; Joanna teaching first course in sf, 50; no posts for female graduates, 86. See also *Epoch*; "View from This Window, The"

Cornillon, Susan Koppelman (aka Susan Koppelman), 45, 47, 90, 153

Cortiel, Jeanne, 184n38, 186n34, 188n72, 196n46, 197n63; confirmation that "The Second Inquisition" is an Alyx story, 183n54; Jai Vedh's fluid sexual identity, 34, 184n34; "killing of a male" (in Joanna's fiction), 131, 195n55; multiple personality disorder in *The Female Man*, 187n55; queer/sexuality reading of "My Dear Emily," 7, 182n28; role play in an early Joanna Russ lesbian story, 196n29; science-fiction as masturbation aid, 184n21; Womanland (in *The Female Man*) as equivalent to the Americas, 188n69

*Country You Have Never Seen, The* (Russ), 26, 27, 47, 50, 114, 121, 135, 136, 138

courtesan, 12

Cramer, Kathryn, 134, 157–61

criticism, 50, 96, 123, 137, 157–58; on absence of sympathetic males in *The Female Man*, 163; of cruelty in a withering review, 141; feminist, 134, 140; feminist movie, 76; hostile male (of Joanna's fiction), 89, 92, 101; of male feminist crimes, 84; political, 45

Cthulhu Mythos, 8, 9, 97, 191n21

cubism, 9, 24

cultural minority, 134

dance, 143, 153; Dragon Dance, 58, 60; excruciating country club dance, 18; family party, locus of condoned sexual predation, 145; harvest dance, 125; high school dance, not proper subject for great writing, 4

Daoist/Taoist, 35, 103

*Darkover* (Zimmer Bradley), 119; *Darkover Landfall*, 101, 191n27, 191n32; "Darkover Newsletter," 102, 192n39; Marion Zimmer Bradley fans, 102; reviewed, 192n37

daydream(s), 17, 27, 58, 99; daydreamlikeness, 75; "Daydream Literature and Science Fiction," 26–27, 97; heroic fantasy as, 112; lawless, 34

death, 16, 28, 41–43, 46, 76, 87, 113, 141, 152; camps, 37; of Chaos, 35, 185n40; "heat death of the universe," 7; penalty, 62, 189n34; personified, 9; Spirit of Death, 105; as a theme, 86, 102–8, 131–32, 145, 190n51

Delany, Samuel R., 3, 11, 48, 77, 155, 158, 159, 166, 185n48, 188n74, 192n42; on *And Chaos Died*, 34, 36, 37, 184n32, 185n42; author of *Triton*, 119–20; comrade in sf theory, 72–75, 92, 189n25; identifying sources for "The Precious Object," 31, 184n27; introduction, first *Alyx* collection, 12, 92; introduction, *We Who Are About To*, 192n42; *Khatru* panelist, 59, 69, 80–88. See also *Dhalgren*

*Demand My Writing* (Cortiel), 7

Depression (historical period), 56, 60

depression (illness), 5, 87, 123, 134, 160; akin to madness, 123; "Everyday Depressions" (short story), 148, 153–54

detective (genre), 28, 46; substantial number of female writers, 168

*Dhalgren* (Delany), 37, 185n48, 185n49; success of, alongside *The Female Man*, 188n74

*Dialectic of Sex, The* (Firestone), 181n9, 187n57; reviewed, 26

Dick, Philip K.: "Open Letter" to Joanna, 89, 90, 92, 93; reviewed, 44; "The Pre Persons," 161

Dickinson, Emily, 8, 113

Disch, Thomas: reviewed, 43, 113, 115–16

divorce: fictional, 30, 64, 146; real life, 11

"domestic revival" (as Cold War reversal of women's emancipation), 5, 40, 60, 71, 76, 183n1

Donawerth, Jane, 71, 186n37, 188n11, 198n3

drama, 3, 4, 45, 73, 98, 158, 161, 192n51; dramatis personae, 100. *See also* play; playwriting; theater

Dworkin, Andrea, 141

ecology, 58, 83, 114, 119; *Gyn/Ecology*, 114, 193n12

Elaine/X (character): coded as avatar of Joanna, 192n48, 192n53; dedicates herself to the "art of dying," 101; identified as "X" in the novel's first half résumé (*Galaxy* magazine), 191n31; nameless until "Elaine" revealed, 106; narrator and protagonist of *We Who Are About To,* 99–108; resists pregnancy by rape, 104. *See also* "Main Street: 1953"

Elgin, Suzette Haden: inventor of a (fictional) "female" language, 196n26; providing the "springboard" for Joanna's *The Two of Them,* 110, 126, 128

Ellison, Harlan, 26, 53, 72, 75, 83, 112, 181n13, 189n33

Eloi, 18, 19, 36, 37, 73, 182n51

Emshwiller, Carol, 10; anthologized stories reviewed, 23, 25, 43; cited as avant-garde sf writer, 49; collection reviewed, 44

*Epoch* (Cornell literary magazine), 9, 79, 80

essay(s), 81, 100, 101, 116, 137, 146, 159, 184n21, 194n37; on *And Chaos Died* (Delany), 37; on C. L. Moore and Women's Science Fiction (Gubar), 135; collected (Russ), 25, 26–28, 34, 45–53, 72–75, 95–97, 117–23, 134,

137–44; on Hugo Gernsback and early sf feminists (Attebery), 188n11; influential (Russ), 91; in *Khatru* symposium, 82–89, 193n16; not revised (Russ), 28; style (Russ), 47; on utopian fiction, 41. *See also specific essays*

essentialism, 139

evaluative, 24, 25, 183n9

exceptional woman, 92, 111, 131, 134

*Extra(Ordinary)People* (Russ), 134, 138, 148–54, 197n58, 197n66; performative, 151, 197n65; publishing history of the stories, 148

*Extrapolation* (journal), 26, 73, 136

Ezekiel, 132, 195n57

faculty wife, 5, 30, 146

fairytale, 37, 42, 66, 107, 125, 144, 195n54; Space Opera as, 47

fandom, 102, 134, 158, 186n25; Seventies Feminism, contentious issue, 70–71

fan-fic (fan fiction), 94, 95; pornographic, 135

fans (sf), 24, 27, 42, 69, 71, 80, 98, 102, 107, 113, 126, 134; assumed to be predominantly young males, 48; college educated, 50; female, rediscovered, 71; heroic fantasy, 124; Jewish male, 76; Joanna's influence on, 72, 93; *Star Trek,* 37, 94; success driven by, 118; fan writers, 70, 110; young, attracted to horror, 96

fantasy (genre), 3, 14, 16, 27, 29, 39, 73, 77, 80, 81, 101, 113, 115, 132, 213, 145, 182n47, 191n20; arcane, 8; avant-garde fiction and, 161; definition and artistic value of, 47, 74, 140, 161; "heroic," 112, 115, 124; relevance to the women's movement, 85, 165–66; scholarship, 135; sword and sorcery, 11, 12, 14, 22

fantasy (mental construct), 31, 82, 151, 186n23; of being Alexander the Great, 5, 47, 50, 76; of being Genghis Khan, 62,

67; of immortality, 103, 186n23, 192n43; of an impossibly generous universe, 102; of killing, 88, 132; of outlawry, 150; of rescuing the self, 109, 145; psychoactive, juvenile, 17–18; sexual, 66, 122, 142; women (or men), as the other sex's fantasy projection, 87

fanzine, 92, 95, 101, 106, 135, 142, 190n6; *Khatru*, 69, 76

father, 2–3, 4, 114, 157, 187nn57–58, 191n27, 193n13; images of, in novels, 103, 105, 128; "nuclear family" figure, 59; in short stories, 80, 99; in "The Second Inquisition," 18–19; young men recruited to war against, 120

female hero, 11, 17, 85, 125, 134; Alyx as, 12, 14, 16, 19

*Female Man, The* (Russ), 4, 8, 10, 31, 40, 41, 56–68, 78, 85, 86, 101, 126, 143, 156, 162–66, 185n5, 187n43, 187n47, 196n40; alienating catalogue of male professionals, 85, 188n71; as "antifiction," 68; astounding lesbian sex, 62; avant-garde techniques in, 75; compared with "When It Changed," 53, 61; congruences with biography and autobiographical short fictions, 146, 181n16, 184n26, 186n36; on everyday sexism, 67; inflexible (social) program, 61; "Manland vs Womanland," 65–66, 134; "many worlds" quantum theory, 57, 187n45; in "Recent Feminist Utopias," 119–20, 193n19; reception and success, 68, 188n74; related to "probability mechanics" stories, 151–53; revisioned in "What did You Do During the Revolution, Grandma?" 134, 151–53, 188n68; sex scene reprised in *On Strike against God*, 197n48; stories related to, 53–54, 76; viewed as a critique of *And Chaos Died* (Delany), 37; violence, 91

*Feminine Mystique, The* (Friedan), 40, 52

feminism, 11, 30, 41, 43, 82, 84, 86, 89, 103, 119, 121–22, 140–44, 158, 188n17; academic, supplanted by "gender studies," 137; antifeminism, 92; as a class struggle, 140; discussed in interview, 162–69; dismissed by young lesbians, 137; eighties, project of assimilation, 123; endangered by essentialism, 139; evolving, in Joanna's novels, 110; failed (fictional), 53; femininists, as a problem for, 142; first engagement (fictionalized), 59–60; future of, 198n4; gratuitous attack on, 44; "lecture," 60; literary and political, 158; male-friendly, 147; political movement, 142; radical, 22, 68, 71, 114, 143; Second Wave, 22, 40–41, 71, 193n12; seventies, 70, 121; tending toward general radicalism, 145; "The Image Of Women in Science Fiction," 47–49; "What Can A Heroine Do? Or Why Women Can't Write," 45–47. *See also* seventies

feminist(s), 4, 5, 11,17, 30, 39, 44, 67, 87, 93, 95, 106, 134, 140, 159; activism, 134, 155; angel, 62; anthologies (sf), 83; antifeminists (sf), 167; *bildungsroman* (Kittatinny), 140; fable ("The Yellow Wallpaper"), 122–23; *Feminist Review*, 114; fiction (Russ), 17; journals, 26, 137; lesbian, 7, 72, 93, 102, 111, 116–17, 134, 135, 139, 140; male feminist, 84; male hostility(sf), 93; manifesto (Russ), 88, 101–5, 190n57; polemic, 63; politics, 132; pornography, 141–44; postfeminist, 92; protofeminist, 12; radical, 3, 26, 38, 71, 88, 141, 159; scholarship, 45, 47, 186n24; *The Secret Feminist Cabal*, 186n25, 188n3, 188n15; seventies, 4, 63, 93, 136, 144, 196n19; sex wars, 141; Susan Wood, 70; teaching, 109; utopia(s), 10, 55, 63, 114, 116–21, 190n2, 193n20; writers, 86, 134, 188n9

feminist science fiction, 40, 45, 55, 79, 106, 116, 117, 110, 132, 141, 144, 155, 158, 160, 169, 187n44, 190n57; antifeminist, 167 fifties, 6, 7, 48, 141, 187n52; conformity, 7; costume in *The Female Man*, 56, 57; housewife, Joanna as an invalid compared to, 134; movies, 48; repression, 96; "that disgusting decade," 185n6; highly sexualized, 127

Firestone, Shulamith, 26, 61, 181n9, 199n57

fix-up, 25, 42, 43, 183n14

*Flash Gordon*, 47

forever house, 6, 66, 144

Friedan, Betty, 40, 53, 64

Galactica, 32

Galactic Suburbia, 49; academic study title, 71

galaxy (astronomy), 85

*Galaxy* (magazine), 21, 78, 96, 101, 191n31, 194n41

"Game of Vlet, A" (Russ), 17

Gearhart, Sally (Miller): author of *The Wanderground*, 39, 117, 193n24; in "Recent Feminist Utopias," 119–20

gender, 14, 45, 48, 49, 72, 95, 136, 149–51, 160; binary, 63; blind, 134, 150; equality, 186n19; future of, 47; gender-bending, 12; gendered work, 119; *Gender Genocide* (Cooper), 95; *Gender Justice* (Kirp), 136; gender studies, 137; pay-gap, 86; performative, 151; politics, 45; reversal (swap, switch) for rhetorical effect, 46, 47, 85, 188n71; role(s), 7, 25, 40, 46, 47, 49, 68, 70, 92, 138; rules, Jewish versus Gentile, 4; sexual gender unknown in Gethen (*The Left Hand Of Darkness*, LeGuin), 49; stereotypes, 7, 119

Genet, Jean, 75, 164

genetics, 57, 58, 127, 184n28; identical, 65

genre (science fiction), 3, 9, 37, 41, 55, 69, 81, 83, 93, 94, 111, 131, 156; academic invasion, 50; aesthetics, 72–75; birth of, 17; British, 47; classification, 25; definition, 72–73; enriched by New Wave, 21; focus, need

to expand, 136; not defined by utopian/dystopian mode, 74; pulps, 27, 51; status of women in, 72; "Trans-Temp" as avatar of, 19; weighted toward male readers, 86; "What If" literature, 47; women instrumental in shaping, 71; writers responding to each other's stories, 110

genres (paraliterature), 7, 26–28, 69, 80, 83, 145, 181n10; accessible to female writers and readers, 123; conventions, 123; definition, 136, 147; detective story, 28, 46, 168; modern gothic, 52–53, 142, 186n33, 118; narrative tricks, 149; plots not limited to one sex, 46; pornography, 27, 51, 141–44, 181n10, 192n42; recurrent characters, 9; sub-genres, 12, 112, 124; Utopian, 41

ghost, 8, 10, 16, 53, 59, 76, 91, 145; conventions of ghost story, 123

Gilman, Charlotte Perkins, 8, 55, 96, 122–23, 195n50; invalidization, 123; racism, 114; rediscovered utopian feminist, 71; reviewed, 114. *See also* "On 'The Yellow Wallpaper'"; *Two of Them, The*; "Yellow Wallpaper, The"

"Gleepsite" (Russ), 53

god, 35, 42, 64, 71, 87, 105, 163, 167, 181n16, 182n38, 184n21, 193n12; beloved comic statues of, 63; "(The) Black God's Kiss," 11; God of the Center, in Daoist fable, 185n40; *The Gods Themselves* (Asimov), 113; *On Strike Against God*, 5, 31, 123, 134, 146–47

godless, 2, 73, 192n52

Golden Age, 57, 58; science fiction, 81

Gomoll, Jeanne, 71, 109, 133, 195n6, 196n19

gothic, 8, 10, 80, 94; gay (male), and proposed lesbian, 153–54; modern, 52–53, 102, 118, 142, 186n33. *See also* genres

Great Mother, 48, 79

Greenlee, Sam, 91, 190n4

gun, 13, 83, 86, 88, 105. *See also* rifle

*Gyn/Ecology* (Daly), 114, 193n12

Hacker, Marilyn, 44, 77, 160; experiences of sexism recounted by Delany, 83

Hartwell, David, 51, 155, 159

helmet, 39; computer, induction technology, 54, 58, 63; media-blocking "Trivia," 15

he-man, 3, 9, 100, 107, 168; in "Alien Monsters," 50–51; in "The Image of Women in Science Fiction," 48

Henderson, Zenna, 10, 48, 186n28

*Herland* (Gilman), 71; early all-female utopian fiction, 55; reviewed by Joanna, 114

heterosexuality, 121, 122, 136, 138, 147

*Hidden Side of the Moon, The* (Russ) (story collection), 9, 11, 29–30, 77–80, 99, 124, 135, 144–45, 184n26

Hitchcock, Alfred, 10

*Homeward Bound: American Families in the Cold War Era* (May), 40, 185n4, 187n52

homosexuality, 29, 31, 35, 42, 142, 152; in *And Chaos Died*, 33–34, 184n34; cryptic, in K/S fantasy, 142; *Journal of Homosexuality*, 137; on Mars, 50; Stonewall riots, 22; suggested in "My Dear Emily," 7; targeted by "Moral Majority," 137, 141; unremarkable in *Woman On The Edge Of Time*, 120

honorary male, 132

honors and awards: Florence Howe for feminist scholarship, 47; National Westinghouse Science Talent Search finalist, 4, 181n14; O. Henry, 80; science fiction, 32, 53, 76, 123, 135, 148; Science Fiction Hall of Fame, 156

horror (genre), 2, 10, 52, 116, 161; covert fear of women, 40; discussed, 96–97; Hammer Horror, 8; *Magazine of Horror*, 9

*How to Suppress Women's Writing* (Russ), 134, 158, 195n5

humanist fantastic, 24, 41

husband, 4, 9, 30, 40, 41, 123, 145, 159, 182n50; in "Alyx" stories, 13–14; atrocious practices of (fictional), 128; divorced (Joanna), 11; earning more than

wives, 47; in gender-swapped version of *A Winter's Tale*, 46; imperative to secure, 4, 63; "Somebody's Trying to Kill Me and I Think It's My Husband," 52–53; toy-boy, 100; trophy, 99

idyll, 56, 112; definition, 41

"Image of Women in Science Fiction, The" (Russ), 25, 47–49, 72, 95; reprint, targeted by male supremacists, 87, 89, 90, 92, 101

Intergalactic Suburbia, 47, 49. *See also* Galactic Suburbia

*In The Chinks of the World Machine: Science Fiction and Feminism* (LeFanu), 70, 136

invalidization, 123, 128

Irene Waskiewicz (character), 111, 126–32, 193n6, 194nn47–49, 195n54, 195n56; autobiographical material (Joanna), 126–27, 131; fantasies of being "Irene Adler," 127; possible perpetrator of "androcide," 132; sexually aggressive, 126

Islamic, 110, 111, 126, 127

Jael (character), 67, 85, 91, 166, 184n26; bat-winged, 53, 186n34; biblical namesake, 65, 188n67; as fourth avatar of Joanna in *The Female Man*, 65–67; named "the best" of the four Js, 67; re-visioned in "What Did You Do During the Revolution, Grandma?" 151–53; Womanland assassin, 187n48

Jai Vedh (character): *And Chaos Died* protagonist, 32–37; "cure for male homosexuality" controversy, 33, 184n32; mystical initiation, 34, 184n36; no fixed physical or sexual identity, 34, 184n34

James, Edward, 24

Janet Evason (character), 10, 46, 47, 55, 91, 138, 166, 184n26; emerging as alternate personality in a crucial incident, 6, 187n55; utopian avatar of Joanna in *The Female Man* 56–67, 187n43; viewpoint character in "When It Changed," 53–54

Moorcock, Michael, 42; "New Worlds" writer, 21, 37; reviewed, 22, 24, 25, 45, 182n47

Moore, Catherine Lucille, 135; "Jirel of Joiry," 11

Moore, Raylyn, 43; *Khatru* panelist, 69, 80–87; reviewed, 112; *The Wizard of Oz*, 80

Moral Majority, 141

Morlocks, 18–19, 36, 73, 182n51

mother, 18–19, 67, 94, 98, 99, 114, 143, 144, 153; in autobiographical material, 79–80, 145; biographical reference, 2–4, 87; figure, 14; Great Mother, 48, 79; nuclear family figure, 59; of science fiction, Mary Shelley as, 51; sf fan as, 71; in *The Two of Them*, 127–29; to the world, 104

motherhood, 114; in all-female societies, 56, 61; "Tiptree" on motherhood, 83, 84

*Motherlines* (Charnas): reviewed, 117; discussed in "Recent Feminist Utopias" 119, 120

murder, 42, 50, 52, 76, 94, 163; androcide, as drastic feminist metaphor, 132, 147, 195n54; classic sf action heroines as murderous, 83, 91; in Joanna's fiction, 15, 18, 36, 66, 91, 102–7, 188n67

music, 20, 21, 22, 30, 38, 101, 107, 151, 183n5, 197n63

musician, 106

musicologist, 100

"My Boat" (Russ), 96, 97–98; tribute to Cicely Tyson, 98

"My Dear Emily" (Russ), 8–9, 17

"Mystery of the Young Gentleman, The" (Russ), 47, 148, 149–50

mysticism/mystical, 1, 136, 196n18; in "Main Street" (Russ), 145

mystification, 42; Marxist sense, 118, 136; "SF and Technology as Mystification," 117–18

myth, 46, 50, 81, 87, 117, 125, 133; creation, 182n42; "Cthulhu Mythos," 9, 97; "The Myth of Matriarchy," 96

mythology, 23, 42, 50

Nabokov, Vladimir, 4, 73, 75, 110, 134, 159, 189n27, 192n1

National Westinghouse Science Talent Search, 4, 181n14

New Wave, 11, 21, 32, 37, 38, 41; in UK, 24

New York, 5, 9, 14, 22, 30, 31, 32, 113, 136, 158, 185n8, 194n32; birthplace, 2; in *The Female Man*, 56, 65, 67, 188n73; state, 146; in stories, 30, 3, 151. *See also* Bronx; Manhattan

*New York Review of Science Fiction, The* (journal), 2, 195n54

Nielsen Hayden, Patrick & Teresa, 158, 197n67

nongenre, 5, 9, 52, 47, 57, 82, 84; articles, 47, 82; *The Female Man* as, 69; feminist, reviews of, 111; fictionalized autobiography, 76; *On Strike Against God*, 5, 123, 144; stories, 30–32

"Nor Custom Stale" (Russ), 1, 5–7

*novum*, 28

nuclear, 6, 7, 44, 66; anti-nuclear war story, 183n1; family, 59; global thermonuclear war, 189n32

Old Earth, 32, 34, 91; agents, 35; as depiction of blighted, broken urban US, 37; listed exports, bound to offend, 35; nightmarish, 36

"Old Pictures" (Russ), 79

"Old Thoughts, Old Presences," (Russ), 80

*On Joanna Russ* (Mendlesohn), 12, 133

*On Strike Against God* (Russ), 5, 31, 123, 134, 146–47, 197nn47–49

"On 'The Yellow Wallpaper'" (Russ), 122–23, 195n50

"Open Letter to Joanna Russ" (Gomoll), 133, 196n19

*Orbit* (anthology series), 11–14, 17, 53, 78; as "chief expression" of the American New Wave, 11; reviewed by Judith Merril, 23

Ourdh, 12–14, 17

*Oxford Book of English Verse* (collection), 2

psychotherapy, 4, 122, 146, 182n45, 193n26
pulp (sf), 11, 27, 51, 71, 81; evolved pulp, 126; no place for an artist, 168

quantum: mechanics, 57; starship, 35, 36. *See also* probability mechanics

rabbit motif, 94
rape, 43, 70, 76, 124, 143, 148, 189n27; in Joanna's fiction, 12, 13, 33, 78, 148; as means of subjugation, 95–96; pleasure of being raped (fictional), 95; pregnancy by, 102–4; as proper material for great writing, 4; "rape isn't sex," 197n58
"Recent Feminist Utopias" (Russ), 117, 118–20
*Red Clay Reader* (journal), 31, 47
reviews/reviewing, 28, 101, 122, 131, 162, 195n12; *A Boy and His Dog* (film), 72, 75; heroic fantasy mocked in, 12, 124; Joanna's style, assessed, 24; by Joanna, in various venues, 22–26, 41–45, 49, 93–94, 111–17, 121, 141, 188n10, 195n12; "Magic Mommas" collection, 141; reviewer's task, 44, 115; scathing, 101, 135; tepid, of *Picnic on Paradise*, 23; why Joanna gave up, 160. *See also* Blish, James; Budrys, Algis; James, Edward; Merril, Judith
re-visioning, 110, 134, 147
revolution: cultural, 21–22; failed (fictional), 104, 106; "The Day Before the Revolution," 151; violent, 93; *Revolution, She Wrote*, Joanna's foreword for, 155; "What Did You Do During the Revolution Grandma?" 78, 148, 151–53, 187n46, 188n68, 194n38
revolutionary: counterrevolutionary, 159; feminist seventies, 136; group, 152; violence, in *The Female Man*, 67, 91
rifle, 147
riot(s), 22; "twenties riots" (fictional), 103

rite of passage, 18, 47
robot, 16, 148, 150, "Robot Revolt," 28
Rubicon, 26, 184n18
Ruritania: as satirical depiction of Modern America in Extra(Ordinary)People, 152, 197n70. *See also* Alan-Bobby Whitehouse
Russ, Joanna: academic career, 11, 22, 134, 137, 157–58; acclaim, 93; anger, 66, 67, 88, 90, 132, 160, 163, 165; autobiographical fictions, 3, 8, 10, 19, 59, 76, 79–80, 91, 106, 110, 126, 130–32, 146–47; birth and childhood, 2–4; depression, 5, 123, 134, 160; early passion for science, 3–4; education, 4–5; and feminism, 11, 22, 26, 40, 41, 43, 56–68, 162; and feminism in sf, 71–72, 80–89, 101–2; and generalized radicalism, 155; health problems, 134, 139, 155; honors and awards, 4, 47, 80, 32, 53, 76, 123, 135, 148, 156, 181n14; Jewish identity, 4, 136; juvenilia (sf), 2; last illness and legacy, 156; lesbian identity, 8, 11, 31, 62, 72, 93, 111, 122, 134, 135, 140–42, 160; marriage and divorce, 5, 11; mysticism, 1, 34, 136, 145, 196n18; and New Wave, 11, 24, 25, 32–37; parents, 2–4, 80, 87, 145; retired, 134, 155; separatism, 120, 136, 139; and Slash fiction (K/S), 95, 135, 140, 142, 144, 158; success, 14, 17, 29, 68; theorist (sf), 3, 26, 72; wilderness years, 10; and women's movement crises, 137, 140–42. *See also entries for specific works*

Sahli, Nancy Ann, 121
Sand, George, 145, 196n45
Sargent, Pamela, 70, 94, 113, 188n17
satire, 29, 47, 74
Schrodinger, Erwin, 57, 59
science, 2, 3, 23, 44, 72–73, 181n14, 187n45, 189n20, 189n21; attracted American women to science fiction, 39; claimed as male territory, 4; "hard," 24, 167, 168, 169;

informing *The Female Man*, 57; lab science, 93; probability mechanics, 78, 151; science/fiction fusion, 7, 57

*Science Fiction Studies* (journal), 72, 95, 96, 117, 193n17, 195n9, 198n3

"Second Inquisition, The" (Russ), 17–19, 111, 183n54, 194n45; elements of, in *The Two of Them*, 127, 132; in *Extra(Ordinary) People*, 154

Second Wave feminism, 22, 40, 41, 71, 193n12

sense of wonder, 1, 2, 10, 71, 156

separatism, 120, 136, 139

seventies, 41, 44, 49, 59, 71, 76, 79, 83, 95, 111, 138, 189n19; butch/femme role-play before, 140; collected letters from, 135; community of women in sf in, 71; feminists and feminism, 4, 70, 93, 102, 121, 136, 142, 144, 196n19; feminist utopians, 63, 116; first contact clichés in, 59; Robert Silverberg as top male literary sf author in, 43; sf theorists in, 3

sexism, 45, 67, 68, 89, 92, 155, 167, 168; biological causation argument, as council of despair, 142; curious form, in *Star Trek* fanfic, 95; endemic in classic sf, 26, 110; extremes of, in *The Female Man*, 163; how to deal with accusations of, 84; interrogation of, 110; *Khatru* chapter on roots of, 87; male, unthinking, 167; rampant in university common rooms, 100; strategies for eliminating, 69

sexist, 69, 95; antisexists, 75; assumptions, 8, 164, 167; James Tiptree's sexist views, 87; nature of the Heroic Quest form, 85; Poul Anderson's sexist attack, 87; society, 118

sexuality, 61, 115, 120, 138, 194n38; Barnard Conference on, 141; lesbian, in "My Dear Emily," 8; lesbian, unproblematic for Joanna in the eighties, 160; queer, in "My

Dear Emily," 7. *See also* homosexuality; heterosexuality; lesbian

"SF and Technology as Mystification" (Russ), 117–18

Shaw, George Bernard, 27, 73, 88, 94, 164

Sheldon, Alice ("Allie"): as Alice Tiptree of the Deepdene Sheldons, 153; *Aurora* anthology, 190n43, 191n24; lesbian identity, 136; relationship with Joanna, 198n73; as Racoona Sheldon, 119; stories discussed, 96, 119–21, 124, 149, 194n21; as Tiptree 87, 188n2. *See also* Tiptree Jr., James

Shelley, Mary, 51, 81, 145; as "Mary Godwin" (fictional), 44

Shelley, Percy Bysshe, 79

short stories (Russ), 5–11, 29–32, 47, 76–80, 97–99, 123–24, 144–46, 155; Alyx cycle, 11–19, 23, 92; autobiographical content, 3, 10, 30–31, 79, 122, 144–45; juvenilia, 2–4; related to *The Female Man*, 53–54

Silverberg, Robert: on *And Chaos Died*, 32, 184n29, 186n21; described as "sossidge factory," 44–45; reviewed, as editor, 54, 79, 116; reviewed, as writer, 43

*Sinister Wisdom* (journal), 116, 124, 135, 140, 141, 145

sixties, 10, 35, 135, 142, 183n5; radicalism, 40, 93, 106; Swinging, 32

Slashfic, 95, 140, 142

Smith, Jeffery D.: as editor of *Khatru* symposium, 88, 190n56; as *Khatru* fanzine editor, 69, 188n1; as moderator in *Khatru* symposium, 80, 81–87, 89

socialism, 48, 89, 155, 159, 160

"Somebody's Trying to Kill Me and I Think It's My Husband" (Russ), 52–53

Space Opera, 47–48, 49

spirit journey, 125

spook, 91–92, 104

*Spook Who Sat By The Door, The* (Greenlee), 91–93, 190n4

vampire, 7, 8, 9, 125, 147, 197n49; psychoanalyst as vampire, 146

*Vertex* (magazine), 87, 144; reprinted "The Image Of Women In Science Fiction" (Russ), 47; responses to the article from Poul Anderson and Philip K. Dick, 89, 90, 92

"View from This Window, The" (Russ), 30–31, 186n36

vignette(s), 8, 17, 57

Wallach Scott, Joan, 136

"Wearing Out of Genre Materials, The" (Russ), 27–28, 110

Wells, H. G., 18, 41, 72, 73, 182n51; Wells/ Verne period, 168

*We Who Are About To* (Russ), 99–108, 110, 111, 132, 139, 145, 190n51, 191n26, 192n36, 192n42; compared with Sam Greenlee's *The Spook Who Sat By The Door*, 91–93; and Marion Zimmer Bradley's *Darkover Landfall*, 101–2, 191n32; punished by male critics, 101; structural problems, 102; value obscured by controversy, 103

*What Are We Fighting For?* (Russ), 155

"What Can a Heroine Do? or, Why Women Can't Write" (also as "Why Women Can't Write") (Russ), 41, 45–47, 82

"When It Changed" (Russ), 53–54, 56, 78, 89, 90, 187n47; compared with *The Female Man*, 61; explicitly feminist, 163; response to the Cornell conference on women in 1969, 53

Whileaway, 54, 65, 66, 67, 91, 120, 138, 151, 153, 166, 186n20, 194n49; as all-female lost colony in "When It Changed," 46, 53, 54, 187n47; as all-female utopian strand in *The Female Man*, 41, 55–65

White, Luise: *Khatru* panelist, 69, 70, 80, 83, 84, 86, 91, 188n7

Wilde, Oscar, 11, 136, 194n48

Wild West, 105

Wilhelm, Kate, 10; belated appreciation for her radical views, 155; *Khatru* panelist, 69, 80, 81, 82, 89; works reviewed, 25, 43, 93–94

Willis, Connie, 188n17

*Window Dressing* (Russ) (play), 5, 181n19

"Window Dressing" (Russ) (short story), 29

Wiscon (sf convention), 134, 155

*Witch and the Chameleon, The* (fanzine), 101

Wittig, Monique, 119, 193n19

Wolfe, Gary A., 12, 15, 18

Womanland, 67, 91, 134, 151–52, 153, 187n48

women's movement, 81, 137, 140, 165, 168–69, 189n19

*Women's Review of Books, The* (journal), 135, 137, 138

Wood, Susan, 70, 109, 116, 189n19

Woolf, Virginia, 20, 46, 124, 139

World War II, 2, 39, 56, 187n51

Yale: *Courant* (journal), 194n31; school of drama, 4, 5, 158, 161

Yaszek, Lisa, 7, 71

"Yellow Wallpaper, The" (Gilman), 96, 126, 195n50; title, referenced in *The Female Man*, 60; referenced in *The Two Of Them*, 129, 195n50. *See also* "On 'The Yellow Wallpaper'"

*Zanzibar Cat* (Russ) (story collection), 7–9, 29, 31, 53–54, 77–78, 97–99, 123, 124, 187n47, 191n24; preparation, 134

"Zanzibar Cat, The" (Russ) (short story), 77, 189n37

Zimmer-Bradley, Marian (MZB); 101–2, 119, 141, 191n27, 192n40, 196n25. *See also Darkover*

GWYNETH JONES is a science fiction and fantasy author and critic. Her fiction includes *Divine Endurance* and the Aleutian trilogy. Her nonfiction includes *Deconstructing the Starships: Essays and Reviews* and *Imagination/Space: Essays and Talks on Fiction, Feminism, Technology, and Politics*. Jones is the winner of two World Fantasy Awards and the Arthur C. Clarke Award, and the SFRA Pilgrim award for lifetime achievement in SF criticism.

## MODERN MASTERS OF SCIENCE FICTION

John Brunner  *Jad Smith*

William Gibson  *Gary Westfahl*

Gregory Benford  *George Slusser*

Greg Egan  *Karen Burnham*

Ray Bradbury  *David Seed*

Lois McMaster Bujold  *Edward James*

Frederik Pohl  *Michael R. Page*

Alfred Bester  *Jad Smith*

Octavia E. Butler  *Gerry Canavan*

Iain M. Banks  *Paul Kincaid*

J. G. Ballard  *D. Harlan Wilson*

Arthur C. Clarke  *Gary Westfahl*

Joanna Russ  *Gwyneth Jones*

THE UNIVERSITY OF ILLINOIS PRESS

is a founding member of the

Association of University Presses.

———————————————————

University of Illinois Press

1325 South Oak Street

Champaign, IL 61820-6903

www.press.uillinois.edu